Client Outcomes in Therapeutic Recreation Services

Client Outcomes in Therapeutic Recreation Services

edited by

Norma J. Stumbo, Ph.D., CTRS
Illinois State University

 Venture Publishing, Inc. • State College, Pennsylvania

Venture Publishing, Inc.
1999 Cato Avenue
State College, PA 16801
Phone   (814) 234-4561
Fax   (814) 234-1651

Production Manager: Richard Yocum
Manuscript Editing: Michele L. Barbin, Valerie Fowler
Cover by Echelon Design

Library of Congress Catalogue Card Number 2003106627
ISBN 1-892132-43-5

Table of Contents

Chapter 1
Outcomes, Accountability, and Therapeutic Recreation 1
Norma J. Stumbo

Chapter 2
The Importance of Evidence-Based Practice in
Therapeutic Recreation 25
Norma J. Stumbo

Chapter 3
Outcomes From a National and Worldwide Perspective 49
John M. Jacobson

Chapter 4
Basing Outcomes on Theory: Theories of Intervention
and Explanation 67
Linda L. Caldwell

Chapter 5
Other Voices, Other Rooms: Consumers' and Healthcare Professionals' Perspectives on Valued Client Outcomes in Therapeutic Recreation 87
Barbara Wilhite, Jan S. Hodges, and Mason Peebles

Chapter 6
The Efficacy of Therapeutic Recreation: Back to the Future 111
Carmen V. Russoniello

Chapter 12
Outcomes Measurement as a Tool for Performance
Improvement 221
Bryan P. McCormick

Chapter 13
Conveying the Possible With Client-Directed Outcomes
and Social Marketing 233
Susan "BOON" Murray

List of Tables and Figures

Preface

Therapeutic recreation (TR) is in the midst of exciting and challenging changes in health and human services. One of the toughest challenges is creating, planning, implementing, and evaluating TR intervention programs that are based on "best practice" and provide maximum accountability to invested persons and parties. These services are designed and delivered to produce outcomes that are valued by, meaningful to, and important to the consumer as well as other service providers. This book represents a synergistic, collective effort to bring the newest information on outcomes, accountability, and evidence-based practice to the field of therapeutic recreation. It does so with a specific focus on the *process* of designing, delivering, and evaluating comprehensive and specific programs (as opposed to specific groups of clients). The actions and decisions described in these chapters apply to all population groups with which therapeutic recreation specialists work.

The book begins with three chapters on background information on outcomes and accountability from national and international perspectives, within and external to the profession of therapeutic recreation. In the next three chapters, past, present, and future directions for outcomes research in therapeutic recreation are highlighted. The next seven chapters address the process of theory selection, program design, assessment, implementation, evaluation, performance improvement, and marketing. The last chapter provides a brief state-of-the-art of outcomes and evidence-based practice in therapeutic recreation. Collectively, these chapters are intended to upgrade and update the outcomes literature within the field and spur professionals into providing higher quality and more meaningful services to all clients. These tasks are not without effort; we are not implying that creating evidence-based practice is easy—but we are saying it is desirable, necessary, and must be taken seriously by every student and professional. Today is the day to start, if even with a small step. We welcome you to open this book, open your mind, and determine how you can best contribute to the outcomes movement within therapeutic recreation. The field and our clients are depending on you.

Acknowledgments

This book represents the collective work of a fabulous group of authors. I am always overwhelmed (and grateful) for the high-quality thinking and writing of my colleagues. This book's seventeen authors, listed on the next page, are an awesome, eclectic, and talented gathering, dedicated to giving readers the most up-to-date and thought-provoking information possible. I am always inspired by their individual and synergistic efforts and am grateful to be among them.

Thanks also to my own professional cheering section: Nancy Navar, University of Wisconsin–LaCrosse; Patricia Malik, Malik Companies, Ltd.; Carol Peterson; and Jan Sneegas; as well as my personal cheering section: Randy Duncan, Nancy Lockett, Barb Busch, and Francis W. Stumbo. Thanks for the encouragement and hours of active listening skills (on your parts!). Love you all.

Thanks also to the Venture crew—Michele, Richard, Valerie, and Kay. Unbelievable skills and patience—you guys are great!

List of Contributors

Candace Ashton-Shaeffer
University of North Carolina at
Wilmington

Linda L. Caldwell
The Pennsylvania State University

Cynthia Carruthers
University of Nevada—Las Vegas

Diane Etzel-Wise
Central Missouri State University

Jan S. Hodges
University of North Texas

Colleen D. Hood
Oklahoma State University

John M. Jacobson
Department of Veterans Affairs

Bryan P. McCormick
Indiana University

Susan "BOON" Murray
University of Wisconsin—LaCrosse

Mason Peebles
University of North Texas

Jo-Ellen Ross
Chicago State University

Carmen V. Russoniello
Eastern Carolina University

Norma J. Stumbo
Illinois State University

Mary S. Wells
Brigham Young University

Mark A. Widmer
Brigham Young University

Barbara Wilhite
University of North Texas

Ramon Zabriskie
Brigham Young University

Brief biographical sketches are located on page 271.

Outcomes, Accountability, and Therapeutic Recreation

Norma J. Stumbo, Ph.D., CTRS
Illinois State University

Accountability. Performance Improvement. Efficiency. Clinical
Guidelines. Outcomes. Efficacy. Outcome Measurement.
Assessment. Evidence-Based Practice. Clinical Control Trials.
Consensus. Effectiveness. Standardization. Best Practices.
Practice-Based Evidence.

To most therapeutic recreation (TR) students and professionals, these terms can seem like a foreign language. However, these terms and many others now are deeply embedded within the lexicon of healthcare providers due to accountability pressures from external regulators, third-party payers, and consumers. The purpose of this chapter is to provide an overview of the burgeoning healthcare outcome movement and TR's responsibility and potential to contribute to it. Background information on the growth of the outcomes movement and related terminology precedes the discussion of important outcomes in healthcare and therapeutic recreation. Important characteristics of outcome measurement and a classification scheme for outcome measurement methods are presented, followed by a presentation of the relationship between outcomes research and evidence-based practice.

   In 1998, Americans spent about one out of every eight dollars on healthcare. That equaled $1.1 trillion dollars or $4,000 for every man, woman, and child in the country, which was approximately a fourfold increase since 1980. In that same time period, personal income doubled, meaning that healthcare expenditures increased at twice the rate of income over those two decades. In 1998, healthcare equaled 13.5% of the national gross domestic product. It is projected that healthcare spending will double again to $2.1 trillion in 2007 (Health Care Financing Administration, 2000; National Coalition on

Healthcare, 2000). It is not surprising then that external accreditation bodies, third-party payers, and healthcare consumers want "proof" that they are getting the most benefit for their treatment dollars—no matter where they are being served within the healthcare system (Stumbo & Hess, 2001).

The healthcare outcome movement represents a major shift in thinking and practice for both providers and consumers. In addressing behavioral health providers, Granello, Granello, and Lee (1999) noted

> Historically, mental health practitioners used professional judg-
> ment and theoretical beliefs to determine client care so long as
> such treatment did not violate state laws and ethical principles…
> however, mental health service delivery has entered an era of
> accountability in healthcare that has shifted the balance of power
> from suppliers to consumers (e.g., clients, employers, third-party
> payers). (p. 50)

Professional judgment, expertise, and clinical experience can no longer be the sole justification for service delivery and evaluation. In the current healthcare environment, the need to determine the cost-effectiveness of interventions requires the use of assessments that produce valid, reliable, and meaningful baseline information; clinical practice guidelines that describe the interventions proven to be most effective for different groups of clients; outcomes measures that are robust, yet sensitive enough to yield dependable, accurate, and incremental data; and methodologically sound research procedures (Mordock, 2000). While professional judgment, expertise, and clinical experience are not neglected, they become only a part of the overall decision-making process that relies heavily on informed, standardized data to best address client needs.

More work is needed within TR services to substantiate and measure outcomes (Riley, 1991b; Stumbo & Hess, 2001). This need is immediate and real in all healthcare professions. Therapeutic recreation specialists (TRSs) would do well to heed the warning issued by Granello, Granello, and Lee (1999) to mental health professionals: "If mental health professionals continue to abdicate their responsibility for measuring outcomes, then it can only be assumed that others, in the government or the insurance industry, will conduct their own outcome research to dictate client care" (p. 51).

Why Have Outcomes Gained Importance?

Many pressures have entered the healthcare picture in the last two decades. Blankertz and Cook (1998) established that these pressures are being felt in every aspect of healthcare and have elevated outcomes to prime importance for providers. According to West (2000)

[M]any sources including payers, government, employers, regulatory agencies, and consumers are exerting significant pressure on healthcare providers to demonstrate that services provided are safe, effective, and produce necessary outcomes at a reasonable cost. Healthcare providers are more involved than ever in assessing outcomes in response to various accountability systems. (p. 81)

The United Kingdom Clearing House on Health Outcomes noted eight global reasons for increased interest in and pressure to measure outcomes:

(a) to eliminate poor/unnecessary practise and promote good practise;

(b) to aid negotiations between purchasers [of healthcare] and providers;

(c) to increase the accountability of services following separation of purchasers and providers;

(d) to develop means to evaluate services for the chronically ill;

(e) to empower consumers and involve them in service evaluation and planning;

(f) to evaluate new services;

(g) to inform priority setting and resource allocation; and

(h) to help set, monitor, and improve standards of care. (1997, p. 1)

Blankertz and Cook (1998) recorded several benefits for agencies focusing on outcomes besides the general notion of demonstrating effectiveness. They felt that outcome measurement contributes to performance improvement (see Chapter 12) and program evaluation (see Chapter 11) through identifying areas of need and areas of strength. Secondly, Blankertz and Cook noted that, done well, outcomes measurement may improve staff morale and job satisfaction through service feedback. Thirdly, they noted that tracking outcomes puts a positive focus on outcome attainment, which may result in higher quality work.

A number of TR authors have echoed similar reasons for establishing outcomes of TR intervention. Among these reasons are

• to verify appropriate and quality services (i.e., treatment effectiveness) rather than just "knowing" and "feeling" in our hearts that valuable services are provided (Caldwell, 2001; Coyle, Kinney, Riley & Shank, 1991; Coyle, Kinney & Shank, 1991; Kloseck, Crilly, Ellis & Lammers, 1996; Lee & Yang, 2000; Scalenghe, 1991; Shank & Kinney, 1991; Shank, Kinney & Coyle, 1993; Stumbo, 2000; Stumbo & Peterson, 2004; West, 2000);

- to measure the relationship between various program and treatment protocols for specific illness or diagnostic categories and the associated outcomes of those treatments (i.e., treatment efficiency; Hodges & Luken, 2000; Hood, 2001; Johnson & Ashton-Shaeffer, 2000; Kloseck, Crilly, Ellis & Lammers, 1996; McCormick & Funderburk, 2000; Riley, 1991a);

- to lay a legitimate claim to a portion of the competitive health-care dollar, and to prove that TR services may lower overall healthcare costs (Kloseck, Crilly, Ellis & Lammers, 1996; Russoniello, 2000; Shank & Kinney, 1991; West, 2000);

- to spur continued acceptance, and enhance growth and support of the profession (Lee & Yang, 2000; Riley, 1991b; Shank & Kinney, 1991; Shank, Kinney & Coyle, 1993); and

- to provide valuable information for the future improvement of programs (Dunn, Sneegas & Carruthers, 1991; Johnson & Ashton-Shaeffer, 2000; Lee & Yang, 2000; West, 2000).

What Are Outcomes?

Central to this discussion is the definition of healthcare outcomes. Several authors have noted that outcomes measures are the documentable changes in client behavior, skills, and/or attitudes that can be attributed to active participation in a TR intervention program (Dunn, Sneegas & Carruthers, 1991; Shank & Kinney, 1991; Stumbo, 1996; Stumbo & Peterson, 2004). Table 1.1 contains a variety of definitions of outcomes, both internal to and external from therapeutic recreation. The majority of these definitions agree that outcomes represent the differences in the client from the beginning compared to end of treatment (and perhaps beyond).

The common element of these definitions is that outcomes are the difference(s) noted in the client from entry into compared to exit from clinical services. Figure 1.1 depicts this difference (Jacobson, personal communication, 2000). Of course most clinicians are hopeful that the changes or outcomes are positive (in the desired direction of treatment) and result directly from active participation within treatment services. Before the measurement issues surrounding these assumptions are discussed, a review of outcomes terminology is provided.

Table 1.1 Definitions of outcomes

Author	Definition
Wade (1999, p. 93)	The (change in a) state or situation that arises as a result of some process of intervention.
McCormick and Funderbunk (2000, p. 10)	Refers to change in a client's status over time.
Blankertz and Cook (1998, p. 170)	Reported as changes in the score between two points of time on individual-level standardized instruments.
JCAHO (1995, p. 717)	The results of performance (or nonperformance) of function(s) or process(es).
Shank and Kinney (1991, p. 76)	The observed changes in a client's status as a result of our interventions and interactions, whether intended or not.... the complications, adverse effects, or short- or long-term changes experienced by our clients represent the efforts of our care....Can be attributed to the process of providing care, and should enable us to determine if we are doing for our clients that which we purport to do.
Riley (1991b, p. 58)	The direct effects of service upon the well-being of both the individual and specified populations; the end result of medical care; what happened to the patient in terms of palliation, control of illness, cure, or rehabilitation.
Scalenghe (1991, p. 30)	Clinical results

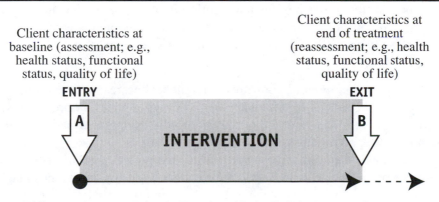

Figure 1.1 Illustration of client outcomes

Important Terminology Related to Outcomes

Each initiative has its own terminology, and outcome measurement is no exception. Although there are other terms in the literature, the following are the most prominent as noted by Stumbo (2000).

Effectiveness characterizes how an intervention works under everyday circumstances in routine clinical practice (Aral & Peterman, 1998; Powe, 1996).

> The effectiveness of an intervention is the impact an intervention achieves in the real world, under resource constraints, in entire populations, or in specified subgroups of a population. It is the improvement in a health outcome achieved in a typical community setting. (Aral & Peterman, 1998; p. 3)

Effectiveness studies attempt to address the degree to which clients improve under treatment as it is actually practiced in the field (i.e., with fewer controls and manipulations than in efficacy research designs; Granello, Granello & Lee, 1999).

Efficacy characterizes how an intervention performs under ideal or more controlled circumstances (Aral & Peterman, 1998; Powe, 1996). "Efficacy is the improvement in health outcome achieved in a research setting, in expert hands, under ideal circumstances" (Aral & Peterman, 1998, p. 3). It usually requires randomization to treatment and control groups, and a specific intervention for the treatment group—that usually has met criteria for a single diagnosis (Granello, Granello & Lee, 1999). In comparing *effectiveness* and *efficacy*, Aral and Peterman explained:

> [E]ffectiveness of an intervention is the product of its efficacy, the penetration or reach of the intervention into the population, and the compliance of the population with the intervention. In general, effectiveness is lower than efficacy, though theoretically, it could be higher. (1998, p. 4)

Effectiveness research compares different healthcare practices or interventions (e.g., medical technologies such as drugs, devices, or procedures) covering the following areas: mortality, morbidity, symptoms, satisfaction, quality of life, preferences, and costs (Powe, 1996).

Outcomes-based management research incorporates similar methods to compare performance under different providers (e.g., physicians, hospitals, clinics, facilities) under the same headings, often for purposes of quality assessment and utilization review (Powe, 1996).

Outcome risk is the probability of a poor outcome that clients bring to the treatment episode; the higher the client's pretreatment risk status, the lower the expected outcome from the episode of care (Hendryx, Dyck & Srebnik, 1999).

Patient outcomes research uses, in additional to more traditional methods, new markers of health status and quality of life, symptoms (particularly those that are bothersome), patient preferences, patient satisfaction, costs, and cost-effectiveness (Powe, 1996).

Near-patient testing (Delaney et al., 1999) or *point-of-care methods* (Dufault & Sullivan, 2000; Hudson, Christenson, Newby, Kaplan & Ohman, 1999) research is performed in locations where treatment decisions are made and care is delivered based on the results of these tests (e.g., research conducted in an outpatient clinic or an emergency room).

Evidence-based medicine or practice means that the practice of medicine should be based on the best available scientific knowledge or evidence of its efficacy (Linde, 1999; Margison et al., 2000). *Practice-based evidence* is the complementary activity in which research reflects routine clinical practice or evidence of its effectiveness (Margison et al., 2000).

Clinical practice improvement is a method for examining the steps of a care process to determine how to achieve the best medical outcomes at the least necessary cost over the continuum of a patient's care (Horn, 1997).

Clinical importance may be contrary to reported statistical significance in the findings of a particular research study but results still would lead to the conclusion of an important difference in patient outcome and in patient health status (Hatala, Holbrook & Goldsmith, 1999). The authors advocate using clinical judgment to determine clinical significance or importance versus statistical significance.

These are the most commonly used terms within the healthcare outcome literature. Many of the concepts are foundational for understanding the mandates of outcome measurement.

Important Outcomes in Healthcare and Therapeutic Recreation

Many authors have attempted to classify outcomes into broader health and functional outcome categories. In general, healthcare outcomes can be divided into five overall categories: (a) clinical status, (b) functional status, (c) well-being or quality of life, (d) satisfaction (Hendryx, Dyck & Srebnik, 1999; McGlynn, 1995), and (e) cost or resource consumption (Johnson, 1993).

Clinical status may include measurements of psychopathology, symptomatology, short-term changes in symptoms or severity of problems or syndromes targeted by services (Hendryx, Dyck & Srebnik, 1999; Mason, 2000). McCormick and Funderburk (2000) cited Granger (1984) and Ware

(1997) to describe clinical status as changes that are measured at the organ level, such as blood pressure, temperature, white blood cell count, respiration, and fitness.

Functional status includes the ability to fulfill social and role functions that reflect broad long-term effects after services have ended and which tend to reflect a person or family's ability to lead a successful, productive, satisfying life. Examples include ADLs; life and self-care skills; safety; stability of living environment; relationship abilities such as marriage, parenting, and sibling interactions; school or employment status; and engagement in at-risk behaviors (Granger, 1984; Hendryx, Dyck & Srebnik, 1999; Mason, 2000; McCormick & Funderburk, 2000; Tully & Cantrill, 1999; Ware, 1997).

Well-being or *quality of life* includes the personal or subjective definition of well-being for the individual. It may involve relative assessment of satisfaction with living conditions, work or school, leisure, finances, and whether basic and fundamental needs are met (Hendryx, Dyck & Srebnik, 1999; Mason, 2000; McCormick & Funderburk, 2000; Russo, Roy-Byrne, Jaffe & Ries, 1997).

Satisfaction measures usually target satisfaction with services received. These assessments may help to determine the patients' opinions whether care is accessible, affordable, effective, and professional (Hendryx, Dyck & Srebnik, 1999; Mason, 2000; McCormick & Funderburk, 2000; Mordock, 2000).

Costs and resource consumption balance the need to reduce costs with unfavorable impacts on the quality of care (Johnson, 1993).

Typical TR Outcomes

Several authors in the field have noted that therapeutic recreation has the capability of identifying outcomes involving clinical status (Lee & Yang, 2000; McCormick & Funderburk, 2000; Russoniello, 2000), functional status (Coyle, Kinney, Riley & Shank, 1991; Lee & McCormick, 2002; Lee & Yang, 2000; McCormick & Funderburk, 2000; Shank & Coyle, 2002; Stumbo & Peterson, 2004), well-being (Stumbo & Peterson, 2004), satisfaction (Coyle, Kinney, Riley & Shank, 1991; McCormick & Funderburk, 2000), and resource consumption (West, 2000).

The following outcomes are typical of those targeted for TR intervention, although most are not fully supported by clinical research nor written in enough detail for measurement purposes (adapted from Coyle, Kinney, Riley & Shank, 1991; Stumbo & Peterson, 2004):

- increased emotional control;
- improved physical condition;

- decreased disruptive behavior in group situations;
- improved short-term and long-term memory;
- decreased confusion and disorientation;
- decreased symptoms of anxiety and depression;
- improved mobility in community environments and situations;
- improved health indicators, such as bone density, heart rate, and joint mobility;
- improved coping and adaptation skills;
- increased awareness of barriers to leisure;
- improved ability to prevent, manage, and cope with stress;
- improved adjustment to disability and illness;
- improved understanding of importance of leisure to balanced lifestyle;
- improved communication among family members;
- increased ability to use assertiveness skills in a variety of social situations;
- improved opportunities for planning, making choices, and taking responsibility;
- improved ability to locate leisure partners for activity involvement;
- improved knowledge of agencies and facilities that provide recreation services;
- improved knowledge of leisure opportunities in the community;
- increased life and leisure satisfaction;
- increased ability to develop and maintain social support networks; and
- improved general psychological health.

Important Characteristics of Outcomes

In order for outcomes to be useful, they must have relevance, importance, and be attainable during the measurement period (Riley, 1991b; Stumbo & Peterson, 2004). Dunn, Sneegas, and Carruthers (1991) noted that within the profession of therapeutic recreation a variety of terms (e.g., objectives, behavioral objectives, performance measures) have been used to define what is currently termed outcome measures (see Chapter 10). What outcomes are relevant? What outcomes carry the greatest importance to clients? What outcomes are attainable during (especially brief) intervention? The answers to these questions may be unique for each individual agency. Stumbo (2000) documented six characteristics of outcomes that are valued and have utility for measurement purposes. These six characteristics include

- Outcomes must be *identified*. This task is of primary importance and must be done before other measurement tasks are undertaken (Johnson & Ashton-Shaeffer, 2000; Stumbo, 2000; Stumbo & Hess, 2001; Stumbo & Peterson, 2004). What outcomes from the TR service are important to the clients seen at this facility? What target outcomes fit within the scope of TR practice that will benefit these clients and fall within the intent of this facility and its other healthcare disciplines?

- Outcomes must be *measurable* (Buettner, 2000; Hodges & Luken, 2000; Stumbo & Peterson, 2004). While most healthcare providers believe their services contribute to the overall, global health and well-being of their clients, these "measures" often are deemed to be too broad and lack meaning in today's healthcare environment. There is greater interest in defining outcomes more specifically and in smaller terms. TRSs need to locate and document outcomes in the five areas previously mentioned: clinical status, functional status, well-being or quality of life, satisfaction with care, and cost/resource utilization. What categories of outcomes or outcome indicators are produced by TR services? What important outcomes of TR services are measurable, and how and when will they be measured? Will these measurements be sensitive to change within a short time period?

- Outcomes must be *achievable* (Hodges & Luken, 2000; Johnson & Ashton-Shaeffer, 2000). Shortened lengths of stay have complicated the accomplishments of most healthcare professionals. With fewer days of inpatient or even outpatient care, it is difficult and sometimes impossible to achieve the outcomes that may have been identified five or ten years ago. What can be accomplished within a patient's two-day or five-day stay? What is important in this person's treatment, and how can it be achieved? It has been a difficult task for most TR professionals to narrow their scope of measurement (and programming) to fit the patient's length of stay.

- Outcomes must be *demonstrable* or *documented* (Buettner, 2000; Stumbo & Peterson, 2004). For example, if a stress management program is to produce measurable changes in the clients' behavior, attitude, or level of stress, the TRS must be able to document that change. Often this means having valid and reliable instruments or tools that measure the level of behavior, attitude, or knowledge that is targeted, and how that changed as the result of care. It also means having a body of research that supports these outcomes (Seibert, 1991).

- Outcomes must be *predictable* or *causal* (Riley, 1991b). That is, there must be a direct relationship between the intervention and the outcome. Using the example of a stress management program, it would be unwise to measure differences in leisure attitudes as an outcome since a change in leisure attitudes is unlikely to be directly attributable to a stress management program.

- Outcomes must be *meaningful* (Buettner, 2000; Devine & Wilhite, 1999; Johnson & Ashton-Shaeffer, 2000; Lee & Yang, 2000; McCormick & Funderburk, 2000; Shank, Coyle, Kinney & Lay, 1995). With all these listed constraints, client outcomes must still be meaningful to the client and his or her recovery or health status, as well as valuable to third-party payers. What important contribution does therapeutic recreation make to the client's success? What unique contribution does therapeutic recreation make to other services on the healthcare team? What outcome changes in the client would make the most difference in his or her life?

Outcomes must be identified, measurable, achievable, documented, causal, and meaningful—no small task for any healthcare profession. The next section discusses the requirements of outcome measurement.

What Is Outcome Measurement?

As simplistic as this may sound, there are two broad concerns in outcome measurement: which outcomes to measure, and how to measure them. Both decisions go hand in hand and often require serious thought and discussion among all those concerned.

Measurement simply refers to the quantification of data in some way, either in absolute terms or in relative terms.

Thus, in order to evaluate the outcome of a process one has to decide and specify what the rehabilitation process is trying to achieve. It is only sensible to measure those factors that the process will or might affect. The measure chosen should focus on the intended area(s) of concern and, as far as possible, should not cover any other extraneous areas. (Wade, 1999, p. 93)

The measurement system may include several steps and decisions. Each one becomes important as it affects other decisions about how, what, and when to measure.

Ensuring that an effective outcome measurement strategy is developed or adopted, identifying who should be responsible for measuring outcomes and maintaining the system, identifying what to measure and how, and producing impactful reports are all important elements that can support collecting outcome data. (Mason, 2000, p. 77)

Careful consideration of the impact of each decision is necessary. "Instrumentation determines the type of data that be obtained, and choices must be made with care....The basic research questions that are being investigated provide guidance as to the type of instrument selected" (Granello, Granello & Lee, 1999, p. 57). Instrumentation or measurement is the "how" after the "what" of outcomes have been determined.

For example, a TRS in a behavioral health partial hospitalization program might ask the following questions:

- To what extent do patients who receive TR intervention improve their ability to plan and carry out leisure involvement?
- To what extent do patients who receive TR intervention improve their ability to socialize with friends and family?
- To what extent are these improvements (if any) sustained over time?
- Do any demographic (e.g., gender, age, family structure) or "treatment risk" factors affect the success rate of the treatment?
- Are patients satisfied with the intervention received?

Outcome measurement then looks for documentable information to demonstrate the effectiveness of TR intervention with these questions in mind. Wade (1999) cautioned "the growth in the outcome measurement industry is rational if it is considered to provide us with better tools to use in various ways" (p. 95). More information on the methods that can be used to gather outcome information is included in the next chapter on evidence-based practice.

Important Characteristics of Outcome Measures

Mason (2000) cautioned that designers not lose sight of the purpose of outcome measurement: "The whole purpose of developing an outcome measurement system is not to measure outcomes, but rather to evaluate services and make changes based on results" (p. 82). In order to stay focused, many authors suggest that agencies establish clear definitions of outcomes, measure them in simple but meaningful ways, and focus on interpretation and use of the information gained.

At the same time that therapeutic recreation strives to more narrowly define its contribution to healthcare services in terms of valued outcomes, it also needs to examine measurement systems that result in dependable evidence that reduces the likelihood of error and increases the likelihood of demonstrating efficacy and effectiveness. Stumbo (2000) and Stumbo and Hess (2001) noted targeted outcomes must be based on solid evidence of *empirically based*, *integrative*, and *standardized* treatment that produces predictable, measurable changes in the client's status.

Newman and Ciarlo (1994) listed eleven principles for selecting outcome measures. These authors stated that outcome measures should

- be relevant to the target group;
- have a simple, teachable methodology;
- use objective (i.e., observable) referents;
- use multiple respondents;
- identify outcomes that are the results of the rehabilitation process;
- have solid psychometric data;
- have a low implementation cost;
- be understandable by a nonprofessional audience;
- involve easy feedback and uncomplicated interpretation;
- be useful in clinical services; and
- be compatible with clinical theories and with practices.

Blankertz and Cook (1998) agreed with several authors in this text that outcome measures should represent the consumer perspective. In addition, they suggested that, for mental health at least, outcome measures should look at individuals who leave treatment as well as those who stay. Others would probably agree this perspective is important in other areas of healthcare besides mental health.

Granello, Granello, and Lee (1999) noted that outcome measures must be cost-efficient and sensitive to meaningful change (i.e., able to measure sometimes small, incremental changes in clients' behavior). Mason (2000) noted they should support accountability and quality of services, the general trend of quantification of services, increased competition for services, and requirements for funding or contractual services, and address the concerns of multiple stakeholders.

Wade (1999) pointed to the potential conflicts between multiple stakeholders, such as providers and purchasers:

> The choice of outcome measures requires full discussion by the service provider and by the service purchaser—often they may have different goals. For example, purchasers often are looking for simple independence in personal activities of daily living and discharge from hospital, or for return to paid employment, whereas providers may have wider interests such as *maximizing leisure participation and social interaction* [emphasis added]. Therefore providers and purchasers may not agree on a suitable measure of outcome because they do not agree on the aims of the service. (p. 93)

Hendryx, Dyck, and Srebnik (1999) agreed that different outcomes may be valued by different stakeholders. Asking the question "What questions am I trying to answer?" (Wade, 1999, p. 94) will aid in focusing and simplifying the outcome measurement process. The answers to this question are likely to be based on the five outcome domains mentioned earlier (i.e., clinical status, functional status, well-being or quality of life, satisfaction, and cost/resource concerns) as well as theoretical orientations to care (see Chapters 4 and 11).

Wade (1999) addressed a common concern in interpreting outcome measurement results within settings that utilize multidisciplinary treatment teams—measuring the degree or extent of contribution of each individual discipline as well as the synergy of the collective whole. He provided a diagram of these contribution complexities (adapted in Figure 1.2) to highlight the difficulties inherent in trying to tease out the individual contributions of each therapy.

Mason (2000) noted that it is essential for agencies to set clear boundaries about what data will be collected and how it will be used. He suggested that, as a beginning, agencies find ways to incorporate outcome measurement into existing operations within the agency. He also noted that measurement systems do not need to be elaborate or extensive to meet the agency's outcome measurement needs. "Outcome measurement systems need not be sophisticated algorithms or complex statistical analyses to be useful" (Mason, 2000, p. 82). He suggested that measurement strategies be limited to a practical few, and in that way, results are more easily interpreted and used. McGlynn (1995) added that data sources typically include administrative data, medical records, and surveys.

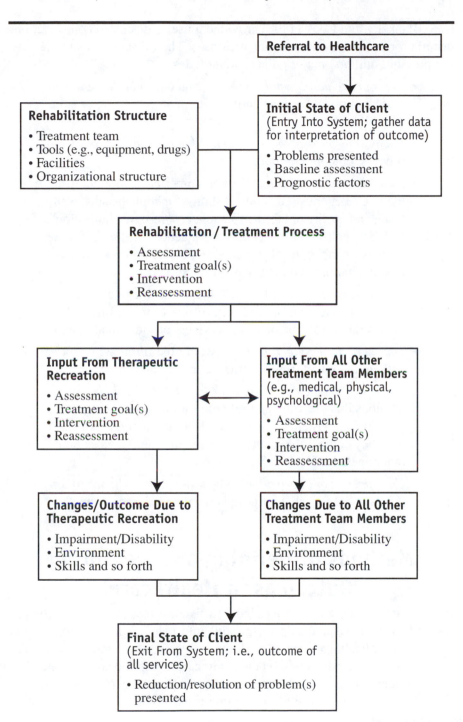

Figure 1.2 Rehabilitation structure, process, and outcome (adapted from Wade, 1999, p. 94)

Blankertz and Cook (1998) provided a useful discussion on selection criteria for outcomes and outcome measures. Their discussion summarizes the previous authors' major points and includes

- *Appropriate unit of analysis:* Is the outcome and measurement system applicable to the entire system, a specific service, or a specific client?

- *Focus of the measurement system:* What is the major concern— process, outcome, or both?

- *Domain(s) to be covered:* What outcomes are important from the five categories (i.e., clinical status, functional status, well-being and quality of life, satisfaction, cost/resource utilization)? Will data collection reflect the consequences of illness in areas such as financial, legal, educational, residential, vocational, hospitalization, and quality of life?

- *Source of data:* From where will the data come (e.g., information systems, clients' self-report, relevant others, survey)? Will it report the outcomes of services for individual clients?

- *Timing of data collection:* Over what time frame will data be gathered—only during treatment, or after discharge?

- *Quality of the measurement instruments:* Will collection methods that are valid and reliable for outcome purposes be used in a consistent manner to collect incremental changes? Are they comparable with those used in other services or at other agencies?

- *Consumer(s) of information:* Who will be the audience(s) for the data and for what purpose is the data being collected?

Methods of Defining and Measuring Outcomes in Healthcare

Patient outcome research, often called effectiveness research, is an evolving research discipline that attempts to provide information about the appropriate application of healthcare practices (Powe, 1996). This information can take a variety of forms, depending on the healthcare discipline and the nature of their services and patients. There have been several classification schemes for outcomes research. The following one is used by Powe (1996) as noted by Stumbo (2000).

Powe (1996) presented eight categories of methods used to measure healthcare outcomes: (a) epidemiological methods, (b) analysis of variations and outcomes in practice, (c) formal literature reviews and meta-analyses,

(d) quality-of-life measurements, (e) decision analyses, (f) patient preference assessment, (g) patient satisfaction assessment, and (h) economic and cost-effectiveness analyses. Many of these categories overlap and can be combined, for example measuring the economic realities of achieving various states of quality of life.

Epidemiology is

a science that studies the frequencies and distributions of disease and health conditions among population groups.…[C]omparison and contrast are used to determine whether groups of people who share a common characteristic (such as people who exercise) experience some condition (such as coronary heart disease) with the same frequency of occurrence as another group (such as sedentary people). (Thomas & Nelson, 1996, pp. 134–135)

Analysis of variations in medical practice and outcomes demonstrate differences in patient management procedures, such as between different facilities or in different geographic regions (Powe, 1996). *Formal literature reviews* and *meta-analyses* are related but separate types of studies. Literature reviews make a formal attempt to synthesize all written literature to find threads of common understanding on a certain procedure or practice. Meta-analyses perform a similar function, but do so through statistical analyses of all the major data points in the sample studies (Thomas & Nelson, 1996).

Powe (1996) identified two categories of *quality-of-life studies*: (a) those using global measures of quality of life that can be applied to different diseases, and (b) disease-specific measures of quality of life. The former can be used to compare between different groups of patients; the latter describes one group's more narrow experiences.

Decision analyses

involve explicit identification of treatment choices, review of evidence-based studies on factors such as prevalence of disease, incidence of complications, and quantitative comparison of those choices through the use of sophisticated computer programs.… [D]ecision analysis is particularly useful for examining trade-offs between clinical outcomes and costs. (Powe, 1996, p. 232)

Patient preference of treatment options (e.g., choosing between a lumpectomy and chemotherapy vs. a mastectomy) and *patient satisfaction* are both difficult to measure with meaning. "Patient involvement in decision making is receiving greater attention because of its potential impact on health outcomes. Patient compliance and satisfaction may be enhanced through involvement" (Powe, 1996, p. 233). Both preference and satisfaction, however, depend on a highly informed patient as a consumer of healthcare.

According to Powe (1996, p. 233) there are three basic types of *economic investigations*: (a) cost-identification studies, (b) cost-effectiveness analyses, and (c) cost-benefit analyses. Cost-identification studies measure the contribution of different types of resources to aggregate healthcare costs. Cost-effectiveness analysis is a method that allows for the enumeration and comparison of costs and benefits of different medical interventions. In cost-effectiveness analysis costs are expressed in monetary terms, and in cost-benefit analysis there is greater interest in clinical outcomes, such as lives saved or complications avoided. In cost-utility analysis, a variant of cost-effectiveness analysis, clinical benefits are commonly measured in quality adjusted life years (i.e., quality of life resulting from the use of one intervention vs. another).

Powe's (1996) classification scheme is but one noted in the healthcare literature. In more recent years, randomized control trials and systematic reviews of randomized control trials have been strongly advocated as superior methods for evidence-based practice. The next chapter will discuss these methods along a continuum of "confidence" that can be placed in the results of outcomes research.

The Relationship Between Outcomes, Outcomes Research, and Evidence-Based Practice

As Lee and Yang (2000, p. 21) noted: "Simply speaking, evidence-based practice attempts to integrate outcome research into practice." Evidence-based practice is the process of applying the results of outcomes research to improve day-to-day TR services to clients. Evidence-based practice is the collective, well-researched wisdom about outcomes that can be expected from standardized clinical intervention. The primary motives behind evidence-based practice are to reduce risk and increase quality of care as much as possible (Lee & McCormick, 2002). This is best achieved through a meaningful, standardized, and integrated research knowledge base.

This book intends to provide TR professionals with ideas and motivation to continue their efforts in outcomes research and evidence-based practice. The following chapters discuss the importance of being systematic in designing, implementing, and evaluating TR services. They stress the importance of first selecting meaningful outcomes, then designing programs and services in ways that can best ensure those outcomes. They also emphasize the contributions toward evidence-based practice that each practicing professional in therapeutic recreation needs to make.

Outcome development within therapeutic recreation does not need to be thought of as an impossible mission or even unreasonably difficult. In fact, it is quite possible. "Although it may be challenging for practitioners to specify and measure client outcomes related to involvement in their programs" (Dunn, Sneegas & Carruthers, 1991, p. 109), more concentrated research in this area is imperative. This requires a paradigm shift to ensure that outcomes are empirically based, integrated, and standardized. Evidence needs to be found that supports that particular interventions have demonstrated desirable consequences (Shank & Kinney, 1991). Challenge can no longer be an excuse, it is time to rise up and "demonstrate accountability for those services that we all have always 'known' and 'felt' in our hearts to be an essential component of quality care" (Scalenghe, 1991, p. 41). How each specialist "practices" therapeutic recreation matters a great deal. Sound decisions that integrate all aspects of assessment, planning, implementation, and evaluation are paramount to being able to produce important, logical, and necessary client outcomes.

Summary

The intent of this chapter was to provide introductory information on outcomes, outcomes measurement, and evidence-based practice. The growing importance of outcomes was presented along with several definitions of healthcare outcomes and related terminology. Also addressed were the five categories of healthcare outcomes (i.e., clinical status, functional status, well-being and quality of life, satisfaction, and cost/resource utilization), and typical TR outcomes. Definitions, characteristics, and methods used to determine healthcare outcomes were discussed, along with their relationship to evidence-based practice. This background information intends to provide a solid foundation for the remaining chapters in this text.

Discussion Questions

1. What forces have popularized the healthcare outcomes movement? How has this impacted the provision of healthcare in the United States and other countries?

2. What TR outcomes may be important in the following settings: oncology? physical medicine and rehabilitation? behavioral health? pediatrics? schools? long-term care? substance abuse?

3. Choose one example from the previous question and describe an outcome measurement plan that fits the criteria given within this chapter. Which are the easier parts to design? Which parts are harder to design?

4. In which areas are therapeutic recreation further ahead in outcomes measurement, and in which are we further behind?

5. What are the primary characteristics of good outcome measurement systems?

6. Describe the relationship between outcomes, outcome measurement, and evidence-based practice.

7. Design a personal professional development plan that includes your contribution to the outcomes movement within TR services.

References

Aral, S.O. and Peterman, T.A. (1998). Do we know the effectiveness of behavioural interventions? *Lancet, Supplement STD's, 351*(9119), 33–37.

Blankertz, L. and Cook, J.A. (1998). Choosing and using outcome measures. *Psychiatric Rehabilitation Journal, 22*(2), 167–174.

Buettner, L.L. (2000). Gerontological recreation therapy: Examining the trends and making a forecast. *Annual in Therapeutic Recreation, 9*, 35–46.

Caldwell, L.L. (2001). The role of theory in therapeutic recreation: A practical approach. In N.J. Stumbo (Ed.), *Professional issues in therapeutic recreation: On competence and outcomes* (pp. 349–364). Champaign, IL: Sagamore.

Coyle, C.P., Kinney, W.B., Riley, B., and Shank, J.W. (Eds.). (1991). *Benefits of therapeutic recreation: A consensus view*. Philadelphia, PA: Temple University Press.

Coyle, C.P., Kinney, W.B., and Shank, J.W. (1991). A summary of benefits common to therapeutic recreation. In C.P. Coyle, W.B. Kinney, B. Riley, and J.W. Shank (Eds.), *Benefits of therapeutic recreation: A consensus view* (pp. 353–385). Philadelphia, PA: Temple University Press.

Delaney, B.C., Hyde, C.J., McManus, R.J., Wilson, S., Fitzmaurice, D.A., Jowett, S., Tobias, R., and Thorpe, G.H. (1999). Systematic review of near patient test evaluations in primary care. *British Medical Journal, 319*(7213), 824–827.

Devine, M.A. and Wilhite, B. (1999). Theory application in therapeutic recreation practice and research. *Therapeutic Recreation Journal, 33*(1), 29–45.

Dufault, M.A. and Sullivan, M. (2000). A collaborative research utilization approach to evaluate the effects of pain management standards on patient outcomes. *Journal of Professional Nursing, 16*(4), 240–250.

Dunn, J.K., Sneegas, J.J., and Carruthers, C.A. (1991). Outcomes measures: Monitoring patient progress. In B. Riley (Ed.), *Quality management: Applications for therapeutic recreation* (pp. 107–115). State College, PA: Venture Publishing, Inc.

Granello, D.H., Granello, P.F., and Lee, F. (1999). Measuring treatment outcomes and client satisfaction in a partial hospitalization program. *Journal of Behavioral Health Services and Research, 26*(1), 50–63.

Granger, C.V. (1984). A conceptual model for functional assessment. In C.V. Granger and G.E. Gresham (Eds.), *Functional assessment in rehabilitation medicine* (pp. 14–25). Baltimore, MD: Williams and Wilkins.

Hatala, R., Holbrook, A., and Goldsmith, C.H. (1999). Therapeutic equivalence: All studies are not created equal. *Canadian Journal of Clinical Pharmacology, 6*(1), 9–11.

Health Care Financing Administration. (2000). *Highlights—National Health Expenditures, 1998* [Online]. Retrieved October 18, 2000, from http://www.hcfa.gov/stats/nhe-oact

Hendryx, M.S., Dyck, D.G., and Srebnik, D. (1999). Risk-adjusted outcome models for public mental health outpatient programs. *Health Services Research, 34*(1), 171–195.

Hodges, J.S. and Luken, K. (2000). Services and support as a means to meaningful outcomes for persons with developmental disabilities. *Annual in Therapeutic Recreation, 9*, 47–56.

Hood, C.D. (2001). Clinical practice guidelines—A decision-making tool for best practice? In N.J. Stumbo (Ed.), *Professional issues in therapeutic recreation: On competence and outcomes* (pp. 189–214). Champaign, IL: Sagamore.

Horn, S.D. (1997). Overcoming obstacles to effective treatment: Use of clinical practice improvement methodology. *Journal of Clinical Psychiatry, 58*, 15–19.

Hudson, M.P., Christenson, R.H., Newby, L.K., Kaplan, A.L., and Ohman, E.M. (1999). Cardiac markers: Point of care testing. *Clinica Chimica Acta, 284*(2), 223–237.

Johnson, D.E. and Ashton-Shaeffer, C. (2000). A framework for TR outcomes in school-based settings. *Annual in Therapeutic Recreation, 9*, 57–70.

Johnson, D.E.L. (1993). Scott & White measures "quality of health" in outcomes studies. *Healthcare Strategic Management, 11*(3), 7–9.

Joint Commission on Accreditation of Healthcare Organizations. (1995). *1996 Comprehensive Accreditation Manual for Hospitals*. Oakbrook Terrace, IL: Author.

Kloseck, M., Crilly, R.G., Ellis, G.D., and Lammers, E. (1996). Leisure competence measure: Development and reliability testing of a scale to measure functional outcomes in therapeutic recreation. *Therapeutic Recreation Journal, 30*(1), 13–26.

Lee, Y. and McCormick, B.P. (2002). Toward evidence-based therapeutic recreation practice. In D.R. Austin, D. Dattilo, and B.P. McCormick (Eds.), *Conceptual foundations for therapeutic recreation* (pp. 165–184). State College, PA: Venture Publishing, Inc.

Lee, Y. and Yang, H. (2000). A review of therapeutic recreation outcomes in physical medicine and rehabilitation between 1991–2000. *Annual in Therapeutic Recreation, 9*, 21–34.

Linde, M. (1999). Theory and practice in the management of depressive disorders. *International Clinical Psychopharmacology, 14*, S15–S25.

Margison, F.R., Barkham, M., Evans, C., McGrath, G., Clark, J.M., Audin, K., and Connell, J. (2000). Measurement and psychotherapy—Evidence-based practise and practise-based evidence. *British Journal of Psychiatry, 177*, 123–130.

Mason, M.M. (2000). Meeting the challenges of data collection in outcome systems. *Education and Treatment of Children, 23*(1), 75–95.

McCormick, B.P. and Funderburk, J. (2000). Therapeutic recreation outcomes in mental health practice. *Annual in Therapeutic Recreation, 9*, 9–20.

McGlynn, E.A. (1995). Quality assessment in reproductive health services. *The Western Journal of Medicine, 163*(3), 19–27.

Mordock, J.B. (2000). Outcome assessment: Suggestions for agency practice. *Child Welfare, 79*(6), 689–710.

National Coalition on Healthcare. (2000). *Healthcare facts: What you need to know* [Online]. Retrieved October 18, 2000, from http://www.nchc.org/know/spending.html#spend

Newman, E.L. and Ciarlo, J.A (1994). Criteria for selecting psychological instruments for progress and outcome assessment. In M. Maruish (Ed.), *Use of psychological testing for treatment planning and outcome assessment* (pp. 30–49). Hillsdale, NJ: Lawrence Erlbaum Associates.

Powe, N.R. (1996). Measuring effectiveness and outcomes of interventions for renal disease. *Current Opinion in Nephrology and Hypertension, 5*(3), 230–235.

Riley, B. (1991a). Introduction. In C.P. Coyle, W.B. Kinney, B. Riley, and J.W. Shank (Eds.), *Benefits of therapeutic recreation: A consensus view* (pp. 1–3). Philadelphia, PA: Temple University Press.

Riley, B. (1991b). Quality assessment: The use of outcome indicators. In B. Riley (Ed.), *Quality management: Applications for therapeutic recreation* (pp. 53–67). State College, PA: Venture Publishing, Inc.

Russo, J., Roy-Byrne, P., Jaffe, C., and Ries, R. (1997). The relationship of patient-administered outcome assessments to quality of life and physician ratings: Validity of the BASIS-32. *Journal of Mental Health Administration, 24*(2), 200–214.

Russoniello, C.V. (2000). Recreational therapy and behavioral medicine: Outcomes and cost effectiveness. *Annual in Therapeutic Recreation, 9*, 71–78.

Scalenghe, R. (1991). The Joint Commission's "agenda for change" as related to the provision of therapeutic recreation services. In B. Riley (Ed.), *Quality management: Applications for therapeutic recreation* (pp. 29–42). State College, PA: Venture Publishing, Inc.

Seibert, M.L. (1991). Keynote. In C.P. Coyle, W.B. Kinney, B. Riley, and J.W. Shank (Eds.), *Benefits of therapeutic recreation: A consensus view* (pp. 5–15). Philadelphia, PA: Temple University Press.

Shank, J. and Coyle, C. (2002). *Therapeutic recreation in health promotion and rehabilitation*. State College, PA: Venture Publishing, Inc.

Shank, J.W., Coyle, C.P., Kinney, W.B., and Lay, C. (1995). Using existing data to examine therapeutic recreation services. *Annual in Therapeutic Recreation, 5*, 5–12.

Shank, J.W. and Kinney, W.B. (1991). Monitoring and measuring outcomes in therapeutic recreation. In B. Riley (Ed.), *Quality management: Applications for therapeutic recreation* (pp. 69–88). State College, PA: Venture Publishing, Inc.

Shank, J.W., Kinney, W.B., and Coyle, C.P. (1993). Efficacy studies in therapeutic recreation research: The need, the state of the art, and future implications. In M.J. Malkin and C.Z. Howe (Eds.), *Research in therapeutic recreation: Concepts and methods* (pp. 301–336). State College, PA: Venture Publishing, Inc.

Stumbo, N.J. (1996). A proposed accountability model for therapeutic recreation services. *Therapeutic Recreation Journal, 30*(4), 246–259.

Stumbo, N.J. (2000). Outcome measurement in healthcare: Implications for therapeutic recreation. *Annual in Therapeutic Recreation, 9*, 1–8.

Stumbo, N.J. and Hess, M.E. (2001). On competencies and outcomes in therapeutic recreation. In N.J. Stumbo (Ed.), *Professional issues in therapeutic recreation: On competence and outcomes* (pp. 3–20). Champaign, IL: Sagamore.

Stumbo, N.J. and Peterson, C.A. (2004). *Therapeutic recreation program design: Principles and procedures* (4th ed.). San Francisco, CA: Benjamin Cummings.

Thomas. J.R. and Nelson, J.K. (1996). *Research methods in physical activity* (3rd ed.). Champaign, IL: Human Kinetics.

Tully, M.P. and Cantrill, J.A. (1999). Subjective outcome measurement—A primer. *Pharmacy World and Science, 21*(3), 101–109.

United Kingdom Clearing House on Health Outcomes. (1997). *About health outcomes* [Online]. Retrieved October 18, 2000, from http://www.leeds.ac.uk/nuffield/infoservices/UKCH/about.html

Wade, D.T. (1999). Editorial: Outcome measurement and rehabilitation. *Clinical Rehabilitation, 13*, 93–95.

Ware, J.E., Jr. (1997). Healthcare outcomes from the patient's point of view. In E.J. Mullen and J.L. Magnabosco (Eds.), *Outcomes measurement in human services* (pp. 44–67). Washington, DC: National Association of Social Workers.

West, R.E. (2000). Outcome measurement as an aspect of recreational therapy practice management. *Annual in Therapeutic Recreation, 9*, 79–100.

The Importance of Evidence-Based Practice in Therapeutic Recreation

Norma J. Stumbo, Ph.D., CTRS
Illinois State University

Sometimes we think that therapeutic recreation (TR) professionals are the only service providers who struggle, trying to adjust to the demands and rigors of healthcare in this new age of accountability and cost containment. However, we are far from alone. Many professions, including medicine, nursing, and physical therapy, are grappling with defining quality, identifying clinical end points (outcomes), using clinical performance measures, and increasing accountability at all points of service. While external forces, such as accreditation agencies like the Joint Commission on Accreditation of Healthcare Organizations (JCAHO), third-party payers, and consumer advocacy groups want patient care to be standardized, cost-effective, and well-researched (Stumbo & Hess, 2001), it has been difficult for healthcare professions to meet these challenges consistently.

Coye (2001) in discussing medicine commented

> The structures, incentives, and forces at work in the U.S. health system produce exactly what we should expect in the quality of care for chronic disease: highly variable patterns of care, widespread failure to implement recognized best practices and standards of care, and the persistent inability of provider systems to achieve substantive changes in patterns of practice. Moreover, after more than two decades of effort to improve clinical care management and to promote the adoption of evidence-based standards, these variations [still] persist. (p. 44)

One effort to reduce wide—and unintended—variations in practice is through the adoption of evidence-based practice—using the best, cumulated evidence possible to inform and enlighten practice. Evidence-based practice improves the predictability and causality of service outcomes and provides regulators, payers, and consumers increased assurance of quality care.

Evidence-based practice, in the largest sense, involves four distinct actions of the part of the healthcare professional:

1. Production of evidence through research and scientific review;
2. Production and dissemination of evidence-based clinical guidelines;
3. Implementation of evidence-based, cost-effective practice through education and management of change; and
4. Evaluation of compliance with agreed practice guidance and patient outcomes—this process is called *clinical audit* (Belsey & Snell, 2001).

That is, through evidence-based service delivery, each practitioner should feel confident that she or he is providing the best possible care that is known to produce the most desirable, intended, and meaningful outcomes. The intent of this chapter is to provide the reader with an understanding of evidence-based practice—what it is, how to do it, and some common problems (and proposed solutions) within other healthcare professions.

What Is Evidence-Based Practice?

"Evidence-based practice can be described as the selection of treatments for which there is some evidence of efficacy" (Denton, Walsh & Daniel, 2002, p. 40). This evidence must be gathered through well-designed and meaningful research efforts with client groups and be applicable to daily practice. In the literature, evidence-based practice also is termed *empirically validated treatment*, *empirically supported treatment*, *empirically evaluated treatment*, *empirical practice*, *research-based practice*, *research utilization*, *evidence-based treatment,* and *evidence-based healthcare* (Chambless & Ollendick, 2001; Denton, Walsh & Daniel, 2002; Evidence-Based Medicine Working Group, 1992; Kendall, 1998; Lee & McCormick, 2002). Table 2.1 displays some common definitions of evidence-based practice.

Bliss-Holtz (1999) documented that the term started as evidence-based medicine in the early 1990s within a group of Canadian physicians called the Evidence-Based Medicine Working Group (1992). These individuals popularized the term that then spread to England largely through the efforts of two physicians, David Sackett and William Rosenberg (cf. Rosenberg & Sackett, 1996; Sackett, 1995a, 1995b; Sackett & Rosenberg, 1995a, 1995b, 1995c; Sackett, Rosenberg, Gray, Haynes & Richardson, 1996). These efforts surfaced from three concerns:

Table 2.1 Definitions of evidence-based practice

Author	Definition
Haynes and Haines (1998, p. 273)	The aim of *evidence-based healthcare* is to provide the means by which current best evidence from research can be judiciously and conscientiously applied to the prevention, detection, and care of health disorders.
Belsey and Snell (2001)	Process of systematically reviewing, appraising and using clinical research findings to aid in the delivery of optimum clinical care of patients.
Sackett, Rosenberg, Gray, Haynes, and Richardson (1996)	*Evidence-based health care* extends the application of the principles of evidence-based medicine to all professions associated with healthcare, including purchasing and management. *Evidence-based medicine* is the conscientious, explicit and judicious use of current best evidence in making decisions about the care of individual patients. The practice of evidence-based medicine means integrating individual clinical expertise and our patients' own values and expectations with the best available external clinical evidence from systematic research.
Walshe and Rundall (2001, p. 431)	*Evidence-based healthcare* is, at its simplest, the idea that care that health professionals provide should be based as closely as possible on evidence from well-conducted research into the effectiveness of healthcare interventions, thereby minimizing the problems of underuse, overuse, and misuse.
Sackett and Rosenberg (1995c)	The ability to track down, critically appraise (for its validity and usefulness), and incorporate this rapidly growing body of evidence into one's clinical practice has been named *evidence-based medicine*.
Tanner (1999, p. 99)	The collection, interpretation, and integration of valid, important, and applicable patient-reported, clinician-observed, and research-driven evidence....The best available evidence, moderated by patient circumstances and preferences, is applied to improve the quality of clinical judgments and facilitate cost-effective healthcare.
Timmermans and Angell (2001)	Reliance on current scientific evidence to reach medical decisions.

(a) many physicians relying on personal judgment rather than research for the treatment of patients;

(b) new knowledge exploding at an almost direct, inverse relationship to the time available to read and absorb it; and

(c) managed care eroding the independence of physician decisions.

Solutions formed by these two groups of Canadian and British physicians included better research evidence for treatment options, better education on how to search for and implement evidence-based interventions, and better utilization of existing research databases (Rosenberg & Sackett, 1996; Sackett et al., 1996).

As such, evidence-based practice involves the systematic collection of data, over time, through near-patient research studies as well as the clinician's reflective approach in applying this information in daily work with clients. Glanville, Haines, and Auston (1998) discussed this relationship:

> There is increasing pressure on healthcare professionals to ensure their practice is based on evidence from good quality research, such as randomized control trials or, preferably, systematic reviews of randomized control trials and trials of other study designs. This pressure comes from various sources. The evidence-based healthcare movement encourages a questioning and reflective approach to clinical practice and emphasizes the importance of lifelong learning. Thus, good access to research-based evidence is necessary. Many governments are encouraging the development of evidence-based medicine because its advantages are understood, especially in terms of improved efficiency in the delivery of healthcare through identification of effective treatments. (p. 200)

Evidence-based healthcare usually involves systematic research—and better yet, the accumulation of systematic research—as applied by conscientious specialists who have the ability to synthesize the research and incorporate it into daily practice decisions with clients. Its aim is to reduce wide variations in practice based solely on clinicians' preferences or personal experiences, eliminating the worst practices, and embracing the best practices (Tanner, 1999).

It has been reported that medical care and mental healthcare have not traditionally been based on research and that has resulted in the overuse, underuse, and misuse of many healthcare interventions (Granello, Granello & Lee, 1999; Walshe & Rundall, 2001). "There is no doubt that many patients receive suboptimal care as a result, and some of them suffer serious, avoidable harm to their health" (Walshe & Rundall, 2001, p. 430). Knudsen, in a 1993 interview, was quoted as saying

> Physicians [are] familiar with mortality and morbidity conferences, hospital-acquired infection rate, length-of-stay information and other crude measurements. But we probably have not prepared as well in terms of true outcome measures, particularly

in collecting that type of information as a regular, ongoing process, nor in collecting information from patients in terms of their functional health status. (Johnson, 1993, p. 8)

Granello, Granello, and Lee (1999) reported similar findings with mental healthcare.

Straus and Sackett (1998) noted how important the specialist's review and evaluation of clinically relevant research is to the improvement of practice:

Evidence-based medicine involves integrating clinical expertise with the best-available clinical evidence derived from systematic research. Individual clinical expertise is the proficiency and judgement that each clinician acquires through clinical experience and practise. Best-available clinical evidence is clinically relevant research which may be from the basic sciences of medicine, but especially that derived from clinical research that is patient centred, that evaluates the accuracy and precision of diagnostic tests and prognostic markers, and the efficacy and safety of therapeutic, rehabilitative, and preventive regimens. (p. 339)

Timmermans and Angell (2001) noted that evidence-based clinical judgment has five important characteristics. Evidence-based clinical judgment: (a) is neither solely evidence nor judgment; (b) requires understanding of the requirements to make a satisfactory clinical decision; (c) increases with opportunity and practice; (d) reduces but does not eliminate clinical uncertainties; and (e) is currently grounded in a Western, allopathic, and professionalized approach to medicine.

Along with dictating that professionals have a familiarity with research methods as well as expertise in patient care, it also is assumed that evidence-based service delivery involves a continual search for new information. Evidence-based healthcare is a process of lifelong, self-directed, problem-based learning in which caring for patients creates the need for clinically important information about diagnosis, prognosis, therapy, and other clinical and healthcare issues (Sackett & Haynes, 1995; Straus & Sackett, 1998).

King and Teo (2000), while addressing nurses, stated that evidence-based practice might help close the gap between research and practice. "The foundation of evidence-based practice de-emphasizes decision making based on opinion, custom, or ritual....Rather, emphasis is placed on applying the best available research findings to specific clinical situations" (p. 597). Bliss-Holtz (1999) agreed that evidence-based practice involves more than research utilization.

For evidence-based practice to advance, better and high-quality evidence from patient-based research is needed, along with more and better ways to incorporate and use this evidence in everyday practice (Richardson, 1997). Rosenberg and Sackett (1996) and Sackett and Haynes (1995) wrote that evidence-based practice can actually be accomplished in three ways: (a) through learning the five steps of evidence-based practice, (b) seeking evidence collected by others, and (c) adopting protocols written by other who have done evidence-based practice research.

In citing Stetler, Brunell, Giuliano, Morsi, Prince, and Newell-Stokes (1998), Bliss-Holtz (1999) noted that evidence-based practice includes performance data from quality improvement efforts, consensus recommendations of recognized experts, and affirmed experience in addition to research findings.

> The clinical experience of the practitioner, particular characteristics or wishes of the patient, and factors external to the practitioner and patient such as the organizational structure will play a substantial part in the implementation of research evidence in practice and orchestrating plans for providing patient care. (King & Teo, 2000, p. 598)

The ultimate expectation of evidence-based service delivery is improved, informed, and more consistent healthcare for all clients.

Evidence-Based Practice Requires Paradigm Shift

Evidence-based practice is demanding new skills from healthcare practitioners. The Evidence-Based Medicine Informatics Project (2001) explained the changes in assumptions made by more traditional practice and evidence-based practice. In traditional practice, a practitioner's unsystematic observations, knowledge of basic disease and pathology processes, medical training, common sense, and clinical experience were enough to be seen as practicing quality medicine. With evidence-based practice, clinical experience needs to be coupled with development of clinical instincts and the understanding of certain rules of evidence to interpret the literature about causation, diagnostic tests, and treatment strategies (Evidence-Based Medicine Informatics Project, 2001).

> Educators define EBM [evidence-based medicine] as a paradigm shift with three tenets: (a) the integration of research based information in clinical practice, (b) the realization that pathophysiology is insufficient for the practice of clinical medicine, and (c) the acquisition of methodological and statistical skills to evaluate studies. (Timmermans & Angell, 2001, p. 344)

Walshe and Rundall (2001) provided a direct comparison of traditional and evidence-based healthcare. Their comparisons are adapted and displayed in Table 2.2 (p. 32).

The next section outlines the five basic steps to evidence-based practice: (a) formulating a clear clinical question from a patient's problem, (b) searching databases for relevant clinical evidence, (c) appraising the evidence, (d) implementing those findings in practice, and (e) evaluating the impact of change in practice.

Steps for Evidence-Based Practice

In general, evidence-based practice involves synthesizing the evidence, developing clinical policy from the evidence, and applying the policy at the right place, in the right way, and at the right time. All of these must be negotiated to form a valid connection between evidence and practice (Haynes & Haines, 1998). There are five steps that aid the specialist in making the connection between research and practice (Sackett, 1997; Straus & Sackett, 1998).

Step 1: Formulate a clear clinical question from a patient's problem.

Every patient presents healthcare problems that need a resolution. One of the ways to work toward a resolution is to convert the clinical problem into a relevant, answerable question (Richardson, 1997; Sackett & Haynes, 1995). Formulating clear, focused clinical questions is a prerequisite to answering them. Four components of a question must be specified:

1. the patient or problem being addressed,
2. the intervention being considered (i.e., cause, prognostic factor, or treatment),
3. another intervention for comparison when relevant, and
4. the clinical outcomes of interest (Belsey & Snell, 2001; Straus & Sackett, 1998, p. 340).

For example, in therapeutic recreation a clinical question may be "Will a middle-aged person with a recent spinal cord injury gain greater stress reduction from yoga or tai chi?" A second example might be "Is a person with a developmental disability more likely to be able to utilize community leisure resources when taught through in-house activities or on community reintegration trips?"

Table 2.2 Paradigm shift from traditional to evidence-based care (adapted from Walshe & Rundall, 2001)

	From Traditional	To Evidence-Based
Research Strategy	National leadership lacking; fragmented funding; poor communication; poor coordination	Growing, strategic national leadership; beginning coordination of research and funding sources; more coherent overall research agenda
Research Direction	Led by higher education researchers due to academic requirements; poor coordination	Led by needs tied to healthcare priorities and focused on major service areas/needs; improved coordination
Research Quality	Ad hoc, piecemeal, small-scale, poorly designed research; not often repetitive; poorly reviewed or managed	Coherent research programs consisting of well-planned, better designed, and higher quality research projects
Research Methods	Frequent mismatches between research questions and research designs; some designs more popular (used) than others	Research questions dictate methods, from experimental to qualitative approaches
Research Outputs	Primary goal is publication in peer-reviewed academic journals	Primary goal is change in clinical practice; publication is one step toward that goal
Dissemination of Research Findings	Journals, textbooks, expert opinions, narrative reviews	Online databases, summaries of evidence, clinical guidelines, systematic reviews, secondary journals
Mode of Access to Research Findings	"Pull" access reliant on clinicians seeking information by accessing libraries, journals, databases, and so forth	"Push" access; relevant research findings delivered to clinicians proactively as close to point-of-care as possible
Practitioner Understanding of Research Findings	Understanding limited to individual research studies/reports	Focus energies on meta-analyses and systematic reviews of relevant, appraised research
Practitioner Attitudes Toward Research	Uninformed, skeptical about methods, motives, and outcomes; lack skills to understand and to critique published research	Informed; involved in using and participating in research; skilled in judging and applying results to one's own practice
Major Influences on Clinical Practice	Practice largely influenced by personal clinical experience, precedence, tradition, expert opinion	Clinical epidemiology; empirical evidence, research
Responsibility for Implementing Research Findings	"Clinician knows best;" decisions left to professional and disciplinary teams with little or no corporate interest or direction in decision making	Viewed as key organizational function; supported by corporate investments; involvement and oversight alongside clinical team in decision making

Step 2: Search databases for relevant clinical evidence.

The second step involves searching for and locating research evidence that helps to answer the question formed in the first step (Sackett & Haynes, 1995). The information should be gained with maximum efficiency and should be as strong as possible. It may come from client assessments and diagnostic tools, established treatment or diagnostic protocols, published research literature, or other sources (Sackett & Haynes, 1995; Straus & Sackett, 1998). Driever (2002) expanded acceptable sources of evidence to include data from multiple other sources, such as quality improvement; evaluation data; retrospective and/or concurrent chart review data; infection control data; international, national, and local standards; and cost analysis. She added that there needs to be rules for evaluating and accepting these as evidence.

Belsey and Snell (2001) and Glanville, Haines, and Auston (1998) noted a variety of literature databases that are helpful to medicine and may, at times, be applicable to therapeutic recreation. Below is a list of evidence-based medicine resources that can be viewed by going to http://www.eboncall.co.uk/.

Evidence-based medicine sites
- Centre for Evidence-Based Medicine, Oxford
- Center for Evidence-Based Medicine, Toronto
- Centre for Evidence-Based Mental Health, Oxford
- HIRU—The Health Informatics Research Unit at McMaster University
- The Centres for Health Evidence
- The Users' Guides to Medical Literature published in JAMA
- The Expanded Users' Guides
- Agency for Healthcare Research and Quality

Data sites
- ACP Journal Club
- Agency for Health Research and Quality (AHRQ)
- Bandolier
- Cochrane Collaboration
- Clinical Evidence
- The National Electronic Library for Health
- The NHS Centre for Reviews and Dissemination at York
- PubMed

Search sites

- The National Electronic Library for Health
- Netting the Evidence: The SCHARR Guide to EBP on the Internet
- SumSearch
- TRIP database

Other useful sites

- The Clinical Assessment of the Reliability of the Exam (CARE; an ongoing Internet-based research project in clinical examination)
- Clinical Practice Guidelines Catalogue (maintained by the Alberta Medical Association)

In the case of medicine, many clinical reviews regarding certain conditions, such as pulmonary disease or bronchitis, can be found within the databases. The best use of these for therapeutic recreation is to understand how the databases work and to be able to use them for retrieval of information pertinent to therapeutic recreation when possible. Oftentimes, therapeutic recreation specialists (TRSs) may need to review more general health literature databases such as those suggested by Lee and McCormick (2002): CINAHL (http://www.cinahl.com), EMBASE (http://www.embase.com), Medline (http://www.ncbi.nlm.nih.gov/PubMed), or the National Library of Medicine Gateway (http://gateway.nlm.nih.gov). Most university libraries offer free access to these and many other databases for current students, faculty, other employees, and alumni.

Step 3: Appraise the evidence.

The third step is to critically appraise that evidence for its validity (i.e., closeness to the truth) and usefulness (i.e., clinical applicability; Sackett & Haynes, 1995). This involves collecting evidence about the tests and research that was reported, including examining how patients were assigned to research groups and the demographic and descriptive characteristics of the patients. At this point, the TRS attempts to determine the quality of the evidence based on the strength of the research design and the treatment(s) given to patients. Critical appraisal of evidence is a method of evaluating and synthesizing the evidence by systematically considering its validity, results, and relevance to the question being considered (Belsey & Snell, 2001).

Belsey and Snell (2001) presented three broad questions to aid this critical analysis:

- Are the results of the review valid?
- What are the results?
- Will the results help locally?

Evidence to answer these questions, as noted in step two, may come from a variety of sources that range in quality. The professional must be aware of the range of research designs that exist to answer the range of research questions—some yield results that are more trustworthy and have greater applicability than others. For example, a randomized control trial in which an adequate number of patients is randomly assigned to the treatment group and the control group, with comparative measures taken at baseline (i.e., pretest) and after treatment (i.e., posttest) is one of the strongest designs. Randomized control trials yield information that generally has high internal validity and clinical applicability. Anecdotal evidence, such as case studies or expert opinions, is less likely to be as trustworthy or as strong as clinical trials. King and Teo (2000) remarked:

> [R]emember that every research design has its specific purpose, strengths, and limitations; the key to evaluating the research is that the appropriate research design has been used to effectively answer the research question. Thus, using these criteria, research using a variety of designs should be potentially helpful to practitioners when searching for empirical evidence for their practice. (p. 597)

Phillips, Bell, Sackett, Haynes, Straus, and McAlister (2002) outlined a complex system of ten levels of the goodness of evidence, within four grade recommendations (i.e., A, B, C, and D). For example, the top two levels within A (highest) are: (a) a systematic review of randomized control trials with homogeneity (similarity) of samples, and (b) an individual randomized control trial with a narrow confidence interval. However, because therapeutic recreation lacks depth and breadth of research studies and literature to need such a complex system (Bedini, 2001; McCormick & Lee, 2001; Widmer, 2001), a simpler classification scheme is available. Belsey and Snell (2001) and Lee and McCormick (2002) noted a five-level scheme:

Level I (Highest): Strong evidence from at least one systematic review of multiple well-designed randomized controlled trials;

Level II: Strong evidence from at least one properly designed randomized controlled trial of appropriate size;

Level III: Evidence from well-designed trials such as nonrandomized trials, cohort studies, time series, or matched case controlled studies;

Level IV: Evidence from well-designed nonexperimental studies from more than one center or research group; and

Level V (Weakest): Opinions of respected authorities based on clinical evidence, descriptive studies, or reports of expert committees. (Belsey & Snell, 2001)

Step 4: Implement and use findings in practice.

The fourth step involves applying the information gained to the question at hand. The specialist is expected to integrate applicable findings with his or her own clinical expertise to determine the best course for treatment (Sackett & Haynes, 1995; Straus & Sackett, 1998). What worked best in other situations that parallel the question at hand? How closely does the research sample match the intended client(s)? What treatment was found to be most efficacious?

Step 5: Evaluate the impact of change in practice.

Although this is listed last, Straus and Sackett (1998) suggested that throughout the process, the specialist evaluate his or her progress, for example: Was the evidence found quickly? Was the evidence effectively appraised? Was the evidence integrated with clinical experience and the patient's unique features? Was there an effective management strategy for implementing the treatment? This is the stage that the specialist asks whether the process and outcome worked for the client for whom the original treatment question was meant to address (Sackett & Haynes, 1995).

The next section introduces some problems and concerns about evidence-based practice. These issues are noted in a wide variety of professions, such as medicine, nursing, and psychology. Therapeutic recreation has much to learn from the initial efforts of other healthcare professions.

Problems and Concerns With Evidence-Based Practice

One of the strongest arguments against evidence-based practice is voiced primarily by physicians and nurses, and is a reaction to the perceived reduction of professional autonomy when evidence-based practice guidelines are implemented (Mitchell, 1999; Rosoff, 2001; Walshe & Rundall, 2001). "In short, physicians and patients fear losing their choices, traditions, and individual preferences" (Eisenberg, 2002, p. 167).

Many in the healthcare community have welcomed this advance of knowledge [evidence-based guidelines], but some see a potential downside for professional autonomy. When more is known about the "right" way to treat a particular condition, there is less latitude for individual judgment. Clinicians, historically accorded wide latitude for the exercise of personal discretion in choosing treatments for their patients, now feel increasing pressure to conform to established norms of treatment…For this reason, EBM is seen by some as packing a one-two punch: Erosion of autonomy going into a treatment situation accompanied by greater risk of liability after the fact. (Rosoff, 2001, p. 327)

However, even with a push for globalization of healthcare, some authors contended that personal autonomy cannot be discounted, and that medical treatment decisions need to continue to be localized:

The challenge is making the evidence available without assuming that global healthcare means identical healthcare; in other words, to globalize the evidence but localize the decision.…Evidence is an important part, but not the only part of effective decision making.…To succeed in globalizing the evidence, policymakers must realize that opportunities to do so will be tempered by three competing core values: choice, efficiency, and equity. In the United States and many Western nations, the ability to choose according to one's own preferences is paramount, allowing citizens the freedom to opt knowingly for treatments that, according to evidence, result in less favorable outcome. In other nations, finding the best way to use scarce resources—efficiency—will govern how research is translated into practice. In still other countries, devoting resources toward those with the greatest unmet needs—equity—will dictate how evidence is used. (Eisenberg, 2002, pp. 166–168)

Marshall, Solomon, and Steber (2001) advocated for consensus building as a method to adopt and practice evidence-based medicine at the local level.

As mentioned in the introduction of this chapter, Belsey and Snell (2001) indicated there are four distinct actions required for the full circle of evidence-based practice. These four areas include:

1. production of evidence through research and scientific review;
2. production and dissemination of evidence-based clinical guidelines;
3. implementation of evidence-based, cost-effective practice through education and management of change; and

4. evaluation of compliance with agreed practice guidance and patient outcomes—this process is called clinical audit.

The following brief review of problems and concerns that have surfaced in other healthcare professions grappling with evidence-based care will be based on these four steps.

Production of Evidence Through Research and Scientific Review

In every profession there are complaints that not enough research is conducted, and research that is done could be stronger and more conclusive. Walshe and Rundall noted that often "the research base is insufficient in many areas of clinical practice because existing research is of poor quality or does not address the relevant research questions, or there is little research available" (2001, p. 435). As noted earlier, Level I research that includes systematic reviews of randomized control trials provide the strongest evidence for practice, while consensual or expert opinions (Level V) are the weakest. Murray, a medical statistician, noted rather harshly that clinical reviews may "reach conclusions along the lines of 'x small and methodologically unsound trials have been published in this area, which collectively tell us nothing of value'" (2000, p. 17). As mentioned in the first chapter of this text, one difficulty is selecting meaningful and relevant outcomes and meaningful measures (Hendryx, Dyck & Srebnik, 1999).

Haynes and Haines (1998) agreed that most research is not complex and rich enough to be of much help. On the other hand, Sackett and Cook (1993) asserted that small clinical trials can be useful in that they may challenge traditional but untested wisdom, they may be of sufficient size to identify the best treatments, and that collectively they can serve as the basis for meta-analyses and systematic reviews.

Another difficulty noted by Murray (2000) is that better practice needs to start while research is being conducted; if the clinician is to wait until convincing results are published, it may be too late. Better practice has to start while research is being conducted.

Williams and Hill (2001) and Eve, Golton, Hodgkin, Munro, and Musson (1996) also reported that significant changes in service delivery will only occur when researchers and clinicians communicate well. Researchers need to listen to clinicians when designing studies so that relevance is maximized, and clinicians also need to listen to researchers and actively engage research in real-world clinical decision making. This active communication is necessary—publishing research is not enough to ensure its incorporation into practice.

Production and Dissemination of Evidence-Based Clinical Guidelines

A second area of concern in evidence-based practice is the development of clinical guidelines translating research into practice (see Chapter 8). Clinical practice guidelines are an important component of the evidence-based practice movement, and seek to promote evidence-based care and to combine quality and efficiency with equity of access in a patient-centered approach (Sharpe, 2002). "Guidelines use existing scientific evidence to champion one course of clinical action over others" (Lescoe-Long & Long, 1999, p. 299).

Several problems, although not insurmountable, have been noted in the development and dissemination of guidelines (Haynes & Haines, 1998). The first problem is that of cost-benefit. Lescoe-Long and Long (1999) noted that when developing a set of practice guidelines, the individuals involved must weigh the anticipated benefits of improved quality and resource savings (associated with mistakes or poor practice) against the resource expenditures connected with developing the guidelines. Considerable time and effort must be expended in creation of clinical guidelines. Additionally Sharpe (2002) noted that some areas of practice may be more amenable to guidelines than others, and may thus be advantageous in terms of resource allocation. Some infrequent but important conditions may get more attention than more frequent but less life-threatening illnesses. Likewise, Hausman (2002) discussed the accessibility and availability of relevant data, social and political considerations of program decision making, and conflicting expectations of clinical research as barriers to the development of clinical guidelines.

Greener and Langhorne (2002) noted both problems and potential solutions to improve clinical guideline creation:

> Issues arose at all stages of the reviews and included: using expertise; planning the review; defining the healthcare problem, patients, outcomes, and intervention of interest; searching for, interpreting, and synthesizing the results of the studies identified; and deriving implications from the review.
>
> Suggestions made to address these challenges include: developing a suitable team of reviewers, using inclusive and broad criteria for inclusion of trials to a review, developing appropriate search strategies, and using caution arriving at conclusions. It is important to be explicit about decisions made during the review process concerning how to handle the challenges. (p. 69)

Haynes and Haines (1998) suggested using services that abstract and synthesize information as well as those that integrate evidence and guidelines with patient care, and producing guidelines for how to develop evidence-based practice guidelines.

Implementation of Evidence-Based, Cost-Effective Practice Through Education and Management of Change

Even if multiple Level I research reviews were conducted and empirically based clinical guidelines were produced, many challenges still exist in seeking adherence to the guidelines (Bero et al., 1998). Mannion and Goddard (2001) felt that clinical outcomes data was rarely used to inform practice, and is more commonly used to support further funding and service development. They attributed poor guidelines uptake to a lack of professional belief in the indicators, arising from perceived problems around quality of data and time lag between collection and presentation of data, limited dissemination, weak incentives to take action, a predilection for process rather than outcome indicators, and a belief that informal information is often more useful than quantitative data in the assessment of clinical performance.

Eve and associates (1996) documented widespread recognition that simply publishing research findings is not enough to ensure that they are carried into clinical practice. These authors felt that practice guidelines will succeed only to the extent that they engage actively with real-world clinical practice, which is more complex than guideline writers sometimes acknowledge. The fact that practice involves economic, administrative, professional, and personal implications also should be considered.

Pollock, Legg, Langhorne, and Sellars (2000) found among 27 physiotherapists, 26 occupational therapists, 22 nurses, 6 speech and language therapists, and 5 other professionals that although attitudes are positive toward evidence-based medicine, the major reported barriers were lack of time, lack of ability/need for training, and difficulties implementing research findings.

Sackett and Haynes (1995) found similar results within the medical profession. They reported a statistically significant negative correlation between physicians' knowledge of up-to-date care and the years that had elapsed since the physicians' graduation from medical school.

Several solutions have been considered in the literature. Because variations in practice due to the above real-world factors will always exist (Eisenberg, 2002), Tanner (1999) suggested that teaching faculty present skills of critical thinking, the ability to read and understand research, and at least an appreciation for quality improvement programs that provide feedback about outcomes of care. Skills that help localize the decision to the patient at hand are also important (Eisenberg, 2002). Sackett and Haynes (1995) and the Evidence-Based Medicine Informatics Project (2001) echoed this sentiment and noted that students from problem-based curricula were better suited to keeping ahead of clinical practice than their traditional medical school colleagues.

Specific training solutions have been noted by several authors, including a three-hour interactive training session concerning databases searches and evidence retrieval (Rosenberg, Deeks, Lusher, Snowball, Dooley & Sackett, 1998), help of knowledgeable librarians (Glanville, Haines & Auston, 1998), and use of a near-patient, mobile evidence cart that contained multiple sources of data and the means to view them on an inpatient unit (Sackett & Straus, 1998).

Evaluation of Compliance With Agreed Practice Guidance and Patient Outcomes

Haynes and Haines (1998) noted that professionals have many difficulties in locating and adhering to clinical guidelines. Among these problems are poor access to best evidence and guidelines, organizational barriers (e.g., lack of time or resources), ineffectual continuing education programs, and low patient adherence to treatment regimens.

Geddes, Game, Jenkins, Peterson, Pottinger, and Sackett (1996) found that approximately 65% of acute psychiatric inpatients in a hospital in Britain were treated according to evidence from randomized control trials or systematic reviews of randomized control trials. On the other hand, Milne, Keegan, Paxton, and Seth (2000) noted in a British study of psychologists that they had consulted guidelines and protocols nearly 60% of the time, but were only minimally influenced by it. However, the latter authors noted that use was increasing and looked promising for British psychologists.

Smith, McMurray, and Disler (2002) evaluated whether recent research complemented the evidence-based medical guidelines on low back pain. After reviewing the literature through a critical analysis, they found the previously written guidelines continued to be supported by more recent low back pain research.

Coye (2001) argued that healthcare will not improve until a business case for quality is achieved. This would mean that healthcare organizations achieving superior quality outcomes could expect to gain a higher price:

> Purchasers would pay a higher premium and insurers would pay higher fees or capitation rates; market share would shift to high performers as purchasers and consumers made choices in response to evidence of better quality; and cost per unit of care would decrease as quality management narrowed variation and improved predictability and the use of resources. None of these conditions characterize healthcare today. (Coye, 2001, p. 45)

Coye (2001) added that continuous quality improvement has been used primarily for administrative procedures and has remained a tactic rather than a core strategy. "Ultimately, neither organized quality improvement efforts by health plans and medical provider groups nor the medical profession's requirements for physicians have been sufficient to ensure the broad adoption for clinical improvements" (Coye, 2001 p. 48). Haynes and Haines (1998) agreed that facilities and organizations need to provide greater incentives to encourage improved patient care and quality improvement programs (see Chapter 12 for a discussion of performance improvement activities). They also called for more effective strategies to improve patient compliance with healthcare recommendations.

Bero and colleagues (1998) suggested that a greater level of attention needs to be given to actively coordinate the dissemination and implementation of evidence-based practice. They recommended paying attention to the characteristics of the message, recognizing external barriers to change, and evaluating the preparedness of professionals to change.

Ways to Address Problems and Concerns

Most of the previous sections provided suggestions on how to overcome the problems associated with evidence-based practice. Bero and colleagues (1998) completed their own systematic review of published research and found that some efforts were more effective than others in promoting evidence-based practice. Their findings are summarized as follows:

Consistently effective interventions to promote behavioral change among health professionals

- Educational outreach visits (for prescribing in North America)
- Reminders (e.g., manual or computerized)
- Multifaceted interventions (i.e., a combination that includes two or more of the following: audit and feedback, reminders, local consensus processes, or marketing)
- Interactive educational meetings (i.e., participation of health-care providers in workshops that include discussion or practice)

Interventions of varied effectiveness to promote behavioral change

- Audit and feedback (or any summary of clinical performance)
- The use of local opinion leaders (i.e., practitioners identified by their colleagues as influential)
- Local consensus processes (i.e., inclusion of participating practitioners in discussions to ensure that they agree that the chosen clinical problem is important, and the approach to managing the problem is appropriate)

- Patient-mediated interventions (i.e., any intervention aimed at changing the performance of healthcare providers for which specific information was sought from or given to patients)

Interventions that have little or no effect

- Educational materials (i.e., distribution of recommendations for clinical care including clinical practice guidelines, audio-visual materials, and electronic publications)
- Didactic educational meetings (e.g., lectures)

Rosoff (2001) noted that

medicine, long recognized as a subtle admixture of science and art, has moved notably in the direction of an exact science as new tools and techniques have been developed to help practitioners of "the healing arts" understand better what works in the treatment of patients. (p. 327)

Nichols (2001) noted similar progress and yet conflict of values within therapeutic recreation. However, when "healthcare professionals use the findings of sound research to help guide their clinical decision making, the outcomes for those for whom they are caring ought to be optimized" (King & Teo, 2000, p. 608).

Summary

As the second chapter of this text, the primary purpose was to introduce the concepts behind evidence-based practice to TRSs who are interested in outcomes, outcome measurement, and efficacious treatment. Several definitions of evidence-based practice were explored along with its origins in British and Canadian medical circles. The paradigm shift from traditional care to evidence-based care was presented along with several ways that it affects research and patient care. The five steps necessary for utilizing research and implementing evidence-based care were outlined, with some notations for TR practitioners and researchers. The last portion of the chapter covered the problems other professions have encountered with evidence-based care and noted some potential solutions. This entire discussion intended both to pique the interests of those who wish to see TR practice evolve as a research-based discipline and to give some clues about how to do so. As such, it provides a backdrop for the remaining chapters of this text.

Discussion Questions

1. What were the original concerns that prompted the creation of evidence-based practice? In what profession(s) were these concerns felt?

2. How do the definitions given for evidence-based practice and evidence-based medicine differ? How are they the same? Write your own definition, incorporating as many of the concepts as possible.

3. What is a paradigm shift? Why is one required to move from traditional patient care to evidence-based care? In what ways are they different? In what ways are they similar?

4. Choose a researchable question from TR practice, and outline what your actions would be for each of the five steps of evidence-based care. What resources would you consult? What sources would you use? How would you help to communicate it to the larger profession? How would you encourage people to adopt it?

5. Review some of the problems encountered in evidence-based care. Present at least two solutions that therapeutic recreation could use to quickly overcome each.

6. What would it take for TR professionals to adopt and embrace evidence-based practice? How would the profession and its clients benefit if we did? What will happen if we don't?

References

Bedini, L.A. (2001). Status of therapeutic recreation research. In N.J. Stumbo (Ed.), *Professional issues in therapeutic recreation: On competence and outcomes* (pp. 335–348). Champaign, IL: Sagamore.

Belsey, J. and Snell, T. (2001). What is evidence-based medicine? Retrieved November 9, 2002, from http://www.evidence-based-medicine.co.uk/

Bero, L.A., Grilli, R., Grimshaw, J.M., Harvey, E., Oxman, A.D., and Thomson, M.A. (1998). Closing the gap between research and practise: An overview of systematic reviews of interventions to promote the implementation of research findings. *British Medical Journal, 317,* 465–468.

Bliss-Holtz, J. (1999). Editorial: The fit of research utilization and evidence-based practice. *Issues in Comprehensive Pediatric Nursing, 22,* iii–vi.

Chambless, D.L. and Ollendick, T.H. (2001). Empirically supported psychological interventions: Controversies and evidence. *Annual Review of Psychology, 52,* 685–716.

Coye, M.J. (2001). No Toyotas in healthcare: Why medical care has not evolved to meet patients' needs. *Health Affairs, 20*(6), 44–56.

Denton, W.H., Walsh, S.R., and Daniel, S.S. (2002). Evidence-based practice in family therapy: Adolescent depression as an example. *Journal of Marital and Family Therapy, 29*(1), 39–45.

Driever, M.J. (2002). Are evidence-based practice and best practice the same? *Western Journal of Nursing Research, 24*(5), 591–597.

Eisenberg, M.J. (2002). Globalize the evidence, localize the decision: Evidence-based medicine and international diversity. *Health Affairs, 21*(3), 166–168.

Eve, R., Golton, I., Hodgkin, P., Munro, J., and Musson, G. (1996). Beyond guidelines: Promoting clinical change in the real world. *Journal of Management in Medicine, 19*(1), 16–25.

Evidence-Based Medicine Informatics Project. (2001). Evidence-based medicine: A new approach to teaching the practice of medicine. Retrieved November 6, 2002, from http://www.cche.net/usersguide/ebm.asp

Evidence-Based Medicine Working Group. (1992). Evidence-based medicine: A new approach to teaching the practice of medicine. *Journal of the American Medical Association, 268,* 2420–2425.

Geddes, J.R., Game, D., Jenkins, N.E., Peterson, L.A., Pottinger, G.R., and Sackett, D.L. (1996). What proportion of primary psychiatric interventions are based on evidence from randomized control trials? *Quality Healthcare, 5*(4), 215–217.

Glanville, J., Haines, M., and Auston, I. (1998). Finding information on clinical effectiveness. *British Medical Journal, 317,* 200–203.

Granello, D.H., Granello, P.F., and Lee, F. (1999). Measuring treatment outcomes and client satisfaction in a partial hospitalization program. *Journal of Behavioral Health Services and Research, 26*(1), 50–63.

Greener, J. and Langhorne, P. (2002). Systematic reviews in rehabilitation for stroke: Issues and approaches to addressing them. *Clinical Rehabilitation, 16*(1), 69–74.

Hausman, A.J. (2002). Implications of evidence-based practice for community health. *American Journal of Community Psychology, 30*(3), 453–467.

Haynes, B. and Haines, A. (1998). Barriers and bridges to evidence-based clinical practice. *British Medical Journal, 317*, 273–276.

Hendryx, M.S., Dyck, D.G., and Srebnik, D. (1999). Risk-adjusted outcome models for public mental health outpatient programs. *Health Services Research, 34*(1), 171–195.

Johnson, D.E.L. (1993). Scott & White measures "quality of health" in outcomes studies. *Healthcare Strategic Management, 11*(3), 7–9.

Kendall, P.C. (1998). Empirically supported psychological therapies. *Journal of Consulting and Clinical Psychology, 66*, 36.

King, K.M. and Teo, K.K. (2000). Integrating clinical quality improvement strategies with nursing research. *Western Journal of Nursing Research, 22*(5), 596–608.

Lee, Y. and McCormick, B.P. (2002). Toward evidence-based therapeutic recreation practice. In D.R. Austin, J. Dattilo, and B.P. McCormick (Eds.), *Conceptual foundations for therapeutic recreation* (pp. 165–184). State College, PA: Venture Publishing, Inc.

Lescoe-Long, M. and Long, M.J. (1999). Defining the utility of clinically acceptable variations in evidence-based practice guidelines for evaluation of quality improvement activities. *Evaluation and the Health Professions, 22*(3), 298–324.

Mannion, R. and Goddard, M. (2001). Impact of published clinical outcomes data: Case study in NHS hospital trusts. *British Medical Journal, 323*, 260–263.

Marshall, T., Solomon, P., and Steber, S.A. (2001). Implementing best-practice models by using a consensus-building process. *Administration and Policy in Mental Health, 29*(2), 105–116.

McCormick, B.P. and Lee, Y. (2001). Research into practice: Building knowledge through empirical practice. In N.J. Stumbo (Ed.), *Professional issues in therapeutic recreation: On competence and outcomes* (pp. 383–400). Champaign, IL: Sagamore.

Milne, D., Keegan, D., Paxton, R., and Seth, K. (2000). Is the practice of psychological therapists evidence-based? *International Journal of Healthcare Quality Assurance, 13*(1), 8–14.

Mitchell, G.J. (1999). Evidence-based practice: Critique and alternative view. *Nursing Science Quarterly, 12*(1), 30–35.

Murray, G.D. (2000). Promoting good research practice. *Statistical Methods in Medical Research, 9,* 17–24.

Nichols, S. (2001). Keynote: Therapeutic recreation practice: Art, science, or magic? In N.J. Stumbo (Ed.), *Professional issues in therapeutic recreation: On competence and outcomes* (pp. 153–158). Champaign, IL: Sagamore.

Phillips, B., Bell, C., Sackett, D., Haynes, B., Straus, S., and McAlister, F. (2002). Levels of evidence. Retrieved November 9, 2002, from http://www.eboncall.co.uk/content/levels.html

Pollock, A.S., Legg, L., Langhorne, P., and Sellars, C. (2000). Barriers to achieving evidence-based stroke rehabilitation. *Clinical Rehabilitation, 14,* 611–617.

Richardson, W.S. (1997). Evidence-based diagnosis: More is needed. *Evidence-Based Medicine, 3,* 5.

Rosenberg, W.M., Deeks, J., Lusher, A., Snowball, R., Dooley, G., and Sackett, D. (1998). Improving searching skills and evidence retrieval. *Journal of the Royal College of Physicians of London, 32*(6), 557–563.

Rosenberg, W.M. and Sackett, D.L. (1996). On the need for evidence-based practice. *Therapie, 51(3),* 212–217.

Rosoff, A.J. (2001). Evidence-based medicine and the law: The courts confront clinical practice guidelines. *Journal of Health Politics, Policy, and Law, 26*(2), 327–368.

Sackett, D.L. (1995a). Applying overviews and meta-analyses at the bedside. *Journal of Clinical Epidemiology, 48*(1), 61–66.

Sackett, D.L. (1995b). Evidence-based medicine. *Lancet, 346*(8983), 1171.

Sackett, D.L. (1997). Evidence-based medicine. *Seminars in Perinatology, 21*(1), 3–5.

Sackett, D.L. and Cook, D.J. (1993). Can we learn anything from small trials? *Annals of the New York Academy of Sciences, 703,* 25–31.

Sackett, D.L. and Haynes, R.B. (1995). On the need for evidence-based medicine. *Evidence-Based Medicine, 1,* 5.

Sackett, D.L. and Rosenberg, W.M. (1995a). On the need for evidence-based practice. *Journal of Public Health Medicine, 17*(3), 330–334.

Sackett, D.L. and Rosenberg, W.M. (1995b). On the need for evidence-based medicine. *Health Economics, 4*(4), 249–254.

Sackett, D.L. and Rosenberg, W.M. (1995c). The need for evidence-based medicine. *Journal of the Royal Society of Medicine, 88*(11), 620–624.

Sackett, D.L., Rosenberg, W.M., Gray, J.A., Haynes, R.B., and Richardson, W.S. (1996). Evidence-based medicine: What it is and what it isn't. *British Medical Journal, 312*, 71–72.

Sackett, D.L. and Straus, S.E. (1998). Finding and applying evidence during clinical rounds: The "evidence cart." *Journal of the American Medical Association, 280*(15), 1336–1338.

Sharpe, N. (2002). Clinical trials and the real world: Selection bias and generalizability of trial results. *Cardiovascular Drugs and Therapy, 16*(1), 75–77.

Smith, D., McMurray, N., and Disler, P. (2002). Early intervention for acute back injury: Can we finally develop an evidence-based approach? *Clinical Rehabilitation, 16*(1), 1–11.

Stetler, C.B., Brunell, M., Giuliano, K.K., Morsi, D., Prince, L., and Newell-Stokes, V. (1998). Evidence-based practice and the role of nursing leadership. *Journal of Nursing Administration, 28*(7/8), 45–53.

Straus, S.E. and Sackett, D.L. (1998). Using research findings in clinical practice. *British Medical Journal, 317*, 339–342.

Stumbo, N.J. and Hess, M.E. (2001). On competencies and outcomes in therapeutic recreation. In N. J. Stumbo (Ed.), *Professional issues in therapeutic recreation: On competence and outcomes* (pp. 3–20). Champaign, IL: Sagamore.

Tanner, C.A. (1999). Evidence-based practice: Research and critical thinking. *Journal of Nursing Education, 38*(3), 99.

Timmermans, S. and Angell, A. (2001). Evidence-based medicine, clinical uncertainty, and learning to doctor. *Journal of Health and Social Behavior, 42*(4), 342–359.

Walshe, K. and Rundall, T.G. (2001). Evidence-based management: From theory to practice in healthcare. *The Milbank Quarterly, 79*(3), 429–457.

Widmer, M.A. (2001). Methods for outcome research in therapeutic recreation. In N.J. Stumbo (Ed.), *Professional issues in therapeutic recreation: On competence and outcomes* (pp. 365–382). Champaign, IL: Sagamore.

Williams, E.N. and Hill, C. (2001). Evolving connections: Research that is relevant to clinical practice. *American Journal of Psychotherapy, 55*(3), 336–343.

Outcomes From a National and Worldwide Perspective

John M. Jacobson, M.S., CTRS
U.S. Department of Veterans Affairs

Improving healthcare outcomes is a worldwide concern because it can lead to higher economic growth and improved welfare of citizens. There is increasing convergence of international clinical and scientific interest in disability and health outcomes research (Andresen, Lollar & Meyers, 2000, p. S1). With healthcare so intertwined with national economies, the growing interest by the international community in disability and health outcomes is not surprising and certainly logical.

The world of healthcare has changed much over the past century. In the 1980s, Paul Starr talked about two historic movements in the development of American medicine: "First, the rise of professional sovereignty; and second, the transformation of medicine into an industry and the growing, though still unsettled, role of corporations and the state" (1982, p. ix). More recently, DeJong stated:

> ...outcomes measures arise, as do the values implicit in them, from a particular social, professional, and economic context. This context is changing largely because of the rise of managed care and capitation payment as the dominant methods of health service delivery and financing in the 1990s. (1997, p. 61)

Thus the political, economic, and social forces of America and the world continue to change the face of healthcare. For those who work in healthcare, it is imperative to learn "what it is (healthcare outcomes) and how to use it wisely, humbly, and graciously in helping patients restore themselves to good health" (Basmagian, 1996, p. 227). The survival of therapeutic recreation (TR) in the 21st century will depend on how well professionals become part of the global movement in healthcare.

This chapter will provide the reader with an understanding of healthcare outcomes from both national and international perspectives. Therapeutic recreation is a part of the rehabilitation community, which is part of the national healthcare community, which in turn is part of the world health community. In today's global economy, it is vital for TR professionals to understand and be a partner with the global healthcare community. This chapter will review some basic outcomes definitions and briefly discuss the recent evolution of outcomes, the importance of their use, who uses outcomes, and the current issues and trends with outcomes.

Definitions of Outcomes

Most healthcare organizations or providers state that they have outcomes, and most hospital and department brochures or websites market their outcomes. Clearly, outcomes are important to payers, consumers, and providers. Following are some key definitions.

Outcomes in healthcare can be looked at as a component of overall healthcare quality within the context of three dimensions: structure, process, and outcome. *Structure* is the framework in which healthcare is practiced. *Process* can be viewed as having the right people, in the right place, doing the right things when they should. *Outcome*, the third dimension, reflects the end result of care.

Paul Ellwood defines outcomes management as a concept and a tool to improve healthcare. The four elements of outcomes management are:

1. Develop standards of care,
2. Systematically measure functioning of patients ongoing along disease-specific lines,
3. Pool clinical and outcomes data on a massive scale, and
4. Analyze the data and disseminate the information. (Ellwood, 1988)

The Australian Health Ministers Advisory Council defines a health outcome as "a change in the health of an individual or group of individuals which is attributable to an intervention or series of interventions" (Eagar, 2000, p. 142). This definition further elaborates on key terms. The first is *attributable*—that the change must be directly due to the health service intervention. *Intervention* is the second term—if we wish to measure outcomes, we need tools to classify and describe healthcare interventions. The third key term is *change*—that there is a difference in health status before and after the intervention.

Rehabilitation outcomes may be defined as changes produced by rehabilitation services in the lives of service recipients (Johnston, Stineman & Velozo, 1997, p. 1). "Outcomes research in medical rehabilitation may be defined as research intended to discover the sustained impact of rehabilitation strategies and treatments on the everyday lives of persons with severe and lasting disabilities" (Johnston, Stineman & Velozo, 1997, p. 2).

TR researchers have defined outcomes as follows:

> Outcomes are the observed changes in a client's status as a result of our interventions and interactions, whether intended or not. Outcomes are the complications, adverse events, or short- or long-term changes experienced by our clients and represent the end results of our care. Outcomes can be attributed to the process of providing care, and this should enable us to determine if we are doing for our clients that which we purport to do. (Shank, Kinney & Coyle, 1991, p. 76)

Thus, simply stated an outcome is a change in a client's current or future health status, which is directly attributable to a specific intervention or treatment plan. Outcome measurement is a systematic approach to evaluating the effects of treatment. Outcomes management is what is done with the information gained from outcome measurement to meet the increasing needs and demands by payers, patients, providers, and other stakeholders to make rational choices.

Evolution of Outcomes

During the last fifty years, the healthcare industry has seen much change. Significant technological developments and breakthroughs have improved the health status of many individuals. From World War II to the late 1960s healthcare expanded. Now with the advent of managed care, we have seen an "economic tug-of-war wherein the payer/financing side of healthcare has steadily overcome the provider/supply side as driving the marketplace force" (Banja & DeJong, 2000, p. 233). When strong fiscal controls emerged during this period, there were concerns about whether or not this type of marketplace culture could meet the ethical ideals of patient-centered care. The healthcare industry of the past primarily concerned itself with structure and process standards (Stumbo & Hess, 2001, p. 45) with minimal interest in outcomes. This was soon to change with the current era of accountability in healthcare.

Interest in outcomes has likely been around for a long time for rehabilitation professionals. However, most of that interest was descriptive. More recently outcomes measurement systems have been more fully developed and standardized. Certainly, early in this period there was minimal agreement among rehabilitation professionals on what should be measured as well as the purposes of measuring outcomes. To some degree, this variation in outcomes measurement between the various rehabilitation settings continues today.

Early attempts to measure rehabilitation outcomes occurred in the 1960s when there was an interest in the Kenny Activities of Daily Living Scale (Melvin, 2001). In the 1970s, the program evaluation requirements of CARF, the Rehabilitation Accreditation Commission, forged the way for rehabilitation facilities in the United States to collect data on their outcomes. In 1980, the World Health Organization's (WHO) International Classification of Impairment, Disability, and Handicap (ICIDH) functional status assessment was the measure of impact of disability (Cohen & Marino, 2000). This was an important beginning of the evaluation of the effectiveness of healthcare on a global scale.

The development of the Uniform Data System for Medical Rehabilitation (UDSmr), which uses the Functional Independence Measure (FIM), was very significant for physical medicine and rehabilitation outcomes. Developed from 1983 to 1987 by a joint task force of the American Congress of Rehabilitation Medicine and the American Academy of Physical Medicine and Rehabilitation in collaboration with eleven other rehabilitation organizations (Hamilton & Granger, 1994), the FIM provides, at this time, the best measure of disability (Cohen & Marino, 2000, p. S27).

Another movement, which brought outcomes to the forefront of healthcare practice occurred within the federal government. For many years, government accountability was merely a budgetary issue, such as determining how public funds were spent, whether an agency kept within its budget, and so forth. As a result of the Government Performance Results Act of 1993, government now must be not only responsible for its actions, but also for the results of its actions. This has created performance measurement systems and performance-based budgeting systems for most government healthcare agencies.

The need to measure outcomes to assess the effectiveness of rehabilitation as a treatment intervention has never been greater as demands for accountability, quality, and improved outcomes have increased. As outcomes continue to evolve in the overall healthcare industry, the need for therapeutic recreation to be a global partner in this effort is paramount. As the profession moves forward we must determine the difference between the effects of our treatment intervention and natural recovery.

The Importance of Outcomes

Why do we need outcomes? First of all, our patients or consumers deserve to know if how we propose to treat a particular problem or dysfunction has any basis, if there are other options, and what the success rate is for those options. For example, with cancer there are many options including surgery, radiation therapy, chemotherapy, and many alternative and complementary treatments. Secondly, if TR professionals cannot empirically demonstrate the contributions of TR intervention and that those contributions are significant to improving function and quality of life, then who would want it? Thus, outcomes are needed for decision making and to demonstrate value.

Ellwood describes outcomes management as "a technology of patient experience designed to help patients, payers and providers make rational medical care-related choices based on more informed insight into what effect these choices have on the patient's life" (1988, p. 1549). Riley states: "Simply said, the outcome measurement movement is dedicated to the goal of providing the best quality healthcare for the least amount of money" (1991, p. 1).

TR professionals must be able to compare changes in status over periods of time for a large number of patients or clients, through assessment of function at appropriate intervals. To understand what function to measure, it is important to understand disability from a global perspective. Once outcomes become measurable, they become manageable. Standardization and unification of such procedures are critical. The positive effect that the Functional Independence Measure has had on physical medicine and rehabilitation is testimony to this.

Who Looks at Outcomes?

We have discussed what outcomes are, how they evolved, and why they are needed from a national and worldwide perspective. Let us now explore some organizations that currently study or use outcomes. As will be seen, many of these are significant players in the healthcare arena which represent both private and public sector entities and are generally independent of each other.

The *Agency for Healthcare Policy and Research* (AHCPR) is well-known for establishing clinical practice guidelines. Through its work in outcomes and effectiveness research, several important developments have been strongly influenced by AHCPR-sponsored work:

- The increasing recognition that evidence, rather than opinion, should guide clinical decision making;

- The acceptance that a broader range of patient outcomes needs to be measured in order to understand the true benefits and risks of healthcare interventions; and

- The perspective that research priorities should be guided in part by public health needs. (Agency for Healthcare Policy and Research, 1999)

Centers for Medicare and Medicaid Services (CMS). To improve care and comply with the law, CMS uses the Outcome and Assessment Information Set (OASIS). OASIS helps home health agencies to determine what patients need, to develop the right plan for their care, to assess that care during the course of treatment, and to learn how to improve the quality of that care. In February 2002, the Center for Medicaid and State Operations introduced the Outcome-Based Quality Improvement Reports based on OASIS data to the 7,000 home health agencies, home health provider associations, state survey agencies, and regional offices. It should be noted that Medicare is the largest purchaser of healthcare in the United States, accounting for 20% of all health-care dollars spent (Chan, Houck, Prela & MacLehose, 2001, p. 474).

The *National Commission on Quality Assurance* (NCQA) sponsored an endeavor to establish a voluntary standardized outcomes measurement system of the Health Plan Employer Data Set (HEDIS), which is used by many HMOs to quantify quality of care.

Accrediting bodies also review outcomes. *CARF, the Rehabilitation Accreditation Commission,* requires an outcomes system in their standards, including measurable effectiveness objectives, efficiency measures, and consumer satisfaction objectives. As a part of CARF's Strategic Outcomes Initiative, the performance indicators project intends to ensure that consumers of rehabilitation services, their advocates, and sponsors have consistent, valid, and reliable information available to them on which to judge the likely quality of programs and to be able to choose services that match their needs (CARF Research and Quality Improvement, 1998, p. 19).

The *Joint Commission of the Accreditation of Healthcare Organizations* (JCAHO) has incorporated patient outcomes into its accreditation process for hospitals and other healthcare organizations through its ORYX initiative performance measures–quantitative measures, which are used to evaluate and improve outcomes or the performance of functions and processes (Skolnick, 1997, p. 1562).

The *National Institute on Disability and Rehabilitation Research* (NIDRR) is a national leader in sponsoring research. NIDRR conducts comprehensive and coordinated programs of research and related activities to maximize the full inclusion, social integration, employment and independent living of individuals of all ages with disabilities. NIDRR's focus includes research in areas such as employment, health and function, technology for access and function, independent living and community integration, and other associated disability research areas.

In 1993, Congress passed and the President signed into law the *Government Performance and Results Act* (GPRA). The broad intent of the legislation is to enhance the effectiveness, efficiency, and accountability of government programs by directing federal agencies to more singularly focus their management efforts on the results that are achieved, and away from such traditional concerns such as staffing and activity levels. Under GPRA, agencies must set goals, measure performance, and report on their accomplishments. They must also ask and answer some basic questions: What is our mission? What are our goals and how will we achieve them? How can we measure performance? How will we use that information to make improvements?

National Institutes of Health (NIH). Established in 1887, the NIH is now one of the world's foremost medical research centers, and the federal focal point for medical research in the United States. The NIH mission is to uncover new knowledge that will lead to better health for everyone. The NIH works toward that mission by conducting research in its own laboratories; supporting the research of nonfederal scientists in universities, medical schools, hospitals, and research institutions throughout the country and abroad; helping in the training of research investigators; and fostering communication of medical information.

Thus many agencies and organizations promote and utilize studies of outcomes. At a more local level, users of outcomes data are consumers, payers, and providers.

Table 3.1 Websites of selected national organizations that look at outcomes

---

Centers for Medicare and Medicaid Services   http://cms.hhs.gov/

National Commission on Quality Assurance   http://www.ncqa.org/

CARF, the Rehabilitation Accreditation Commission   http://www.carf.org/

Joint Commission of the Accreditation of Healthcare Organizations
          http://www.jcaho.org/

National Institute on Disability and Rehabilitation Research
          http://www.ed.gov/offices/OSERS/NIDRR/

Government Performance and Results Act
          http://www.whitehouse.gov/omb/mgmt-gpra/gplaw2m.html

National Institutes of Health   http://www.nih.gov/

Current and Emerging Issues With Global Outcomes

Recently, a number of new trends and initiatives have developed that will affect the future use of outcomes in healthcare in the United States, and in some cases, the world. Additionally a number of important institutions or organizations have become very prominent in the national outcomes scene. These organizational entities and developments are relevant to client outcomes for therapeutic recreation, as well as for partnering or involvement on a larger scale. What follows is a description of several of these issues and organizations, and their role in outcomes management in healthcare now and in the future.

Evidence-based medicine. Basically, this term refers to the conscientious, explicit and judicious use of current best evidence in making decisions about the care of individual patients. The practice of evidence-based medicine means integrating individual clinical expertise and our patients' own values and expectations with the best available external clinical evidence from systematic research (Sackett et al., 1996). The previous chapter discussed evidence-based practice in detail.

National Institute on Disability and Rehabilitation Research (NIDRR). NIDRR's lengthy research agenda includes a health and function focus and research related to rehabilitation outcomes. In NIDRR's Long-Range Plan for Health and Function, specific research priorities are listed for rehabilitation outcomes (National Center for the Dissemination of Disability Research, 2002). These include

- expansion of outcomes evaluation approaches to include outpatient and long-term follow-up information,
- development of outcomes measures that include measures of environmental barriers,
- evaluation of methods that translate outcomes findings into quality improvement strategies,
- analysis of barriers and incentives to consistent use of health and medical rehabilitation outcomes measures in payer-driven and consumer choice service models, and
- refinement of measures of rehabilitation effectiveness.

Health-Related, Quality-of-life Outcomes Measures. A growing body of outcomes research relates to quality-of-life issues. Health-related quality of life (HRQOL) incorporates multiple components, such as role functions, social issues, well-being, and generally involves the patients' own perspective

(Andresen, Lollar & Meyers, 2000, p. S30). TR professionals will want to be involved with, or at least be aware of, such research activities.

Rehabilitation Outcomes Research Center (RORC). This new center was established early in 2002, and is jointly funded by the Department of Veterans Affairs through their Health Services Research and Development, and Rehabilitation Research and Development Services, and is affiliated with the University of Florida's Brooks Center for Rehabilitation Studies.

> The mission of the Rehabilitation Outcomes Research Center for Veterans With Central Nervous System Damage is to enhance access, quality, and efficiency of rehabilitation services through interdisciplinary research and dissemination activities. The RORC will develop a national database of outcomes for individuals with stroke, develop and test outcomes related to newly emerging rehabilitation therapies based on principles of neuroplasticity and innovative technologies, and provide scientific evidence that will promote informed clinical policy in rehabilitation. The Center will ultimately optimize care and functional recovery for veterans with central nervous system damage. (Rehabilitation Outcomes Research Center, 2002)

World Health Organization International Classification of Functioning, Disability and Health. In November 2001, the World Health Organization (WHO) released a new publication which classifies the functioning, health, and disability of people across the world, and which challenges mainstream ideas about how we understand health and disability (World Health Organization, 2001b). The International Classification of Functioning, Disability and Health (ICF) has been accepted by 191 countries as the international standard to describe and measure health and disability.

There are several purposes of the ICF:

- to provide a scientific basis for understanding and studying health and health-related states, outcomes, and determinations;

- to establish a common language for describing health and health-related states in order to improve communication between different users, such as healthcare workers, researchers, policymakers, and the public, including people with disabilities;

- to permit comparison of data across countries, healthcare disciplines, services, and time; and

- to provide a systematic coding scheme for health information systems. (WHO, 2001a, p. 5)

The ICF focuses on how people live with their health conditions and how these can be improved to achieve a productive, more fulfilling life. Thus, the ICF focuses on all people, not just those with disabilities. Furthermore, the ICF takes into consideration the social aspects of disability and provides a mechanism to document the impact of the social and physical environment on a person's functioning.

A very simplified overview of the concepts of the ICF is presented in Table 3.2. The ICF has two parts, each with two components. The first part is Functioning and Disability, with the components bodily functions and structures, and activities and participation. The second part is Contextual Factors,

Table 3.2 An overview of International Classification of Functioning (WHO, 2001a, p. 11).

	Part 1 Functioning and Disability		Part 2 Contextual Factors	
Components	Body functions and structures	Activities and participation	Environmental factors	Personal factors
Domains	Body functions Body structures	Life areas (tasks, actions)	External influences on functioning and disability	Internal influences on functioning and disability
Constructs	Change in body functions (physiological) Change in body structures (anatomical)	*Capacity* Executing tasks in a standard environment *Performance* Executing tasks in the current environment	Facilitating or hindering impact of features of the physical, social, and attitudinal world	Impact of attributes of the person
Positive Aspect	Functional and structural integrity	Activities participation	Facilitators	not applicable
	Functioning			
Negative Aspect	Impairment	Activity limitation Participation restriction	Barriers/ hindrances	not applicable
	Disability			

with the components environmental factors and personal factors. Each component can be expressed in both positive and negative terms and consists of various domains. As a classification, ICF does not model the process of functioning and disability:

> It can be used, however, to describe the process by providing the means to map the different constructs and domains. It provides a multi-perspective approach to the classification of functioning and disability as an interactive and evolutionary process. It provides the building blocks for users who wish to create models and study different aspects of this process. In this sense, ICF can be seen as a language. (WHO, 2001a, pp. 10, 18)

Thus, Table 3.2 can be seen as representing an individual's functioning in a specific domain which is a dynamic interaction or complex relationship between the health condition and contextual factors.

As a health and health-related classification system, it is expected that the ICF will be used by insurance companies for evaluation of managed healthcare, social policy, and general legislative development. It may be useful for health prevention and promotion programs, and disability advocacy groups, and to study healthcare systems for both evaluation and policy formation (WHO, 2001a, p. 6).

There are nine domains in the activities and participation component of Functioning and Disability. As seen in Figure 3.1 (p. 60), one of these domains is community, social, and civic life. This domain deals with the actions and tasks required to engage in organized social life outside the family, in community, social, and civic areas of life (WHO, 2001a, p. 168). While other domains, such as interpersonal interactions and relationships, have applicability to therapeutic recreation, community, social, and civic life is the most logical domain for involvement of therapeutic recreation specialists (TRSs).

Within each domain are qualifiers: performance and capacity. The performance qualifier describes what a person does in his or her current environment, whereas the capacity qualifier describes a person's ability to execute a task or an action (WHO, 2001a, p. 123). There is a coding system for use of this classification, which is beyond the scope of this chapter. For further information about this classification system, readers are encouraged to read *International Classification of Functioning, Disability and Health: ICF*, published by the World Health Organization, 2001. Information on ordering this publication may be found at: http://www3.who.int/icf/icftemplate.cfm. This should be an area of much interest to TR clinicians and researchers, especially the development of the coding system and its applicability to the profession.

Many federal agencies and organizations that deal with outcomes from a world or national perspective are embracing the ICF as a useful tool to

	Domain	Qualifiers	
		Performance	Capacity
d1	Learning and applying knowledge		
d2	General tasks and demands		
d3	Communication		
d4	Mobility		
d5	Self-care		
d6	Domestic life		
d7	Interpersonal interactions and relationships		
d8	Major life areas		
d9	Community, social, and civic life		

Figure 3.1 Activities and Participation: Information Matrix (WHO, 2001a, p. 14) *Reprinted with permission of the World Health Organization. All rights reserved.*

measure outcomes. Numerous projects are in planning stages for making this classification system more user friendly and accessible to busy clinicians in both the United States and worldwide, and to crossvalidate it with established instruments.

The *National Committee on Vital and Health Statistics* (NCVHS) recently completed its report, "Classifying and Reporting Functional Status," which was approved by the full committee at its June 2001 meeting and submitted to the Secretary of the Department of Health and Human Services in July 2001. The purpose of the report is to put functional status "solidly on the radar screens of those responsible for health information policy, and to begin laying the groundwork for greater use of functional status information in and beyond clinical care" (NCVHS, 2001, p. 1). The report looks at the current and potential uses of functional status information and why this information should be included in clinical and administrative records to support optimal decision making for health. In this report it is important to note that the International Classification of Functioning, Disability, and Health (ICF) is recommended as a code set for reporting functional status information. "In the Committee's view, the ICF is the only existing classification system that could be used to code functional status across the age span" (NCVHS, 2001, p. 13). The conclusion of the report urges the U.S. Department of Health and Human Services to continue to collaborate with the World Health Organization regarding use of the ICF.

Healthy People 2010. The purpose of *Healthy People 2010* is to increase the quality and years of healthy life for all Americans and to eliminate health disparities (National Center on Birth Defects and Developmental Disabilities [NCBDDD], 2001, p. 1). The goal of the chapter on disability and secondary conditions in *Healthy People 2010* is to "promote the health of people with disabilities, prevent secondary conditions, and eliminate disparities between people with and without disabilities in the U.S. population" (NCBDDD, 2001, p. 7). The recommendations of the disability and secondary conditions chapter include to develop a research agenda relating to optimal disability measures, which are based on the WHO's International Classification of Functioning, Disability, and Health (NCBDDD, 2001, p. 149). The ICF gives a conceptual framework for understanding the interaction of the person and the environment, as well as providing a classification system for data on the dimensions of the disability process.

The *Center for Measuring Rehabilitation Outcomes at Boston University* is a federally funded rehabilitation research and training center dedicated to promoting rehabilitation effectiveness through improving the quality and use of outcome measures. The Center is working on several specific projects that include the development of a new generation of relevant, adaptable, responsive, and efficient rehabilitation outcome measures; the investigation of the effectiveness of rehabilitation services; and the impact of specific interventions on rehabilitation outcomes (Boston University, 2001). At the January 9, 2002, Interagency Subcommittee on Disability Statistics Conference (within the National Center for the Dissemination of Disability Research), Center staff described their work as pushing "the boundaries of outcome assessment for use in rehabilitation" (Jette & Haley, 2002). The meeting's minutes further state that key factors driving their work include the growing pressure to distinguish the effects of rehabilitation outcomes across diagnostic groups and care settings, the need to develop outcome tools feasible for routine clinical assessment, and pressures to distinguish the effects of rehabilitation from the natural course of recovery.

Most outcome instruments in rehabilitation emphasize activities of daily living (ADL) skills. The Boston University project intends to move the concept of traditional rehabilitation beyond ADLs toward advanced community movement skills by using the ICF conceptual framework. Thus, patient-based assessment would be looking at the patient's actual participation in the ICF participation domain. The new system will be based on the WHO's comprehensive model of health and the consequences of disease and will use the ICF model in the development of test items to measure activity and participation.

The progress of these new ventures into outcome measurement will be important for TRSs to track in the future.

Conclusion: National and World Outcomes Issues and Therapeutic Recreation

The need for adequate outcomes monitoring with increasing demands for accountability, quality care, and improved outcomes has never been greater. Commitment to outcomes is critical if TRSs want to move the focus from cost to value for money.

For therapeutic recreation, the challenge is to demonstrate the value derived from the effectiveness of daily clinical and operational decisions. To do this requires using measures of disability that produce consistent results from TRSs using the same measures and over a specific time span. Such systems must be built to satisfy the needs of purchasers of healthcare services. If such systems are not designed and based on outcomes that show the sustained impact of TR strategies and treatments, then they will be of minimal value. Therapeutic recreation has many different kinds of outcomes measures. Are there any which are used universally? Were such measures developed to meet the needs of professional providers, or of those who are paying for services? Are they in agreement with nationally recognized and adapted outcomes measures, or reflective of national standards or classification systems? Perhaps TR assessment tools need to be aligned with an accepted worldwide classification system such as the ICF.

Therapeutic recreation must be an active partner in the larger global community of healthcare, and in the universal drive for consistent, valid outcomes measurement. This is a great opportunity for therapeutic recreation as healthcare outcomes are evolving to include what happens to patients once they return to the community. The ICF appears to be the driver of outcomes measurement for the very near future. The TR profession can have a role in the development of protocols and tools that are grounded in ICF classifications. The ICF classification provides "a potentially powerful tool for evidence-based advocacy" (WHO, 2001a, p. 243). ICF will most likely be the tool used worldwide for measuring effectiveness of interventions. It is time to move from the perceived benefits of therapeutic recreation to what the measured outcomes are as defined and validated by the world healthcare community by translating the ICF classification system into TR practice.

Discussion Questions

1. There are many definitions of outcomes. Some are research oriented; others are from the perspective of clinicians. If you were asked to give a definition of an outcome, how would you respond in your own words?

2. The increased interest in outcomes toward the end of the 20th century has been said by many to be attributable to an era of accountability in healthcare. What factors caused this need for accountability?

3. Outcomes are used by many different people, such as consumers, third-party payers, providers, researchers, and so forth. Describe why you think each of these (and other) groups are interested in outcomes. For which group do you think a knowledge of outcomes is most important and why?

4. This chapter discusses the new International Classification of Functioning, Disability and Health (ICF). Do you think it is important for the nation and the world to classify disability uniformly? Why or why not?

5. When a therapeutic researcher studies outcomes of therapeutic recreation, what do you think should influence the choice of outcomes measures: (a) what is personally interesting to the researcher, (b) what the professional organization says is important, (c) what consumer groups think are important to know, or (d) what the larger healthcare community says is important? Why?

6. How can TRSs become more visible partners in healthcare outcomes decisions and policies on a national and international scale? Do you think it is important for you to be involved in more global healthcare initiatives and projects? If so, how would you do that?

References

Agency for Healthcare Policy and Research. (1999). *The outcome of outcomes research at AHCPR: Final report* (AHCPR Publication No. 99-R044). Washington, DC: AHCPR Publications Clearinghouse.

Andresen, E.M., Lollar, D.J., and Meyers, A.R. (2000, December). Disability outcomes research: Why this supplement, on this topic, at this time (Suppl. 2). *Archives of Physical Medicine & Rehabilitation, 81,* S1, S30–S39.

Banja, J.D. and DeJong, G. (2000, February). The rehabilitation marketplace: Economics, values, and proposals for reform. *Archives of Physical Medicine & Rehabilitation, 81,* 233–239.

Basmagian, J. (Ed.). (1996). *Clinical decision making in rehabilitation: Efficacy and outcomes.* New York, NY: Churchill Livingstone.

Boston University, Sargeant College of Health and Rehabilitation Services. (2001). *Center for Rehabilitation Effectiveness* [Brochure]. Boston, MA: Author.

CARF Research and Quality Improvement. (1998, August). *Performance indicators for rehabilitation programs, Version 1.1: Working paper for comment.* Tucson, AZ: Author.

Chan, L., Houck, P., Prela, C.M., and MacLehose, R.F. (2001). Using Medicare databases for outcomes research in rehabilitation medicine. *American Journal Physical Medicine & Rehabilitation, 81,* 474–480.

Cohen, M. and Marino, R. (2000, December). The tools of disability outcomes research functional status measures (Suppl. 2). *Archives of Physical Medicine & Rehabilitation, 81,* S1–S2, S21.

DeJong, G. (1997). Value perspectives and the challenge of managed care. In M.J. Fuher (Ed.), *Assessing medical rehabilitation practices: The promise of outcomes research* (pp. 61–90). Baltimore, MD: Brooks Publishing.

Eagar, K. (2000, September). *An overview of health outcome measurement in Australia.* Paper presented at meeting of the Mental Health Research and Development Strategy Outcomes Conference. Wellington, New Zealand.

Ellwood, P. (1988). Shattuck lecture: Outcomes management: A technology of patient experience. *New England Journal of Medicine, 318*(23), 1549–1556.

Hamilton, B.B. and Granger, C.V. (1994, May). Disability outcomes following inpatient rehabilitation for stroke. *Physical Therapy, 74*(5), 494–503.

Jette, A.M. and Haley, S. (2002, January 9). *Expanding the frontiers of rehabilitation outcomes assessment.* Paper presented at the teleconference of the Interagency Subcommittee on Disability Statistics. Washington, DC. Retrieved from http://www.ncddr.org/icdr/isds/01_09_02.html

Johnston, M.V., Stineman, M., and Velozo, C.A. (1997). Outcomes research in medical rehabilitation: Foundations from the past and directions for the future. In M.J. Fuhrer (Ed.), *Assessing medical rehabilitation practices: The promise of outcomes research* (pp. 1–42). Baltimore, MD: Brooks Publishing.

Melvin, J. (2001). Outcomes research in rehabilitation: Scope and challenges. *American Journal of Physical Medicine and Rehabilitation, 80*(1), 78–82.

National Center on Birth Defects and Developmental Disabilities (NCBDDD). (2001, December). *Healthy people 2010—Chapter 6, Vision for the decade: Proceedings and recommendations of a symposium* (pp. 1–11, 148–149). Atlanta, GA: Centers for Disease Control and Prevention.

National Center for the Dissemination of Disability Research (NCDDR). (2002). NIDRR's long-range plan—Health and function, section two: NIDDR research agenda. Chapter 4: Health and Function. Retrieved June 28, 2002, from http://www.ncddr.org/rpp/hf/lrp_ov.html

Rehabilitation Outcomes Research Center. (2002). *Mission*. Retrieved June 28, 2002, from http://www.stroketoolbox.com/rorc/Mission.htm

Riley, B. (1991). Introduction. In C.P. Coyle, W.B. Kinney, B. Riley, and J.W. Shank (Eds.), *Benefits of therapeutic recreation: A consensus view* (pp. 1–15). Philadelphia, PA: Temple University,.

Sackett, D.L., Rosenberg, W.M., Gray, J.A., Haynes, R.B., and Richardson, W.S. (1996). Evidence-based medicine: What it is and what it isn't. *British Medical Journal, 312,* 71–72.

Shank, J., Kinney, W., and Coyle, C. (1991). Monitoring and measuring outcomes in therapeutic recreation. In Riley, B. (Ed.), *Quality management: Applications for therapeutic recreation* (pp. 69–88). State College, PA: Venture Publishing, Inc.

Skolnick, A. (1997 November 19). Joint Commission begins tracking outcome data. *Journal of the American Medical Association, 278*(19), 1562.

Starr, P. (1982). *The social transformation of American medicine*. New York, NY: Basic Books.

Stumbo, N.J. and Hess, M.E. (2001). The status of client outcomes in selected programs as measured by adherence to the therapeutic recreation accountability model. *Annual in Therapeutic Recreation, 10,* 45–56.

U.S. Department of Health and Human Services, National Committee on Vital and Health Statistics (NCVHS). (2001, July). *Classifying and reporting functional status* (pp. 1–16), Washington, DC: Author.

World Health Organization. (2001a). *International classification of functioning, disability and health (ICF)*. Geneva, Switzerland: Author.

World Health Organization. (2001b, November 15). *WHO publishes new guidelines to measure health*. [Press Release WHO 48]. Retrieved June 28, 2002, from http://www.who.int/inf-pr-2001/en/pr2001-48.html

Basing Outcomes on Theory:
Theories of Intervention and Explanation

Linda L. Caldwell
The Pennsylvania State University

Some readers may recall the classic 1967 movie *The Graduate* starring Dustin Hoffman. In one of the scenes, a wealthy friend of the family was giving career advice to Hoffman's character, Benjamin, at his graduation party. The dialog went something like this:

"Son, do you want to know where the future lies?"

"Yes...."

"Plastics!"

That was certainly a prescient comment. Today, if someone asked me about the future of therapeutic recreation (TR), one of my first remarks would be "Evidence-based practice!" That remark, however, is not as prophetic as the previous comment, because the call for evidence-based practice has been resounding for some time.

There is an important movement in health, education, developmental psychology, social work, and many other fields to encourage practitioners to use *evidence-based, blue ribbon*, *blueprint*, or *gold standard* programs (see Greenberg, Domitrovich & Bumbarger, 2001). These *best practices* all have one thing in common: they are based on science. In more and more cases, funding for programs and services is predicated on whether or not there is science behind the intervention.

Evidence-Based Intervention

What does being based on science mean? There are many important aspects to "science," but three will be mentioned, and two will be the focus of the chapter. Three important aspects of science-based programs are (a) having a sound evaluation (e.g., based on rigorous research methods), (b) being based on a good theory(ies), and (c) being able to clearly link outcomes to the program. In fact, one cannot have science without theory, and implementing a sound evaluation also implies a theoretical foundation. The focus of this chapter is on how to use theory to develop program outcomes.

It is important to realize, however, that no matter how good the science is, the intervention or program will not be successful unless there is a strong dynamic between the practitioner, service recipient, and the program. That is to say that professional judgment, in conjunction with the individual who receives the service, is the final arbiter of what works and what does not. It is a common misunderstanding that programs based on science must be adhered to strictly as developed. Interventions based on science are developed to be somewhat flexible, if warranted and justified, and can be modified to fit the cultural or situational context. Why somewhat flexible? Here is where it is important to understand the interplay between science and practice.

Evidence-based interventions have been evaluated for their success in producing desired outcomes. There are various levels of scientific rigor and various types of evaluations to keep in mind, however. Gold standard programs have been tested and replicated across contexts (e.g., urban, rural, predominantly African American) and have had both efficacy and effectiveness trials. *Efficacy trials* are evaluations based on an experimental design done under ideal situations. That is, a highly trained intervention specialist delivers all programs, and all experimental and treatment conditions are held constant. The idea behind this type of evaluation is that if the program is going to work, the best chances of seeing evidence of success are in this type of controlled design. *Effectiveness trials* are also evaluations based on experimental design, but this time practitioners who have been trained in the program run the intervention. The main difference here is that in efficacy trials, practitioners are well-acquainted with the theory of the program and have been highly involved with the intervention. In effectiveness trials, practitioners have been primarily trained in the intervention during a short training period and are less trained in the theory behind the program. Thus, the program is evaluated for effectiveness under less controlled and stringent guidelines, which approximates a more realistic context.

In both cases, practitioners are expected to understand the theory behind what they do—a point that will be discussed further in a moment. For a program to reach gold standard level, it should have had both efficacy and effectiveness trials. As well, these trials should have been replicated under various conditions in various contexts. The number of people who participated in these trials would be large—large enough that scientists have confidence in the results. One could therefore have some faith in these programs since they have been as rigorously tested. Thus, the more one deviates from that which has been tested, the less one is certain about the effectiveness of the program. In many fields, staying true to the intervention as intended is termed *implementation fidelity*. This does not mean, however, that one is not justified on practical grounds for deviating from the program. This is where one returns to the point that the practitioner must be well-versed in the theory and science behind the program in order to make good practice judgments about *what* should be changed and *why*.

In therapeutic recreation, it is not always possible to have gold standard programs on which to rely. For example, the leisure-based intervention may need to be highly idiosyncratic and designed specifically for an individual in a particular context. Or, these gold standard programs simply do not exist to meet the specific needs of the therapeutic recreation specialist (TRS) or client. Important work is being done in the area of clinical practice guidelines, however (e.g., Hood, 2001, 2003). These guidelines are based on a combination of science and practice, and offer the practitioner suggested procedures for intervention. Clearly in therapeutic recreation, more evidence-based interventions are needed. In the absence of evidence-based interventions and clinical practice guidelines, however, it is still important to base programs and interventions on theory. Therefore, the remainder of this chapter addresses this issue. Following a discussion of theory and intervention, a practical example will be provided.

Interplay of Theory and Practice

As implied in the previous discussion, theory and practice are very much intertwined and *not* at opposite ends of a continuum. Theories stem from practice and are modified by practice (e.g., Marrow, 1969). Practice puts the theory into action. Thus, theories are very "practical." A theory helps to specify what worked and why. It helps to understand what goes on within an individual or groups of individuals, and it suggests rules for effective intervention. Theories can specify critical factors (i.e., outcomes) to target for change, suggest program and intervention strategies (i.e., how to effect change), and guide the evaluation. In sum, theories explain mechanisms by which programs produce their effects.

TRSs know that leisure-based interventions are about change—intentional change. Theory-based practice requires theories of why things have or should have changed (i.e., theory of explanation) as well as how change can be facilitated (i.e., theory of intervention; Schuman & Schwarz, 1998). Using theories of intervention and explanation are important in understanding pathways of change (e.g., Thyer, 2001). In the best situation, the theories of intervention and explanation should be specified beforehand (i.e., prospectively), providing the TRS with complete knowledge about what he or she is supposed to do, why he or she is taking action, and what he or she can expect to happen. Sometimes, however, one has to retrospectively review and try to understand program effects. While it is helpful and important to look back and try to explain why things occurred the way they did, a prospective road map of anticipated outcomes and a corresponding intervention is the strongest strategy.

For example, most readers have probably made a cake sometime in their lives. Let us use this analogy of making a cake and having a birthday party to illustrate points about theory and outcomes. This is a trivial example, but it conveys issues similar to what might be faced in TR intervention. While TR services are goal oriented, often a specific rationale or theory prospectively linking intervention with intended outcomes is missing.

Consider this scenario. Evan loves to cook and wants to make a cake for his coworker Shakeh for her birthday. He intends to arrange an end-of-the-day office party for the celebration. Evan has observed that Shakeh has been feeling a bit down lately, but he does not know exactly why. He suspects that the reason is because she has been overstressed at work and has expressed feeling out of touch with her coworkers. So Evan decides to make her his specialty cake from scratch. In his kitchen, he finds the recipe, assembles the ingredients and tools, and makes the cake. The next day, he and his coworkers sing Happy Birthday to Shakeh and they eat the cake, tell jokes and share stories to catch up on each other's lives. Shakeh appears to relax and have a wonderful time with her coworkers.

A few weeks after Evan's party, he notices that Shakeh has more energy than she seemed to have during the month or so before the party, she interacts more with her colleagues, and she seems less stressed. This observation causes him to ponder the success of his cake and the party. First, he was happy to note that his modifications to the cake recipe worked well (he added honey and decreased the amount of milk). Second, it became clear during the party conversation that Shakeh considered her coworkers to be a substitute family since she was far away from her own family. Because Evan is an aspiring graduate student, he consulted his social psychology textbook to try to find a fuller explanation of why Shakeh seems less stressed. He referred to a stress-coping model that suggested the leisure-based social support Shakeh gained at the party helped her considerably.

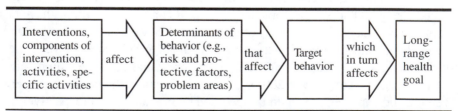

Figure 4.1 Behavior, Determinant, Intervention (BDI) Logic Model, Version 1

What does this scenario have to do with theory and practice? Using a logic model to diagram this process will help understand what transpired. A logic model is a map of the mechanisms of change. It specifies the causal pathways of how interventions cause behavior and outcomes. In the literature there are many types of logic models, and although different terminology is used, the process and the intent of each is the same.

Figures 4.1 and 4.2 depict a basic logic model—the behavior, determinant, intervention (BDI) logic model. Two versions are provided to introduce different terms that one might encounter. The main thing to remember is that these models convey the same information despite differences in terminology. It is important, however, that all users of this model understand the terminology and use terms in the same way. Choice of which type of model to use is up to the TRS—use whatever best fits one's own comfort level and situation. The reason there are two outcomes boxes is to represent that most interventions or programs have direct outcomes as a result of the immediate intervention as well as more indirect or longer-term outcomes that occur. In fact, there could be additional outcomes boxes added, suggesting a longer-term perspective on a chain of effects. This chapter contains the terminology in Figure 4.2, in particular because this author likes the implication that short-term outcomes mediate between the intervention and long-term outcomes. That is, short-term outcomes are the direct link between the intervention and long-term outcomes. The reason the long-term outcomes occur is because the short-term outcomes happened first, as a direct result of the intervention. Evan's scenario can help the reader understand the basic use of a logic model.

In Evan's case, he constructed a two component, leisure-based intervention to produce a change in Shakeh (see Figure 4.3, p. 72). He believed his intervention would affect stress level and lack of social support (i.e., mediators) and in turn affect Shakeh's longer term level of relaxation, coping, and camaraderie (i.e., distal outcomes). He might have predicted an impact outcome—better interaction with individuals she serves. In the terminology of Figure 4.2, Evan would say that the cake and social party had an influence on Shakeh's level of relaxation, coping, and sense of camaraderie because his intervention affected her stress level and sense of social support.

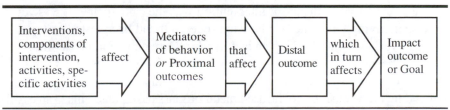

Figure 4.2 Behavior, Determinant, Intervention (BDI) Logic Model, Version 2

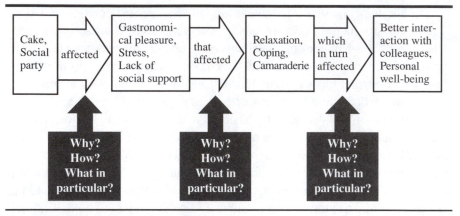

Figure 4.3 Evan's BDI Logic Model

Applying Theory

How does theory fit into logic models that depict an intervention and its out-comes? Weiss (1997) stated, "Theory-based evaluation examines conditions of program implementation and mechanisms that mediate between processes and outcomes as a means to understand when and how programs work" (p. 41). Understanding how to use theory is complicated by the fact that people have distinguished among categories of theories and different terms are used to describe theories. So far the terms *theories of intervention* and *theories of explanation* have been proffered. A theory of intervention may also be called a program theory, a theory of action, or an internal theory. The main question addressed here is: Among all of the things going on in the intervention, what were the most important factors that caused the outcomes and why? The shaded boxes in Figure 4.3 ask the, "How did this work" questions of Evan's intervention. Practitioners need to know the active ingredient in their inter-vention. What is the link between the intervention and the mediating outcome? How is the program to be run? These are important theory-of-intervention questions. We will return to theories of explanation later in the chapter.

Theory of Intervention

One aspect of Evan's theory of intervention was the cake recipe. It was very precise in giving guidelines for how to proceed. It had been tested and repli-cated in various contexts. If Evan had lived in Denver, Colorado (a different context) he would no doubt have followed the recipe's suggestions for high-altitude cooking. He may have changed the amount of time to bake the cake depending on whether or not he used metal or glass cake pans. This is an excel-lent example of a "gold standard" intervention (recipe) being used flexibly by the practitioner because (a) Evan was a good cook and understood the theory behind his actions (i.e., interaction of ingredients), and (b) the recipe had been tested in various contexts and gave guidelines for modifications when appropriate. A good theory not only describes what happens and why, but also suggests what may happen to whom given the circumstance and why.

Cake making was only one aspect of Evan's intervention. He also had a naïve or practitioner-based theory of how to change Shakeh's outlook and coping skills. He knew how important coworkers were to Shakeh, and he structured a social situation to bring together her coworkers in a way that would boost her sense of belonging. Indeed, the mediating outcome of the logic model for this scenario was that Shakeh appeared less stressed and expressed that she felt much closer to her colleagues. In this situation, however, Evan still does not know *exactly* what caused the reduction in stress. Was the cake most important? Was it being in a social situation with coworkers?

In fact, he did not really stop to specify *exactly* what mediators he wanted to target and what distal outcomes he wanted to influence. If he had, he might address the questions: Did he want to increase her culinary delight, decrease her level of stress, increase her coping skills, offer social support, or facilitate a sense of belonging? Would it matter if he wanted to increase her ability to communicate with her colleagues, but instead decreased her level of stress? Because he did not exactly specify what he wanted the mediating outcomes to be prospectively, it would have been difficult for him to describe the necessary actions to be taken to achieve the desired long-term results. That is, beyond the recipe for the cake, he had no theory of intervention. Should the party have been a surprise? Should a recently retired coworker have been invited? Was there an interaction between the cake and the social gathering (i.e., would one have been as effective without the other)? Was it more powerful to have them combined?

Furthermore, did he even think about what the impact outcome(s) might be? Would this leisure-based intervention affect Shakeh's long-term ability to handle stress or work with people? Would there be unanticipated outcomes? Would she call her parents to come for a visit? Would she be inspired by his cake and want to take up a new hobby of baking?

Of course this example is not a real TR intervention, and in a real-life casual situation like this we would not expect Evan to be so deliberate in planning the party for Shakeh. This example does, however, illustrate how there is often a breakdown in understanding what happens in an intervention to cause outcomes. The oft-referred to black box of intervention or programming still looms in this picture in terms of specifying outcomes (as depicted in Figure 4.3). Note that this is not the case for the cake as it was produced using a very solid theory (i.e., recipe) with predictable outputs—this process has a very good prospective intervention theory. It was clear to cream the egg yolks and sugar first, next add the egg whites, then add the sifted dry ingredients. Following the recipe thus would ensure a successful outcome—delicious cake.

In reality, it is of course difficult to reduce what occurs in leisure-based interventions to a simple recipe, and that is not the intent nor implication of this discussion. Rather, it tries to illustrate how important it is to attempt to connect exactly what is done in practice (i.e., intervention, program, action or internal theory) with exactly what occurs (i.e., outcomes). A systematic and reasoned explanation of this process is critical to fully understanding how to affect change in the most autonomy enhancing and effective way possible.

Theory of Explanation

Remember that theories of intervention help link specific aspects of a program to the immediate, mediating outcomes. A theory of intervention (i.e., internal theory, action theory, program theory) identifies the mediators of behavior or attitude to target for the intervention (e.g., stress level). A theory of explanation (i.e., external theory) is a "larger" or more encompassing theory that explains and links how specific aspects of the program work together to influence the more distal outcomes. It is less a theory about how the program works specifically and more a general theory of explanation. A theory of explanation goes hand in hand with a theory of intervention, and in fact *suggests* what the specific linkages are between intervention and outcomes. It is, however, more "theoretical" and it is up to the TRS to translate it into action.

Evan tried to understand how the intervention produced outcomes by *retrospectively* using stress and coping theory as his theory of explanation. Remember that the best (i.e., gold standard) interventions are those that can clearly and prospectively articulate that both intervention and explanation theories are linked to all levels of outcomes. While applying a theory of explanation retrospectively is helpful in modifying an existing intervention or developing a new one, it is much stronger to have based the entire logic model on a theoretical framework before the intervention implementation.

Theories of explanation are also very important for another reason. Often it is not possible to measure outcomes at all levels. In fact, in most leisure-based interventions, the TRS can only measure (i.e., assess) mediating outcomes due to time and resource constraints. Unfortunately, because of this therapeutic recreation as a practice in general has lacked a vision of how powerful leisure-based interventions can be. Typically intervention outcomes are limited to "immediate" outcomes with no thought that these outcomes actually mediate between the intervention and more distal outcomes. This is problematic because it limits outsiders' (e.g., stakeholders, consumers, allied health professionals) perspectives of the importance of therapeutic recreation. It is perhaps natural or understandable that this is the state of affairs because most TRSs see their efforts focused on assessment, intervention, and immediate results of the intervention. That is, most TRSs are focused on what is happening "at the moment" and do not forecast or expect more distant, long-term outcomes. Using a logic model and theory of explanation will help not only broaden the perspective of the power of leisure-based interventions, but it will also help TRSs articulate how they fit into their broader context. It answers the query "so what?" The distal or impact goals to focus on will likely be those that are of interest to most colleagues and stakeholders.

Theories of explanation also *theoretically* link distal outcomes with intervention and mediators. That is, theories supply a reasonable description and explanation of how mediators link to distal and impact outcomes, even if this link cannot be tested. Sometimes one can only focus on mediating outcomes, but one should be able to link what one does theoretically with those more long-term outcomes.

Theories of explanation are comprised of either broad, comprehensive metatheories or on very specific theories. Usually they are "well-known" and are backed by research studies. In Evan's case, he referred to stress-coping theory (e.g., Hood & Carruthers, 2002; Wills & Shiffman, 1985) to explain how his leisure-based intervention was effective (see Figure 4.4, p. 76). In his case he reasoned that his intervention helped Shakeh realize that she needed to balance demands of work with her available resources. His intervention also produced a leisure experience (i.e., distraction or diversion) where she felt a renewed connection to her friends (i.e., social support). Imagine if Evan used leisure-based stress-coping theory at the beginning to construct his intervention. Would his intervention have changed? Would he have been better able to target the determinants (i.e., mediators) or predict the outcomes? Would he have been more efficient and effective in producing the desired outcomes?

Relationship of Theory and Outcomes

Which comes first, the theory or the outcome(s)? Although there is no right answer to that question, for the most part, choice of outcomes precedes choice of theory. It is poor practice to choose a theory because it sounds good or interesting or you learned about it in school, and then determine compatible outcomes. It is an equally poor custom to base practice on available interventions at your disposal. Most readers are probably familiar with the old adage: If the only tool you have is a hammer, everything looks like a nail.

Most leisure-based interventions are developed to solve a problem or to effect a change at either a group or an individual level. The TRS should ask, "How does that desired change articulate with long-term goals desired by others, including the individual(s) being served?" As shown in Figure

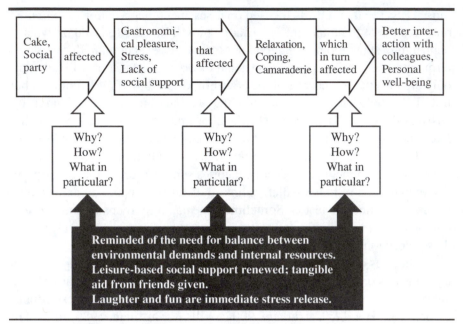

Figure 4.4 Using theory to explain Evan's intervention

4.5, the TRS should consider the valued outcomes in his or her context. This is not to say that leisure alone is not a valued outcome, because it is. But leisure experience and behavior can almost always be linked with longer-term outcomes (e.g., coping). Theory will help to specify those mediating variables that the leisure intervention can influence. The bulk of this book focuses in some way or another on those questions. We will return to this point in the discussion of a specific example later in the chapter.

Although the process in Figure 4.5 is depicted in a linear manner, this is not to say that practice does not affect theory, because it does. Practice is critical to the development and continued refinement of theory. Furthermore, the choice of mediating outcome(s) is a dialectic between organization context (i.e., mission of agency), professional judgment, and theory as a tool to link outcome(s) with intervention. Often theories are in the "back of one's mind" when choosing outcomes.

Drug Prevention Example

A concrete example of the preceding discussion comes from the National Institute of Drug Abuse's (NIDA) five-year strategic plan "Bringing the Power of Science to Bear on Drug Abuse and Addiction." The strategic plan contains the following statement:

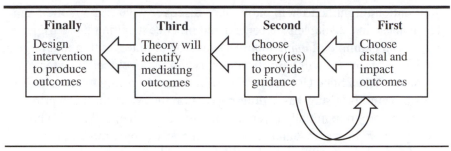

Figure 4.5 Developing outcomes using theory

Understanding what determines vulnerability to substance abuse is crucial to the development of effective prevention programming. At this point, there is no evidence that a single, unique factor determines which individuals will abuse drugs; rather, drug abuse appears to develop as the result of a variety of genetic, biological, emotional, cognitive, and social risk factors that interact with features of the social context. Thus, both individual-level factors and social context-level factors appear to make an individual more or less at risk for drug abuse and influence the progression from drug use to drug abuse to drug addition. (NIDA, 2002, p. 1)

This statement implies numerous risk and protective factors (i.e., determinants or mediators) to target, as well as numerous outcomes that could accrue from leisure-based intervention. The goal of a *primary* prevention intervention[1] would be to prevent the onset of any substance use. One type of primary prevention program is termed *universal*. Universal prevention programs would target *all* people in the population of interest. For example, a school-based leisure education program that focuses on teaching young adolescents to use their free time in healthy and personally meaningful ways might be one plausible intervention for an entire school district. The focus would be on instilling a sense of personal responsibility for one's actions. *Indicated* primary prevention programs might have a similar outcome (i.e., prevent onset of substance use), but they would focus only on youth who have indications of potential drug use (e.g., parents who use drugs). In this case, the program theory (i.e., intervention theory) would be different than that of the universal prevention program.

A *secondary* prevention program's outcomes would be vastly different, because these programs target a group of people who have already experienced the problem condition (in this case, substance use). Here the ultimate goal would be to reduce further risk associated with drug addiction and promote behavior change (i.e., no further use). An outcome of a leisure-based intervention might be to help individuals discover what triggers their sub-stance abuse in a social leisure context and practice handling those triggers.

As an example of using theory to develop an intervention that targets specific outcomes, I will describe an intervention developed by a team at the Pennsylvania State University[2]. The *TimeWise: Learning Lifelong Leisure Skills* program is leisure-based drug-prevention intervention. It is a primary prevention program initially given to rural grade 7 students, with two booster sessions given in grades 8 and 9. Next I will apply a logic model to this pro-gram and describe its theory and development. The program was developed in response to recognition that most substance abuse prevention programs ignore the importance of leisure, and the team felt that a leisure-based inter-vention would be an important part of any school-based effort to reduce substance use among youth. The *TimeWise* intervention was designed to focus on two distal outcomes: decrease the number of students who initiated substance use, and increase participation in positive leisure activity. The impact goal was to contribute to positive youth development and decrease the likelihood of future addiction. Notice that these outcomes and goals are very general and are ones that educators, parents, and health professionals would also have as their distal outcomes.

Through a process of literature review, discussions with colleagues (including practitioners), and past research efforts of the team, they identified a general causal pathway linking leisure-related variables (mediating out-comes), the initiation of substance use, and the selection and maintenance of healthy leisure activities. Choosing one theory on which to base the interven-tion, however, was impossible. Despite the usefulness of theories to represent human behavior and experience, it is often difficult for one or two theories to explain human behavior and experience. Life is just too complex. Logic models can combine or use multiple theories and offer more complex ways to examine behavior and experience. In this case the team identified several "main" theories and a number of subtheories that would (a) help explain the causal chain and (b) provide specific guidance for the intervention itself. The basic logic model of the program is depicted in Figure 4.6.

The team did not enter into this process naïvely, nor was its choice of outcomes "out of the blue." In Figure 4.6 there is an arrow from step one to step two. In reality, because of the team's collective professional expertise and knowledge, they adopted the distal outcomes and impact goals knowing they had a good arsenal of theories to help specify the intervention theory and the intervention itself. Reading and keeping abreast of a wide array of literature helps one understand theories of human behavior that could be useful in linking intervention with outcomes. This is much easier to do in the academic community than the practitioner community; practitioners are challenged to find the time to read and keep up with literature on a variety

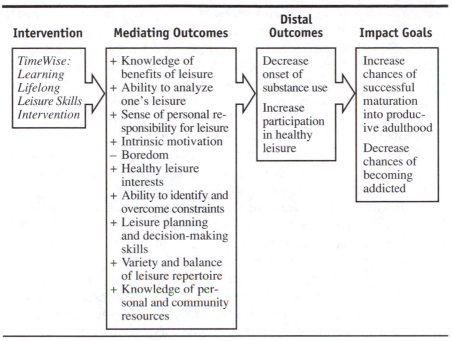

Figure 4.6 *TimeWise* Logic Model

of topics. Networking with others (including academics) and making reading a part of the job description would be helpful in meeting this challenge. Believe it or not, once one gets used to reading theory and thinking about application, it becomes easier and less time-consuming.

The metatheory of selective optimization with compensation (SOC) reflects the overall theoretical orientation of *TimeWise*. The application of SOC is based on how Lerner, Freund, Stefanis, and Habermas used SOC to understand how youth attempt to regulate their own lives as they interact with the external environment (i.e., context). Specifically, Lerner and colleagues stated that SOC allows the study of

> …how a youth decides what "to do," how he or she "does" (what is selected), and how he or she may either "keep at it" or identify alternative routes to healthy functioning in the face of failure or loss. Thus, selection, optimization, and compensation denote processes of goal-selection, goal-pursuit, and goal-maintenance/alternation, respectively. (2001, p. 32)

The processes of SOC are very important to sustained activity engagement, particularly in the rural context where *TimeWise* was applied, as SOC gives guidance to youth's understanding how to set realistic goals and maintain pursuit of those goals. SOC, being a metatheory, provided a good "large" conceptualization for the team's intervention, and team members were able to bring in other theories as they were helpful. Figure 4.7 identifies specific aspects of the intervention, links the intervention directly with mediating outcomes, and links both with theory. Two lessons (of the six) are highlighted in Figure 4.7. These lessons focus on motivation (mainly using Ryan and Deci's [e.g., 2000] conceptualization) and boredom and interest development (mainly using theories of optimal arousal and boredom [e.g., Caldwell, Darling, Payne & Dowdy, 1999]) and initiative development (Bronfenbrenner & Morris, 1998; Larson, 2000). Other contributing theoretical perspectives are introduced in Figure 4.7. The example in Figure 4.7 comes from the *TimeWise* intervention but is not a complete summary due to space.

After the team was comfortable with the theoretical conceptualization and logic model, they were faced with the challenge of developing the intervention itself. Theory guided both the sequence of the intervention as well as specific activities. Although it was a creative challenge, having the theory already specified made it much easier to determine the goals and objectives of each lesson and to create activities that were developmentally appropriate.

It should be noted this intervention was pilot tested and practitioner judgment was an essential part of refining the intervention. As the reader will note, a number of theories were used in these two lessons. As well, some of the theories identified (e.g., motivation) were used across lessons, which provided for continuity and integrity of the intervention.

The theories used to develop this intervention also linked mediating outcomes with distal outcomes, although the empirical support for these links is not as strong, and thus the theory of explanation is more "theoretical." Ideally, evidence-based intervention would have a stronger, more empirically based theory of explanation. Figure 4.8 (p. 82) suggests a possible overarching theory of explanation to link the *TimeWise* intervention with its mediating and distal outcomes.

To evaluate the effectiveness of *TimeWise*, the team used an experimental design having both a control and experimental group. They gave all students a pretest and a series of posttest questionnaires over three years to assess students' knowledge, attitudes, and behaviors that directly related to the mediating outcomes (e.g., levels of motivation, levels of boredom) and the distal outcomes (e.g., frequency of consumption of alcohol, number of new leisure interests developed). Thus the theories of intervention and explanation, as diagrammed in the logic model (Figure 4.6), influenced all aspects of the leisure-based intervention. In this case, the assessment was the questionnaire. Hopefully readers can see how theory and use of a logic model can identify factors (i.e., mediators) on which to base one's assessment. Once a theoretically based intervention is developed, it is easy to determine *what* to assess as well as the items to use in the assessment. If Evan was using a

Intervention Activities	Mediating Outcomes Students will:	Theoretical Bases
Lesson Two: My Motivation Analyze time use—Examine time diary Use motivation scenarios to introduce motivation concepts Describe why understanding one's motivation is important Label leisure time using the five motives	Increase knowledge of five leisure motives Increase ability to analyze one's own motivations Understand that some types of motivation can lead to unhealthy choices such as drinking alcohol, using drugs, or smoking cigarettes Understand that the type of motivation can affect one's quality of experience	This lesson is primarily based on intrinsic motivation and the theory of self-determination (e.g., Ryan & Deci, 2000; Vallerand, 1997). Beyond becoming self-aware, the lesson moves students to become more intrinsically motivated in their leisure rather than acting because they are amotivated, externally driven, driven by the need to fit in or be popular with their friends (introjected motivation). Students are taught that more benefits accrue if they can do more things in their leisure time that are intrinsic or identified (see Ryan & Deci, 2000; Vallerand, 1997). Students are cautioned, however, that they must be responsible and that there are times when they must do things that their parents and friends want them to (external and introjected motivation). This complex balance is addressed, with the message that always doing things to please friends or even parents will not lead to pleasurable, healthy, and beneficial leisure.
Lesson Three: Avoiding Boredom and Developing Interests Analyze what is boring and interesting about current activities and determine why Write and perform a rap song about boredom (or avoiding boredom) Complete a new activity interest sheet Discuss difference between having long-term and short-term interests	Increase understanding of what makes things boring and interesting Develop long-term interests Learn how to avoid boredom and make things more interesting Increase understanding of attitudes and stereotypes that keep interests from being developed	Optimal arousal and boredom (e.g., Caldwell, Darling, Payne & Dowdy, 1999; Csikszentmihalyi, 1990; Mannell & Kleiber, 1997) are two concepts behind this lesson. Chronically high levels of boredom in leisure lead to participation in unhealthy and destructive leisure activities (Caldwell et al., 1999; Iso-Ahola & Crowley, 1991). Two other main concepts are intrinsic motivation (e.g., Ryan & Deci, 2000; Vallerand, 1997) and initiation (Bronfenbrenner & Morris, 1998; Larson, 2000). Personal awareness of interests, including how to develop and maintain long-term interests, are important ways to overcome boredom. Sustained involvement in intrinsically motivating activities leads to positive developmental outcomes.

(arrows between columns labeled "affects" and "because")

Figure 4.7 Specifying a theory of intervention for *TimeWise*

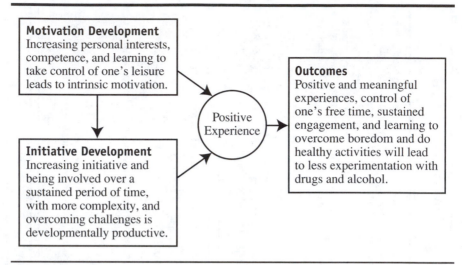

Figure 4.8 Theory of explanation for *TimeWise*

scientifically backed, leisure-based intervention, he would have assessed, at the least, Shakeh's levels of stress and appraised her coping skills. Positive resources (e.g., physical, psychological, social, lifestyle) and negative demands (e.g., problem-focused and emotion-focused coping) would have been assessed (e.g., Hood & Carruthers, 2002).

TimeWise has been tested only on a rural group of youth in central Pennsylvania. While the development team has confidence that the theory of explanation is applicable across cultures and across contexts, modifications to both intervention theory and activities will be needed to transfer this intervention to other contexts. It would be best to empirically test its effectiveness, but the sound theoretical basis at least gives the next user confidence that "in theory" the intervention is sound.

Summary

Theory, practice, and research combine to build strong leisure-based interventions. Although there is a strong argument for evidence-based interventions, these are not always possible or desired in all situations. Despite that, even small, highly idiosyncratic programs can benefit from using logic models to specify a theory of intervention and explanation.

As stated at the beginning of this chapter, gold standard programs based on theory should be flexible, and allow the TRS to modify and adapt the intervention to be age-specific, developmentally appropriate, and culturally sensitive, and to address the specific needs of the people served. Gold standard programs, as with clinical practice guidelines, are based on common characteristics of people known to have similar problems. Theory is used to determine how best to construct the intervention.

Endnotes

[1] For those not familiar with prevention or prevention terminology, consult Caldwell (2000) or Simeonsson (1994).

[2] Although Caldwell was the lead investigator on the NIDA grant that led to the development of *TimeWise*, there were many important contributors to this intervention: Dr. Cheryl K. Baldwin, Tanya Boone, Susanne Dubrouillet, Justin LeWinter, John Persing, Shelly Steiner, and Richard Wylie.

Discussion Questions

1. Why are theories of intervention and explanation important in therapeutic recreation?

2. Think about a program with which you are familiar. Can you describe its theories of intervention and explanation?

3. Suppose you were given the luxury of all the resources you needed to develop the best TR intervention you could. Use the process described in Figure 4.5 to construct a theory of intervention, such as depicted in Figure 4.4. Make sure you identify the theories you will use. *Hint*: Do not get stuck starting with the intervention—start by identifying the outcomes and theory. Match the intervention to the theory and outcomes.

4. Keeping the same outcome(s) you identified in Question 3, identify another theory that would help you achieve the outcome and plan an intervention. Develop another intervention based on that theory. Compare and contrast the two interventions you just developed. You should be able to see how the use of different theories can change the way you offer a program or design an intervention. Discuss how you would make the decision of which theory or intervention to use.

5. Identify scholarly theories with which you are familiar. What do these theories offer to TR programming?

6. What can you do to increase your skills in using theory to develop coherent programming?

References

Bronfenbrenner, U. and Morris, P.A. (1998). The ecology of developmental processes. In R.M. Lerner (Vol. Ed.) and W. Danon (Series Ed.), *Handbook of child psychology Vol. 1: Theoretical models of human development* (pp. 993–1028). New York, NY: Wiley.

Caldwell, L.L. (2000). Beyond fun and games? Challenges to adopting a prevention and youth development approach to youth recreation. *Journal of Park and Recreation Administration, 18*, 105–122.

Caldwell, L.L., Darling, N., Payne, L., and Dowdy, B. (1999). "Why are you bored?" An examination of psychological and social control causes of boredom among adolescents. *Journal of Leisure Research, 31*, 103–121.

Csikszentmihalyi, M. (1990). *Flow: The psychology of optimal experience.* New York, NY: Harper and Row.

Greenberg, M.T., Domitrovich, C., and Bumbarger, B. (2001). The prevention of mental disorders in school-aged children: Current state of the field. *Prevention and Treatment, 4*, 1–48.

Hood, C.D. (2001). Clinical practice guideline—A decision-making tool for best practice. In N.J. Stumbo (Ed.), *Professional issues in therapeutic recreation: On competence and outcomes* (pp. 189–214). Champaign, IL: Sagamore.

Hood, C.D. (2003). Standardizing practice and outcomes through clinical practice guidelines: Recommendations for therapeutic recreation. In N.J. Stumbo (Ed.), *Client outcomes in therapeutic recreation services* (pp. 149–164). State College, PA: Venture Publishing, Inc.

Hood, C.D. and Carruthers, C.P. (2002). Coping skills theory as an underlying framework for therapeutic recreation services. *Therapeutic Recreation Journal, 36*, 137–153.

Iso-Ahola, S.E. and Crowley, E.D. (1991). Adolescent substance abuse and leisure boredom. *Journal of Leisure Research, 23*(3), 260–271.

Larson, R. (2000). Toward a psychology of positive youth development. *American Psychologist, 55*, 170–183.

Lerner, R.M., Freund, A.M., Stefanis, I.D., and Habermas, T. (2001). Understanding developmental regulation in adolescence: The use of the selection, optimization, and compensation model. *Human Development, 44*, 29–50.

Mannell, R.C. and Kleiber, D.A. (1997). *A social psychology of leisure.* State College, PA: Venture Publishing, Inc.

Marrow, A.J. (1969). *Practical theorist: The life and work of Kurt Lewin.* New York, NY: Basic Books.

National Institute of Drug Abuse (NIDA). (2002). *NIDA strategic plan: Bringing the power of science to bear on drug abuse and addition.* Retrieved September 11, 2002, from http://www.drugabuse.gov/StrategicPlan/Strategy1.html

Ryan R.M. and Deci, E.L. (2000). Self-determination theory and the facilitation of intrinsic motivation, social development, and well-being. *American Psychologist, 55*, 68–78.

Schuman, S.P. and Schwarz, R.M. (1998). Using theory and research to improve your practice. Paper presented to International Association of Facilitators, Santa Clara, CA. Retrieved September 11, 2002, from http://www.iaf-world-org/IAF98/schwars.html

Simeonsson, R.J. (1994). Promoting children's health, education, and well-being. In R.J. Simeonsson (Ed.), *Risk, resilience and prevention: Promoting the well-being of children* (pp. 3–12). Baltimore, MD: Paul Brooks.

Thyer, B.A. (2001). What is the role of theory in research on social work practice? *Journal of Social Work Education, 37*, 9–25.

Vallerand, R.J. (1997). Toward a hierarchical model of intrinsic and extrinsic motivation. In M.P. Zanna (Ed.), *Advances in experimental social psychology, Vol. 29* (pp. 271–360). San Diego, CA: Academic Press.

Weiss, C.H. (1997). Theory-based evaluation: Past, present and future. In D.J. Rog and D. Fournier (Eds.), *Progress and future directions in evaluation: Perspectives on theory, practice, and methods* (pp. 41–56). San Francisco, CA: Jossey-Bass.

Wills, T.A. and Shiffman, S. (1985). Coping and substance abuse: A conceptual framework. In S. Shiffman and T.A. Wills (Eds.), *Coping and substance use* (pp. 1–24). San Diego, CA: Academic Press.

Other Voices, Other Rooms:
Consumers' and Healthcare Professionals' Perspectives on Valued Client Outcomes in Therapeutic Recreation

Barbara Wilhite, Ed.D., CTRS, CPRP
University of North Texas

Jan S. Hodges, Ph.D., CTRS
University of North Texas

Mason Peebles, M.S., CTRS
University of North Texas

This chapter borrows the title of Truman Capote's first novel, *Other Voices, Other Rooms*, to illustrate the authors' orientation in addressing outcome research in therapeutic recreation (TR). Capote's title alludes to a time marked by new and different voices and approaches in literature. Similarly, this chapter investigates valued client outcomes in therapeutic recreation from two perspectives not always sought in TR practice and research efforts: (a) consumers— the professed beneficiaries of our research and service efforts, and (b) other healthcare professionals—potential collaborators in TR research and practice. By focusing on these voices and approaches, the authors vary from previous reviews of outcomes research in therapeutic recreation (e.g., Bedini & Wu, 1994; Schleien & Yermakoff, 1983; Witt, 1988).

The specific purpose of this chapter is two-fold. First is to highlight research focused on interventions and interactions conducive to consumer outcomes. Second is to draw attention to research that demonstrates a more integrated and holistic view of outcomes by featuring the voices of consumers and other healthcare professionals.

Involving Consumers

By concentrating on consumers' voices and the research of other healthcare professionals, the authors are responding to two needs that have of late received much attention. First is the need to focus TR interventions and interactions on outcomes valuable to individuals with disabilities (Coyle, Boyd, Kinney & Shank, 1998; Hodges & Luken, 2000; Jacobson, Carruthers & Keller, 2001; Rehabilitation Accreditation Commission, 2000; Stumbo &

Hess, 2001). When consumers are viewed as active participants in care along-side healthcare professionals, achieving valued outcomes can be enhanced. A vital function of outcome-based research, then, is to increase self-care competence and empower consumers to be active partners in healthcare (Kemper, Lorig & Mettler, 1993). Consumers can benefit both from the results of research as well as from their involvement in the research process itself (Jacobson, Carruthers & Keller, 2001).

Moving Beyond Single Discipline Research

A second need is to stimulate collaboration in TR research between and across disciplines (Iso-Ahola, 1988; Malkin, Coyle & Carruthers, 1998; Sable, Powell & Aldrich, 1993/94; Shank, Coyle, Boyd & Kinney, 1996). While several reviews of client outcomes, issues, trends, and research agenda items in therapeutic recreation have been conducted (e.g., Carruthers, 1997/98; Compton, 1984; Compton & Dieser, 1997; Malkin, Coyle & Carruthers, 1998), these reviews look primarily at research conducted by TR professionals and whose results have most often been included in recreation- or TR-specific publications. In *Benefits of Therapeutic Recreation: A Consensus View* (Coyle, Kinney, Riley & Shank, 1991) presented one of the most extensive outcome-based research reviews to date that was not limited to the activities of TR professionals or to dissemination in our own discipline-specific publications. In a later summary of this work, Shank, Kinney, and Coyle (1993) suggested that strategies for increasing efficacy research in therapeutic recreation should include forging cooperative relationships and activities with professionals in other disciplines. In interdisciplinary research (between disciplines), professionals work in close collaboration to address common outcomes. Transdisciplinary research (across disciplines) involves sharing knowledge and resources to address a common outcome (Malkin, Coyle & Carruthers, 1998). In transdisciplinary research, TR professionals may function as the primary facilitator or coordinator of an outcome-based research project that involves other disciplines. Interdisciplinary and transdisciplinary approaches are likely to increase as healthcare professionals focus their efforts on achieving widely valued client outcomes (Jacobson, Carruthers & Keller, 2001; Shank, Coyle, Boyd & Kinney, 1996; Stumbo & Hess, 2001). These two foci—involving consumers and moving beyond TR-specific research—will help TR professionals to ensure the appropriateness and accountability of outcomes they seek to achieve.

Revisiting a Research Agenda for Therapeutic Recreation

To delineate an updated research agenda for therapeutic recreation, a Delphi study was conducted (Wilhite, Keller, Collins & Jacobson, in press). Respondents (N=131) were members of the National Therapeutic Recreation Society (NTRS) during April 2000. Top-ranked research agenda items emphasized the effect of therapeutic recreation and leisure functioning on global healthcare outcomes such as client health status, independent functioning, community integration/reintegration, rehabilitation outcomes, and quality of life. Also ranked among the top agenda items was the need to investigate the effect of frequency and duration of contact with clients on TR outcomes. These outcomes were embraced by a wide spectrum of practitioners, educators, and researchers.

Recently, therapeutic recreation and other healthcare professionals have had much to say about the need to address the changing nature of the environment in which healthcare services are provided and the changing nature of the populations served (Coyle, Boyd, Kinney & Shank, 1998; Hoffman, 2003; Landrum, Schmidt & McLean, 1995; Riley & Skalko, 1998). Therefore, the agenda items that ranked low in this study also revealed interesting insights. For example, some of the lowest priority agenda items related to at-risk youth and the reduction of delinquent behaviors. The researchers expressed concerns about the absence of outcomes pertaining to new or emerging populations, such as individuals with HIV/AIDS, children with failure to thrive syndrome, individuals who are homeless, people experiencing chronic pain, or people with terminal illness. Research outcome priorities pertaining to new or emerging settings, such as outpatient, adult day services, in-home care, hospice, corrections, or schools, were likewise limited. Existential or psychosocial client outcomes such as social support, optimism, sense of control, isolation, and loneliness did not appear often. Research agenda items relating to prevention of further functional limitations and promotion of health, multicultural issues, the everyday life and leisure experiences of people with disabilities, and social and environmental limitations were also notably absent. Coyle and her colleagues (1998) and Riley and Skalko (1998) have suggested that if therapeutic recreation is to remain viable, it is vital to address outcome priorities that are valued by these emerging consumers and that "expand the range of settings in which TR professionals work" (Riley & Skalko, 1998, p. 69). Wilhite and her colleagues (in press) concluded, therefore, that the lack of these agenda items was problematic. The research agenda items identified in this study provided the authors with an additional lens through which to examine outcomes research.

A Selected Review of Outcome-Based Literature

For this review, outcomes were defined according to the definition proposed by Shank and Kinney (1991) and paraphrased here: observed short- or long-term changes in a client's status as a result of interventions and interactions or some aspect of providing and receiving services. These outcomes can be intended or not—beneficial or adverse. Using the classification scheme for TR research suggested by Shank and colleagues (1996), outcome-based literature was reviewed in three major areas: (a) functional limitation outcomes (e.g., physical, psychological, cognitive, social), including prevention of further functional limitations (directed toward consumers and/or society); (b) experiences of individuals with disabilities (e.g., establishing and maintaining social support networks, adjusting to disability, maintaining or redefining recreation activities, leisure satisfaction); and (c) societal limitations (e.g., social inclusion, environmental supports, attitude formation). Movement toward evidenced-based approaches to decision-making in healthcare began in the early 1970s and expanded greatly in the 1990s (Malkin, Coyle & Carruthers, 1998; Patrick, 2001). Therefore, in this review, attention focused on outcome-based studies published in the 1990s or later with a select few from earlier years. Selection criteria emphasized: (a) articles authored by one or more professionals from a discipline other than therapeutic recreation, including articles coauthored by consumers or TR professionals; (b) articles that reported outcomes of these professional interventions and interactions with consumers, or reported outcomes that could be attributed to some aspect of the process of providing and receiving services; (c) articles that had specific implications for TR practice in the areas of functional limitations, experiences of people with disabilities, and societal limitations; and (d) articles not previously highlighted or that had received minimal attention in other reviews. In each of the outcome areas reviewed, the selected articles show diversity with regard to outcomes, consumer groups, service settings, research methods, and year of publication.

The primary electronic databases used in this literature review were EBSCOhost, PsychInfo, and FirstSearch. EBSCOhost searches across a broad range of sources in health, education, social science, humanities, business, and technology. EBSCOhost also searches across other electronic databases such as Medline, Sociological Abstracts, and ERIC. PsycInfo, formerly known as PsycLit, searches documents in psychology and related disciplines such as psychiatry, education, medicine, nursing, behavior analysis, sport, and social work. FirstSearch indexes articles from journals in science, technology, business, medicine, social science, humanities, and popular culture.

Outcome-Based Literature Related to Functional Limitations

The largest number of outcome-based articles reviewed related to improving and/or maintaining the functional independence of consumers. Professionals from physical education, physical therapy, occupational therapy, nursing, psychology, rehabilitation, and recreation collaborated on intervention programs designed to promote psychological, social, leisure, physical activity outcomes, and healthy behaviors in consumers.

The first study presented does not feature a specific intervention. It is an important study to begin with, however, as it provides justification from outside therapeutic recreation for emphasizing leisure lifestyle and developing leisure-specific interventions. Five professionals with backgrounds in neurology, psychiatry, and psychology, including two physicians, collaborated on a prospective research study to determine whether leisure activities modify the risk for dementia (Scarmeas, Levy, Tang, Manly & Stern, 2001). A total of 1,772 community-dwelling individuals without dementia aged 65 years or older were identified and studied. A number of standardized neurologic and neuropsychological measures were performed for up to seven years (mean 2.9 years) through face-to-face visits. A structured interview was used to elicit self-reported leisure participation in 13 preselected activities. Even when factors such as ethnic group, gender, education, occupation, and health limitations were controlled, subjects with high leisure activity had 38% less risk of developing dementia. The researchers suggested that engagement in leisure activities might reduce the risk of dementia by providing a reserve that delays the onset of clinical manifestations of the disease. They concluded that life-enhancing recreation and leisure interventions might reduce the risk of developing dementia.

Nour and colleagues (2002) investigated the impact of a home-based leisure education program designed and implemented by professionals from gerontology, physical education, and recreation. The program, designed to be consumer-centered, encouraged and supported individuals' efforts to self-manage leisure. Fourteen persons, age 55 and older and recently discharged from a rehabilitation program following onset of stroke, were involved in a study of the effect of leisure education on depression and quality of life. The participants, four females and ten males, had a mean age of 71. Race was not reported. The pretest-posttest experimental design included a control and treatment group. One group participated in a 12-step leisure education program (see Carbonneau, Hélie & Quellet, 1994) during one-to-one weekly interventions. The control group participated in casual visits for one hour per week. Data were collected upon admission to the study, during the first session at home, and at the completion of the last session, ten weeks later.

The leisure education group scored significantly better on posttest measures than the control group for total, physical, and psychological quality of life, but not for level of depression. After reviewing field notes, researchers concluded that favorable pretest depression scores and the program's "buffering effect" (p. 60) for participants without significant social support most likely explained the findings regarding level of depression. Researchers suggested that further studies were needed to explore potential psychological benefits of the leisure education program for participants without family and other natural supports. As with the study by Scarmeas and colleagues (2001), healthcare professionals outside therapeutic recreation provided a rationale for leisure activity as a goal to reduce functional limitations. These researchers concluded by calling for the involvement of "experienced leisure practitioners" (p. 62) to provide leisure education interventions.

Depression was the focus of another study investigating functional outcomes for older adults. Fitzsimmons (2001) examined the use of a prescribed TR–nursing intervention, wheelchair biking, for treatment of depression in older adults in a long-term care setting. Fitzsimmons, a geriatric nurse practitioner and clinical nurse specialist, collaborated with a CTRS to design and implement the pretest-posttest experimental study. This study, conducted in a Veterans Home, consisted of 39 participants; 5 women and 14 men in the treatment group and 6 women and 14 men in the control group. Mean ages for the treatment and control group were 81 and 80, respectively. Race of participants was not reported.

The intervention used a modified tandem wheelchair bicycle. The one-hour program involved groups of three to five participants in a two-part session. Part one featured group reminiscing about bike riding and related events. Part two involved a 15-minute wheelchair bicycle ride assisted by a therapist; most rides occurred outdoors. Participants were engaged in the program five days a week for two weeks. Results indicated a highly significant decrease in posttest depression means for the treatment group ($p < .000$). Depression scores for the control group did not demonstrate a significant change although they did increase slightly from pretest to posttest. In discussing the findings, researchers noted a "cultural difference" (p. 22) between male and female participants with men much more eager to participate in the biking intervention than women. Interestingly, the women who participated showed a greater decrease in depression scores than the men. Fitzsimmons concluded:

> Armed with the knowledge that psychosocial interventions can be effective in treating depression may prevent...nurses from automatically resorting to the medical model of pharmacological treatment. This may be accomplished by working closely with the therapeutic recreation specialist and by writing or requesting orders for recreational therapies. (2001, p. 22)

Although symptoms of depression noted in the aforementioned study did not appear to limit efforts to elicit consumer voice, it may be challenging for outcome-based interventions to reflect the voices of consumers when cognitive limitations are severe. In a research endeavor that included professionals from nursing, therapeutic recreation, gerontology, and psychology, Kolanowski, Buettner, Costa, and Litaker (2001) reported a study in which knowledgeable informants provided information about the premorbid personality of older adults with dementia residing in a nursing home. This information helped facilitators match personally meaningful and relevant activities with individuals' skill levels. Kolanowski and associates reported that subjects (N = 10) demonstrated increases in participation and positive affect measures, and decreases in dementia behaviors such as screaming, wandering, and physical aggression. They concluded that in persons with dementia "informant ratings of premorbid personality show promise as an effective, more comprehensive way of assessing style of interest" (Kolanowski, Buettner, Costa & Litaker, 2001, p. 232).

Other studies under review focused on psychological and social outcomes achieved by adults with physical disabilities, and by children and adults with mental illness. In a collaboration between psychology and therapeutic recreation, Farias-Tomaszewski, Jenkins, and Keller (2001) determined the outcomes of a 12-week therapeutic horseback-riding program for adults with a variety of physical disabilities. A one-group pretest-posttest design was used to assess changes in levels of global and physical self-efficacy, and self-confidence. Participants included 22 adults with physical disabilities ranging in age from 17–61 with a mean age of 40. Fifteen female and seven male participants, all of whom were white, took part in the riding program at three separate facilities. Researchers did not report the number of riding sessions per week or the length of the sessions.

Measures of global self-efficacy, physical self-efficacy, and behavioral self-confidence in riding ability were assessed on the first day of riding class, and again on the last day. Physical and self-efficacy measures were self-administered. Two separate raters—the riding instructor and a research assistant—completed behavioral observations and ratings on the level of confidence riders exhibited while on the horses. Researchers reported that the programs used in the study had very similar orientations regarding the goals of treatment. Therefore, participants from each site were pooled and analyzed as one group. Analyses revealed a significant increase in physical self-efficacy, but not in global self-efficacy. Behavioral ratings of self-confidence made by both raters increased significantly from pretest to posttest. Researchers also sought informal feedback about benefits of the riding program. Reported psychosocial benefits included improvements in mental well-being, the opportunity to meet and socialize with others, to recreate, and to gain a sense of achievement. The researchers urged healthcare professionals to use referrals to therapeutic riding programs in their treatment planning with persons who have physical disabilities. During conclusions, the researchers emphasized the exploratory nature of the study and called for future research to replicate and extend the present findings.

Of the articles reviewed, few focused on children at risk. Rawson and Barnett (1993), both affiliated with a children's center, hypothesized that the use of a short-term intensive camping experience would decrease levels of anxiety in children with learning and/or adjustment problems. Anxiety in excessive amounts is debilitating and interferes with learning, achievements, and relationships. These interferences are particularly devastating for children with learning and behavioral limitations (Rawson & Barnett, 1993).

Children ages 8 to 12 years old were involved in a ten-day residential therapeutic camp program. Children referred to the program came predominantly from low socioeconomic backgrounds and single-parent homes, and were considered to be socially and/or culturally deprived. Groups of children (seven to nine children per group) were arranged by age and sex so that younger and older campers and boys and girls participated separately. Each child was pretested 24 hours after arrival at camp and posttested 24 hours before departure from camp to determine change in anxiety levels. Anxiety data were collected from participants across seven sequential ten-day camp sessions (N = 191).

The camping experiences were highly structured. Mornings began with activities such as nature studies and crafts in which the children succeeded on an individual basis. Afternoon activities such as building tree houses or log cabins provided opportunities to succeed as a team. Evening sessions featured group competitive activities. Therapeutic characteristics of the program included a highly structured teaching approach, a token economy system, adult and peer modeling, verbal and nonverbal praise and recognition, individual tutoring, and daily group counseling.

The researchers found a statistically significant decrease in anxiety from pretest to posttest. This change was consistent regardless of the child's sex or age. Unfortunately, the limits of the study prevented the researchers from concluding that the camping intervention, in whole or in part, caused the desired outcome. They speculated, however, that highly structured and supportive environments, like this camping intervention, could decrease levels of anxiety, and that this change can be measured in this population.

Professionals from psychosocial rehabilitation and therapeutic recreation collaborated to study the effect of a TR program on appropriate behaviors of six individuals with schizophrenia (Pestle, Card & Menditto, 1998). According to these researchers, inappropriate behavior (e.g., laughing, pacing, rocking) often exhibited by individuals with schizophrenia may be especially prevalent when these individuals reside in institutional settings. Through learning-based interventions, individuals with schizophrenia can learn appropriate social and interpersonal skills (Paul, Stuve & Menditto, 1997). Six residents with schizophrenia or schizoaffective disorder living in a large state mental hospital were the focus of this investigation. Included were three females and three males ranging in age from 37 to 57 years with a mean age of 46.

TR sessions consisted of active (e.g., volleyball, Frisbee softball, aerobics) and passive (e.g., trivia, crafts, board games) activities based on residents' assessments. TR activity sessions were implemented according to learning-based intervention principles that included behavioral assessment and reinforcement procedures, and direct skills training. Participation was voluntary.

A time-series research design with repeated measures was used to investigate change in behavior scores. Observers recorded participants' behaviors using the Time Sample Behavioral Checklist (Paul, 1987). Observational data for the six participants were recorded over a 15-month period. Total number of observations per participant during this 15-month period ranged from 60 to 80. Total appropriate behavior scores, calculated from the categories of physical position, facial expression, and concurrent activities, increased over time for all six participants. As the 15-month study period progressed, study participants learned to exhibit appropriate behaviors more often, with a leveling off of scores in the final months of the study. The researchers' conclusion emphasized the value of using social-learning techniques during TR interventions and in conducting these interventions over time.

Outcome-Based Literature Related to the Experiences of Individuals With Disabilities

How individuals adapt to functional limitations that affect roles, family, work, and community life (Shank, Coyle, Boyd & Kinney, 1996) constitutes outcome studies that pertain to the experiences of individuals with disabilities. The authors were particularly interested in outcome studies that helped healthcare professionals better understand these experiences. An innovative study published in 1980 allowed patients direct input into their treatment plan to effect a positive change in their behavior, inspire commitment to achieve specific treatment goals, and offer a more effective means of communicating. In this study, a TRS and physician working in the inpatient unit of a mental health hospital devised a method whereby adolescent patients wrote information in progress notes alongside information written by the therapist (Fisher, 1980). Thirty-nine adolescents ages 13 to 17 (no other demographic information was provided), who were inpatients for three months or longer, participated in TR groups ranging from "very basic—dealing with reality testing—to high level—dealing with group process and organizational skills" (p. 150). Groups met three to five times a week. After each group, patients wrote chart notes about their behavior and feelings. The TRS then wrote a note alongside the patients'. This process was repeated until patients were discharged. Patients were informed that their writing would be visible to all healthcare staff, including their physician. Communication and understanding between patients and the specialist was enhanced with patients expressing a variety of feelings and establishing treatment goals. The researcher reported that progress notes were no longer "only a recording mechanism, but they had become a therapeutic treatment modality" (p. 150).

In another study concerned with the experiences of people with disabilities during treatment, possible racial bias and its effect on patient-therapist interactions was assessed (Flaherty & Meagher, 1980). The study, conducted in the late 1970s by a psychiatrist and a psychologist, consisted of a retrospective chart audit of 66 African American and 36 white male inpatients diagnosed with schizophrenia. The clinical setting was described by the researchers as a "fishbowl-like exposure and required interracial communal living" and "a place where the issue of racial bias cannot be ignored" (p. 680). The professional staff was almost exclusively white and the majority of nurses' aides were African American.

Data were collected on the use of as-needed tranquilization, seclusion, and restraints; the ordering of occupational therapy and therapeutic recreation; the level of privilege over time; and the length of stay. The researchers felt that bias would be indicated by more restrictive measures, fewer privileges, and longer lengths of stay. They also collected data on patient characteristics that might provide plausible alternative explanations for racial bias (e.g., age, marital status, employment status). Statistically significant differences were found with African American patients receiving more as-needed tranquilization, more seclusion and restraints, a lower privilege level, less therapeutic recreation and occupational therapy, and shorter lengths of stay. Although researchers could not completely rule out other factors in accounting for these differences, they concluded that indication of racial bias existed. Furthermore, they believed that the clearest measure of staff bias was the difference in rate of ordering therapeutic recreation and occupational therapy. "Although physicians report that they order these therapies routinely unless a patient is too dangerous or psychotic to participate, it is a striking fact that they are more 'routinely' ordered for white patients" (p. 681).

Based on their experience with the staff, researchers felt that the bias indicated by study results was due primarily to subtle stereotyping, and greater familiarity with and preference for white patients. Staff expressed openness to considering both the existence of racial bias and measures needed to reduce this bias. The recruitment of African American professionals and trainees was seen as a key step to addressing this bias.

Outcomes of a community-based intervention designed for individuals with serious mental health problems who perceived deficiencies in their social relationships were reported by Petryshen, Hawkins, and Fronchak (2001). The social recreation program, developed and implemented by therapeutic recreation and mental health professionals, served individuals 18–65 years of age described as socially isolated and living with a serious and persistent mental health problem. Maintaining satisfactory relationships—companionships, friendships, and intimacy—was quite difficult and a source of intense distress for these consumers (Petryshen, Hawkins & Fronchak, 2001). Principles of inclusion, such as opportunities for empowerment and self-determination, guided the program. Program strategies were intended to address both individual and social/environmental concerns such as community resources, social skills building, relationship development, healthy lifestyles (e.g., exercise, weight, sleep), volunteer activities, and community forums on understanding mental illness. About 200 group activities were offered per year; participation was voluntary. Measures of loneliness, self-esteem, quality of life, and participation were administered at intake and after 12 months in the program. Within subject change over time was examined.

Thirty-six individuals (22 women and 14 men) were included in the evaluation; the mean age was 43. Marital status, educational background, and living situation of participants varied. Race was not reported. On average, individuals reported low life satisfaction and high loneliness at the time of intake. Consumer participation during the study period varied considerably. The median number of activities completed was 18 per year. Regarding participation, a significant effect of gender was revealed. Men participated in a greater range of activities than women. No other demographic variables significantly affected participation. Statistically significant improvements on all outcome measures were observed. Specifically, individuals reported more life satisfaction, less loneliness, higher self-esteem, higher social functioning, and increased satisfaction with both social relations and leisure activities. Only one outcome, changes in satisfaction with social relationships, was observed to be significantly associated with levels of program participation. Consumers who participated in more program activities reported greater improvements in their satisfaction with social relationships. These research findings not only validated and helped to explain the effectiveness of this particular intervention, but they also helped to justify leisure lifestyle as a viable outcome of therapeutic interventions. The researchers hoped that this study would serve as a framework and impetus for the continued development and evaluation of community-based social recreation.

Fewer opportunities to experience play and leisure, and to maintain or redefine these experiences over time, exist for individuals limited in their ability to communicate preferences and choices (Dattilo & Light, 1993). A researcher from therapeutic recreation and a communication disorders specialist teamed up to examine outcomes achieved when significant others are trained to promote communication with individuals using augmentative and alternative communication (AAC) systems. A single-subject multiple baseline design, replicated across three dyads, was used. The three dyads were composed of two women with severe motor and speech impairments who used AAC systems, and three adult facilitators known to them. Two facilitators were associated with one participant (the first two dyads) and one facilitator was associated with the other (the third dyad). Facilitators were involved in four one-hour sessions designed to teach interaction strategies to increase participation by the participant using an AAC system and promote greater reciprocity within the dyad. Instructional sessions occurred within the facilitators' daily routine and involved participants in order to encourage generalization to natural environments (Dattilo & Light, 1993).

Observations of the dyads were conducted during baseline, training, and postintervention phases. Data were collected via a video camera and analyzed by three observers. Data were coded as communicative initiations or responses of each dyad partner. Data revealed that all three dyads demonstrated positive changes in their communication patterns marked by an increase in conversational participation and control of participants. Researchers concluded that facilitator instruction could help consumers using AAC systems to assume more active roles in their communication and demonstrate increased self-determination.

Unruh, Smith, and Scammell (2000), researchers from the field of occupational therapy, examined how gardening may be used to face illness or personal crisis and live optimally. In their qualitative pilot study, these researchers explored the personal meanings attributed to being in one's garden and to the experience of gardening in the daily lives of people living with a diagnosis of cancer. These researchers also hoped to determine if the experience of gardening was compatible with attention restoration theory (Kaplan, 1995).

Three women with breast cancer volunteered to participate in the study. The women, ages 35, 52, and 57, all reported gardening as a leisure pursuit. Two of the participants had gardened before their diagnosis while one began gardening about the time of her diagnosis. Two semistructured interviews, one to two hours in length, were conducted about one week apart. These interviews were tape recorded, transcribed, and augmented by field notes. Additionally, in the second interview, the participants completed a quantitative measure derived from attention restoration theory (Hartig, Korpela, Evans & Garling, 1996).

The researchers concluded that the outcomes of gardening for the women, which included aesthetic pleasure, interaction with living things, meeting personal needs (e.g., accomplishments, satisfaction), reflecting about life, and coping, were multidimensional and at times gardening may have led to a state of flow. The researchers concluded that gardening could serve as a vehicle that made it possible for the participants to momentarily "escape" day-to-day life and reflect on the meaning of life both in a broad sense and with respect to their own personal crisis. The researchers suggested further, "gardening may thus serve in the role of spiritual enabler making it possible to find meaningfulness in life under extreme circumstances" (p. 76). Additionally, the study results revealed that quantitative data supported the interview data and the conclusion that gardening was essential in helping the women cope with the stress of cancer. As a result, the researchers suggested that attention restoration theory is a useful framework for understanding the meaning of gardening and should be explored further. The researchers concluded by imploring healthcare professionals to seek a better understanding of the spirit and the ways in which personally significant activities such as gardening may meet the spiritual needs of people experiencing adversity and thus contribute to their well-being and quality of life.

Outcome-Based Literature Related to Societal Limitations

Structural or attitudinal constraints imposed on consumers by the effects of social and public policies were the focus of outcome studies related to societal limitations. In the first study featured in this area, Dupuis and Pedlar (1995) point out the urgent need that exists for policymakers, administrators, and program designers to recognize the concerns of family caregivers along with consumers. For example, as a result of increases in both the prevalence and incidence of dementia, demands on caregivers have also increased. Even when loved ones with dementia reside in institutional settings, family members can experience guilt and inadequacy. Visits can prove to be difficult and have the opposite effect of what is intended. In a collaborative effort between family studies and therapeutic recreation, Dupuis and Pedlar (1995) reported the impacts on family members involved in a resident-family therapeutic music program. The resident-family music intervention was part of an original study investigating its effects on the psychological well-being of older adults with dementia (Dupuis & Pedlar, 1993). Resident-family music sessions were an hour in length and scheduled for a set time twice a week. Each session followed the same structure and this structure remained consistent for the duration of the intervention period. Early in the original study, the researchers noted that the program appeared to be having unanticipated effects on family members. To investigate these effects, data were collected and analyzed in the present study using qualitative research methods including structured observations, in-depth interviews, and field notes. Outcomes of the program experienced by family members included (a) enhanced quality of visits, (b) social support received from other caregivers, (c) increased coping and less guilt, and (d) more positive perceptions of their family member. Opportunities for family members to contribute to their relative's life and care through positive shared leisure experiences helped to maintain their own well-being (Dupuis & Pedlar, 1995).

Vandercook (1991), a special educator and community integration specialist, examined the degree to which leisure skills demonstrated with an instructor would generalize when consumers participated in those same activities with a peer. The study also examined whether social interaction of the two peers and attitudes of the peer without disabilities would be enhanced if competence in leisure skills was demonstrated. The primary participants in the study were five high school students with severe mental and physical disabilities; two males and three females, ages 18 to 21. Five same-age students without disabilities were also involved in the study. A bowling alley close to the high school was selected, and the activities of bowling and pinball were targeted.

A multiple-probe baseline design across activities was conducted for each student with severe disabilities. Instruction featured task analysis, a decreasing assistance procedure, rules for fading instructional prompts and reinforcers, and natural cues and consequences. The students with disabilities bowled and played pinball with the same peer once per week for four months. Performance was recorded by teaching staff.

All five students with severe disabilities were able to acquire the leisure skills of bowling and pinball and were able to generalize these skills to participation in the community with their nondisabled peer. Cooperative participation scores were positively correlated with skill level for both members of the dyad. Attitudes of the five students without disabilities toward students with disabilities were initially positive and became even more positive by the end of the study. Researchers concluded that systematic instruction on age-appropriate leisure activity directed toward students with disabilities is a successful strategy for enhancing subsequent interactions with their nondisabled peers during these activities. Further, skill demonstration facilitates cooperative participation by both peers and augments attitudes of the peer without disabilities.

Peer Education and Advocacy through Recreation and Leadership (PEARL) was initiated to train and support persons with mental illness as advocates for inclusion (Gammonley & Luken, 2002). The study measured changes in empowerment, quality of life, and community activity involvement. Participants were primarily white (n = 24) with five African-Americans and one Native American; most were single (n = 18).

TRSs, social workers, psychiatric nurses, consumer advocates, and psychosocial rehabilitation providers designed and implemented the training program. The 30-hour program was based on direct skills teaching procedures

(Nemec, McNamara & Walsh, 1994) and was conducted over 15 sessions of about two hours each. Session topics progressed from getting to know other trainees and peer advocacy principles to skill development in communication, advocacy, and activity planning. Upon completion of training, participants assumed roles as personal advocates for their own, as well as for their peers', involvement in community activities. Project staff supported the advocates for a minimum of six months with stipends for transportation and participation costs, monthly follow-up group sessions, and mentoring.

Data were collected before group training, at the conclusion of group training, and six months following training. Data from empowerment, quality of life, and community activity involvement measures were analyzed using descriptive and nonparametric tests. Seventeen of thirty advocates increased the frequency of making telephone calls to gain information about community resources during the training phase and maintained a level higher than baseline during follow-up. Significant gains during training and maintenance during follow-up were observed in self-reported quality of life. Comfort around other people was stable through training but increased significantly during follow-up as advocates practiced their skills. A primary goal of increasing community activity involvement was achieved with 27% of the advocates involved in community activities at baseline and 77% involved at follow-up. Support was found for the purposeful use of recreation and leadership activities to enhance inclusion and increase quality of life for individuals with mental illness.

Looking to the Future

What has been learned from this brief review of completed outcome-based research that can be applied to future research in therapeutic recreation? The discussion in the following paragraphs considers this research relative to valued outcomes, consumer groups, and service settings.

In general, the limited number of outcome studies that met this review criteria was somewhat disappointing. However, scant numbers increased considerably from the mid-1990s to the present. This observation suggests that researchers are paying attention to recent calls for advancing outcome-based research in healthcare disciplines. As outcome-based studies become more prevalent, researchers are challenged to address methodological limitations observed in this review, such as lack of control groups and limited sample size, so that results may be viewed with greater confidence. The diversity of settings indicated in these studies—inpatient, outpatient, community-based, in-home—suggests that healthcare disciplines are embracing a full continuum of service venues. Perhaps this observation will provide TR professionals more encouragement to identify desired consumer outcomes, design interventions, and initiate studies in these service settings.

It was also gratifying to observe a variety of intervention processes being investigated. Yet, only one study was found that vigorously examined the effect of frequency and/or duration of involvement in interventions on outcomes (cf. Pestle, Card & Menditto, 1998). Since this variable is considered a priority research agenda item in therapeutic recreation (Wilhite, Keller, Collins & Jacobson, in press), future studies should be designed so that the influence of this variable can be determined.

Outcome-based research related to older adults and individuals with mental health needs was more readily discovered than research related to other populations. Within the parameters of this review, outcome-based research relating to consumer groups such as at-risk children and adolescents, individuals with mental retardation, or individuals with chronic illness or disease was limited. Even when considering the more recently published literature, the authors were not able to locate outcome studies related to less traditional consumer groups such as individuals with HIV/AIDS, individuals who are homeless, or individuals with terminal illness. Hoffman (2003) pointed out that there has been a gap between the healthcare system and its potential constituencies. Coyle, Boyd, Kinney, and Shank (1998) stated that therapeutic recreation and other healthcare professionals must demonstrate leadership in these emerging areas, or opportunities to maintain the support of the healthcare system and of those who consume these services will be lost.

We were likewise surprised that we were able to locate only a few outcome-based studies that directly or indirectly addressed interactions between specialists and consumers, or reported outcomes attributed to the process of providing and receiving services. For example, while a study published in 1980 boldly investigated and reported racial bias in patient-therapist interactions, many of the other studies we reviewed did not even report race or ethnicity demographics let alone consider these a primary variable. The researchers in the 1980 study concluded that their approach to measuring racial bias was somewhat simplistic, but felt it was a useful beginning. In reflecting on the literature reviewed here, we have found that this beginning is one that has been largely ignored in the past 20+ years. Additionally, since 95% of the NTRS respondents in a Delphi study investigating TR research priorities were white, we claim further that professionals of color continue to be underrepresented in therapeutic recreation. The influence of gender on outcome achievement received more attention than race or ethnicity in the studies reviewed, yet was still limited. We concur with Jacobson and her colleagues (2001) that the failure to adequately recognize and investigate the influence of these and other aspects of cultural identity, such as family, class, sexuality, and spirituality, limits our understanding of desired outcomes and effective interventions.

A bias toward functional outcomes, in therapeutic recreation as well as in other healthcare disciplines, has been indicated (Shank, Coyle, Boyd & Kinney, 1996; Sylvester, 1996). As noted earlier, this was the area most often targeted in the outcome studies reviewed for this chapter. We were heartened, however, because this emphasis went beyond physical functioning to include outcomes related to psychological, social, and cognitive functioning. Studies that addressed outcomes related to prevention of further functional limitations were not found. This finding suggests that opportunities exist for TR researchers and practitioners to promote the long-term consequences of both psychosocial and physical health.

Shank and his colleagues (1996) suggested that outcome research pertaining to the experience of individuals with disabilities or to social and environmental limitations and supports for inclusion is especially well-suited to interdisciplinary and transdisciplinary research collaborations. However, in the studies reviewed, these two outcome areas were less often the focus of research than were functional outcomes. A notable exception was the work of Unruh, Smith, and Scammell (2000) that explored the relationship between gardening, spiritual well-being, hardiness, and resilience. This research emphasis can lead to a more holistic perception of people with illness or disability by acknowledging their spirit. At the same time, it underscores potential spiritual dimensions of leisure and the linkage between spirituality and well-being. We echo the sentiment expressed by Shank and his colleagues that these are outcome areas in which therapeutic recreation can be proactive—leading the way to expand and promote a concept of life quality that moves beyond functional limitation.

A number of articles included the consumer voice. Yet, the involvement of consumers rarely included identifying socially valued outcomes, designing studies, or interpreting findings. Additionally, this review confirmed that a need exists for studies that move beyond anecdotal reports of consumer outcomes so that consumers' understanding and appreciation of outcomes can be more rigorously validated.

Finally, we were encouraged to see other disciplines supporting the role of leisure and recreation with regard to improving independent functioning and enhancing quality of life. TR researchers can take advantage of the findings reported by researchers and professionals from outside therapeutic recreation and use them to seek support for collaborative outcome studies of TR interventions. In addition, TR professionals should strive to publish the results of outcome studies in the journals of other healthcare disciplines, not just in recreation- or TR-specific journals, so that opportunities to educate, inform, and foster collaboration with these disciplines may be increased.

Closing Thoughts

We reviewed outcome research related to therapeutic recreation from the perspective of other healthcare professionals, and to the extent possible, from the perceptions of consumers. Shank and his colleagues (1996) reminded us it is essential that "TR researchers and practitioners not lose sight of the unique contribution and focus that is TR practice" (p. 190). It has not been our intent to disregard this imperative. Rather, by heeding the voices of consumers and other healthcare professionals, TR researchers and practitioners may be better prepared to identify highly valued outcomes of these consumers and professionals; outcomes that may represent broader health and human concerns than typically addressed in single-discipline research efforts. This knowledge can serve TR professionals in three ways.

One, this information can help professionals identify areas of shared concern and interest where collaboration in outcomes studies is desired. TR professionals and practitioners may thus feel empowered to initiate dialog and propose group research efforts. Two, knowing more about the research agendas of other healthcare disciplines provides opportunities for TR research-ers and practitioners to exert positive influence in areas that are of priority to our consumers and professionals, yet are being minimized or neglected by other healthcare professionals. Prepared with the knowledge of TR research priorities and existing research activities in other disciplines, TR professionals may be able to challenge biases and begin to address important research needs. Three, as we learn more about the interests and priorities of other stakeholders—consumers, caregivers, and professionals—the areas in which therapeutic recreation's input and impact is needed can be identified. The input of "outsiders" makes available a view of therapeutic recreation that may not be understood by those within (Richter & Kaschalk, 1996). It is here that TR professionals should concentrate efforts to increase the knowledge, credibility, and visibility of therapeutic recreation as a viable healthcare intervention. These perspectives and educational efforts may even help us to understand ourselves better (Richter & Kaschalk, 1996).

We conclude this chapter by acknowledging that we are not without our biases. Our own voices—our own unique point of view—influenced our perspective of research and our interpretation of the information provided. Perhaps the most valuable benefit of the chapter is that readers will take the time to reflect carefully and thoughtfully on their beliefs or interpretations and take action accordingly.

Discussion Questions

1. Choose a setting in which TR interventions could be implemented and a group to whom these interventions could be directed. Identify possible outcomes of TR interventions in the areas of (a) functional limitations, (b) experiences of individuals with disabilities, and (c) societal limitations.

2. What does research tell us about priorities in the three outcome areas listed in question one?

3. The authors claim that the concerns of consumers and professionals of color continue to be underrepresented in therapeutic recreation. Discuss this claim identifying evidence that supports or refutes it. Consider further how other aspects of cultural identity (e.g., family, class, sexuality, gender, spirituality) affects TR professionals' understanding of desired outcomes and effective interventions.

4. Discuss how consumers could be more fully involved in the design and implementation of outcome-based research. What are the potential benefits of such an approach? Costs or concerns?

5. Discuss three research methods that have been used to study TR outcomes.

6. In what ways can therapeutic recreation and other healthcare professionals collaborate to produce outcome studies? What are the benefits of such collaborations?

References

Bedini, L. and Wu, Y. (1994). A methodological review of research in *Therapeutic Recreation Journal* from 1986 to 1990. *Therapeutic Recreation Journal, 28*(2), 87–98.

Carbonneau, H., Hélie, C., and Quellett, G. (1994). *Évaluation d'un programme d'éducation au loisir.* Trois-Rivières, QC: Université du Quebèc à Trois-Rivières.

Carruthers, C. (1997/98). Therapeutic recreation efficacy research agenda. *Annual in Therapeutic Recreation, 7,* 29–41.

Compton, D. (1984). Research priorities in recreation for special populations. *Therapeutic Recreation Journal, 18*(1), 9–17.

Compton, D. and Dieser, R. (1997). Research initiatives in therapeutic recreation. In D. Compton (Ed.), *Issues in therapeutic recreation: Toward the new millennium* (2nd ed.; pp. 299–325). Champaign, IL: Sagamore.

Coyle, C., Boyd, R., Kinney, W., and Shank, J. (1998). The changing nature of therapeutic recreation: Maintaining consistency in the face of change. *Parks & Recreation, 33*(5), 57–63.

Coyle, C.P., Kinney, W.B., Riley, B., and Shank, J. (Eds.). (1991). *Benefits of therapeutic recreation: A consensus view.* Ravensdale, WA: Idyll Arbor.

Dattilo, J. and Light, J. (1993). Setting the stage for leisure: Encouraging reciprocal communication for people using augmentative and alternative communication systems through facilitator instruction. *Therapeutic Recreation Journal, 27*(3), 156–171.

Dupuis, S.L. and Pedlar, A. (1993). Reclaiming identity through music: An examination of the effects of a music program on the psychological well-being of older adults with dementia of the Alzheimer's type. In K. Fox (Ed.), *Proceedings of the Seventh Canadian Congress on Leisure Research* (pp. 194–198). Winnipeg, MB: University of Manitoba Printing Services.

Dupuis, S.L. and Pedlar, A. (1995). Family leisure programs in institutional care settings: Buffering the stress of caregivers. *Therapeutic Recreation Journal, 29*(3), 184–205.

Farias-Tomaszewski, S., Jenkins, S., and Keller, J. (2001). An evaluation of therapeutic horseback riding programs for adults with physical impairments. *Therapeutic Recreation Journal, 35*(3), 250–257.

Fisher, F. (1980). Self-charting for patients in recreation therapy. *Adolescence, 15*(57), 149–154.

Fitzsimmons, S. (2001). Easy rider wheelchair biking: A nursing-recreation therapy clinical trial for the treatment of depression. *Journal of Gerontological Nursing, 27*(5), 14–23.

Flaherty, J.A. and Meagher, R. (1980). Measuring racial bias in inpatient treatment. *American Journal of Psychiatry, 137*(6), 679–682.

Gammonley, D. and Luken, K. (2002). Peer education and advocacy through recreation and leadership. *Psychiatric Rehabilitation Journal, 25*(2), 170–178.

Hartig, T., Korpela, K.M., Evans, G.W., and Garling, T. (1996). Validation of a measure of perceived environmental restorativeness. *Göteborg Psychological Reports, 26*, 1–64.

Hodges, J.S. and Luken, K. (2000). Services and support as a means to meaningful outcomes for persons with developmental disabilities. *Annual in Therapeutic Recreation, 9*, 47–56.

Hoffman, B. (2003). Healthcare reform and social movements in the United States. *American Journal of Public Health, 93*(1), 75–85.

Iso-Ahola, S.E. (1988). Research in therapeutic recreation. *Therapeutic Recreation Journal, 22*(1), 7–13.

Jacobson, S., Carruthers, C., and Keller, M.J. (2001). Keynote: A sociohistorical perspective on therapeutic recreation research. In N.J. Stumbo (Ed.), *Professional issues in therapeutic recreation: On competence and outcomes* (pp. 317–334). Champaign, IL: Sagamore.

Kaplan, S. (1995). The restorative benefits of nature: Toward an integrative framework. *Journal of Environmental Psychology, 15*, 169–182.

Kemper, D.W., Lorig, K., and Mettler, M. (1993). The effectiveness of medical self-care interventions: A focus on self-initiated responses to symptoms. *Patient Education Counseling, 21*, 29–30.

Kolanowski, A.M., Buettner, L., Costa, P.T., and Litaker, M.S. (2001). Capturing interests: Therapeutic recreation activities for persons with dementia. *Therapeutic Recreation Journal, 35*(3), 220–235.

Landrum, P.K., Schmidt, N.D., and McLean, A. (1995). *Outcome-oriented rehabilitation: Principles, strategies, and tools for effective program management.* Gaithersburg, MD: Aspen.

Malkin, M.J., Coyle, C.P., and Carruthers, C. (1998). Efficacy research in recreational therapy. In F. Brasile, T. Skalko and J. Burlingame (Eds.), *Perspectives in recreational therapy: Issues of a dynamic profession* (pp. 141–164). Ravensdale, WA: Idyll Arbor.

Nemec, P.B., McNamara, S., and Walsh, D. (1994). Direct skills teaching. In W.A. Anthony and L. Spaniol (Eds.), *Readings in psychiatric rehabilitation* (pp. 172–190). Boston, MA: Center for Psychiatric Rehabilitation.

Nour, K., Desrosiers, J., Gauthier, P., and Carbonneau, H. (2002). Impact of a home leisure educational program for older adults who have had a stroke. *Therapeutic Recreation Journal, 36*(1), 48–64.

Patrick, G. (2001). Clinical research: Methods and mandates. In N.J. Stumbo (Ed.), *Professional issues in therapeutic recreation: On competence and outcomes* (pp. 401–418). Champaign, IL: Sagamore.

Paul, G.L. (Ed.). (1987). *Observational assessment instrumentation for service and research—The time-sample behavioral checklist: Assessment in residential treatment settings (Part 2)*. Champaign, IL: Research Press.

Paul, G.L., Stuve, P., and Menditto, A.A. (1997). Social-learning program (with token economy) for adult psychiatric inpatients. *The Clinical Psychologist, 50*, 14–17.

Petryshen, P.M., Hawkins, J.D., and Fronchak, T.A. (2001). An evaluation of the social recreation component of a community mental health program. *Psychiatric Rehabilitation Journal, 24*(3), 293–298.

Pestle, K., Card, J., and Menditto, A. (1998). Therapeutic recreation in a social-learning program: Effect over time on appropriate behaviors of residents with schizophrenia. *Therapeutic Recreation Journal, 32*(1), 28–41.

Rawson, H.E. and Barnett, T. (1993). Changes in children's manifest anxiety in a therapeutic short-term camping experience: An exploratory study. *Therapeutic Recreation Journal, 27*(1), 22–32.

Rehabilitation Accreditation Commission. (2000). *Managing outcomes: Customer-driven outcomes measurement and management systems—A guide to development and use*. Tucson, AZ: Author.

Richter, K.J. and Kaschalk, S.M. (1996). The future of therapeutic recreation: An existential outcome. In C. Sylvester (Ed.), *Philosophy of therapeutic recreation: Ideas and issues Vol. II* (pp. 86–91). Arlington, VA: National Recreation and Park Association.

Riley, B. and Skalko, T.K. (1998). The evolution of therapeutic recreation. *Parks & Recreation, 33*(5), 64–71.

Sable, J., Powell, L., and Aldrich, L. (1993/94). Transdisciplinary principles in the provision of therapeutic recreation services in inclusionary school settings. *Annual in Therapeutic Recreation, 4*, 69–81.

Scarmeas, N., Levy, G., Tang, M., Manly, J., and Stern, Y. (2001). Influence of leisure activity on the incidence of Alzheimer's Disease. *Neurology, 57*, 2236–2242.

Schleien, S.J. and Yermakoff, N. (1983). Data-based research in therapeutic recreation: State of the art. *Therapeutic Recreation Journal, 17*(4), 17–26.

Shank, J.W., Coyle, C.P., Boyd, R., and Kinney, W.B. (1996). A classification scheme for therapeutic recreation research grounded in the rehabilitative sciences. *Therapeutic Recreation Journal, 30*(3), 179–197.

Shank, J.W. and Kinney, W.B. (1991). Monitoring and measuring outcomes in therapeutic recreation. In B. Riley (Ed.), *Quality management: Applica-*

tions for therapeutic recreation (pp. 69–88). State College, PA: Venture Publishing, Inc.

Shank, J.W., Kinney, W.B., and Coyle, C.P. (1993). Efficacy studies in therapeutic recreation research: The need, the state of the art, and future implications. In M. Malkin and C. Howe (Eds.), *Research in therapeutic recreation: Concepts and methods* (pp. 301–328). State College, PA: Venture Publishing, Inc.

Stumbo, N.J. and Hess, M.E. (2001). On competencies and outcomes in therapeutic recreation. In. N.J. Stumbo (Ed.), *Professionals issues in therapeutic recreation: On competence and outcomes* (pp. 2–20). Champaign, IL: Sagamore.

Sylvester, C. (1996). Instrumental rationality and therapeutic recreation: Revisiting the issue of means and ends. In C. Sylvester (Ed.), *Philosophy of therapeutic recreation: Ideas and issues Vol. II* (pp. 92–105). Arlington, VA: National Recreation and Park Association.

Unruh, A.M., Smith, N., and Scammell, C. (2000). The occupation of gardening in life-threatening illness: A qualitative pilot project. *Canadian Journal of Occupational Therapy, 67*(1), 70–77.

Vandercook, T. (1991). Leisure instruction outcomes: Criterion performance, positive interactions, and acceptance by typical high school peers. *The Journal of Special Education, 25*(3), 320–339.

Witt, P.A. (1988). Therapeutic recreation research: Past, present and future. *Therapeutic Recreation Journal, 22*(1), 14–23.

Wilhite, B., Keller, M.J., Collins, J.R., and Jacobson, S. (in press). A research agenda for therapeutic recreation revisited. *Therapeutic Recreation Journal.*

The Efficacy of Therapeutic Recreation: Back to the Future

Carmen V. Russoniello, Ph.D., TRS/CTRS
East Carolina University

When the right thing can only be measured poorly, it tends to cause the wrong thing to be measured only because it can be measured well. And it is often much worse to have a good measurement of the wrong thing—especially when, as is so often the case, the wrong thing will in fact be used as an indicator of the right thing—than to have a poor measurement of the right thing.
                                                    —Tukey (1979, p. 786)

This chapter provides an overview of outcome measurement and its relationship to evidence-based practice. Current methods associated with establishing evidence-based practice standards are reviewed. A similar process evolving in therapeutic recreation (TR) is reviewed and methods to advance this process are suggested. The chapter also reviews a number of efficacy studies from disciplines shaping the future of healthcare. These findings add further evidence to the claim that therapeutic recreation is efficacious and provide a foundation for future evidence-based studies and practice.

Outcomes Movement

It has been noted that the measurement of healthcare outcomes has become a "movement" and yet, paradoxically, large, seemingly insurmountable barriers impede any substantial progress (Lyons, 1999). These tensions are felt throughout the healthcare professions and often stymie outcome-oriented studies and practice. Five powerful tensions that are helping shape the current movement of outcome measurement are

1. The federal government is moving toward a report card approach at the same time that our educational system is learning that report cards may not facilitate education.

2. There is support at the national level for standardization while there is a growing emphasis on local control of service delivery, particularly in the public sector.

3. Everybody is talking about outcomes, but they remain an unfunded mandate.

4. Behavioral healthcare is moving toward disease state management; at the same time there is a growing recognition of the potential importance of nontraditional services.

5. Outcomes are to be used both for accountability and quality improvement. (Lyons, 1999, p. 12)

Some examples of these tensions include the current use of aggregate data from collection systems such as the Functional Independence Measure (FIM; Keith, Granger, Hamilton & Sherwin, 1987) and the Global Assessment of Functioning Scale (GAF; American Psychiatric Association, 2000). This data is now being used by governmental regulatory and accreditation agencies as an outcome indicator (i.e., report card approach). Another example (accountability vs. quality improvement) is when administrators use profit to determine outcome, but cannot envision how improving care is related to this outcome.

Outcome measures in healthcare can be broken into four areas: cost and use, clinical outcomes, patient satisfaction, and quality of life. To a large extent patient satisfaction and quality of life are by-products of successful clinical outcomes. Unfortunately, healthcare organizations have become adept at measuring and monitoring cost and use, but much less skilled at the three patient-centered outcome areas (Bergman, 1995). Patient-centered (clinical) outcomes, however, are the cornerstone of a caring profession. Long and Fairfield (1996) argued that there has been enormous difficulty differentiating between outcomes related to purchasing care (comparing one practice or hospital with another) and those associated with individual care. Because of this, healthcare professions and governmental agencies have been charged, either implicitly or explicitly, with developing guidelines to help healthcare professions understand how to identify, monitor, and accurately prescribe treatments to derive specific outcomes. Ethical and moral obligations, upheld the by healthcare professions, dictate that investigations are directed toward increasing the specificity of services (i.e., prescription of treatment) thereby increasing overall effectiveness. While other outcomes are important, the success of a healthcare service is contingent on meeting patient-centered outcomes.

Evidence-Based Practice

One effective way to ensure success at deriving patient-centered outcomes is through the systematic development of evidence-based practice. Identifying and testing outcomes to develop evidence-based practice is a daunting task for any profession to undertake but is essential to the growth and development of a profession. According to Ben Massey, President of the American Physical Therapy Association, efficacy-based practice is the standard used by clinicians and payers. Yet, astoundingly, he asserts that only 20% of clinical practice in any field (e.g., medicine, nursing, occupational therapy) can be supported by research findings. As a result of this shortcoming the profession has to go with lesser degrees of evidence (e.g., anecdotal) until more rigorous experiments can be conducted (Wolski, 2002).

In order to guide the development of evidence-based practice it is important to begin by establishing standards for research methodology that help with the development of empirical support for treatments. For instance, a task force on methodology and empirically supported treatments in psychophysiology and biofeedback (Moss & Gunkelman, 2002), recently created a template consisting of five categories to help classify evidence and develop evidence-based practice. The five categories are

1. Not Empirically Supported,

2. Possibly Efficacious,

3. Probably Efficacious,

4. Efficacious, and

5. Efficacious and Specific.

Other considerations and ethical standards provide guidance to practitioners and other interested parties who want to know whether a treatment is efficacious. According to Moss and Gunkelman this is a proactive approach to help guide "committees that will be reviewing studies in the area of clinical psychophysiology and biofeedback for the purpose of producing 'white papers' and efficacy reviews" (2002, p. 19). Physical therapy has undertaken a similar approach by recently convening a panel to develop evidence-based clinical practice guidelines on selected rehabilitation interventions (Philadelphia Panel, 2001)[1]. It is important to note, however, that the physical therapy profession is not waiting for this important process to establish itself. Instead the American Physical Therapy Association is implementing a variety of strategies to address the 80% of practice that still needs validation. For instance, they have implemented a national program called Hooked on Evidence in which practitioners are encouraged to write summaries and post them in online databases. A huge benefit of this effort will be the ability of practitioners to easily review summaries about similar cases from practitioners around the nation (Wolski, 2002). They also will be able to use these to identify, and then test, common practices that seem to work.

Another strategy is their participation in an alliance with occupational and speech therapies. The main goal of the Physical Therapy, Occupational Therapy, and Speech Therapy Trialliance is to determine consistent patient outcomes across disciplines and pool resources to increase clout in influencing external audiences like Congress (Wolski, 2002). This method is similar to others used by other healthcare professions such as mental health (Barkham et al., 1998) to begin the drive toward evidence-based practice. A similar proactive approach by TR's professional associations is needed to guide the profession toward evidence-based practice.

Outcome Development in Therapeutic Recreation

Outcome theory and practical applications of clinical outcomes are not new in therapeutic recreation. Riley (1987) provided an overall structure for an evaluation process of TR services. Huston (1987) applied these principles to clinical practice. The use of outcomes (Riley, 1991), including their measurement, has also been explored (Dunn, Sneegas & Carruthers, 1991; Shank & Kinney, 1991; Stumbo, 2000). These reviews have provided the field with effective processes and techniques with which to identify outcomes and to evaluate treatment success. This book intends to extend those efforts.

Temple University's *Benefits of Therapeutic Recreation: A Consensus View* made a significant contribution to the profession by helping identify health outcomes that could be attributed to TR services (Coyle, Kinney, Riley & Shank, 1991). The experts invited to the conference were charged with the identification of common outcomes from research within the profession as well as in related areas. The goal was to build a typology that could set the stage for the next level of outcome specificity. Six global benefits emerged from this comprehensive review:

1. Physical health and maintenance,
2. Cognitive functioning,
3. Psychosocial health,
4. Growth and development,
5. Personal and life satisfaction, and
6. Societal and healthcare system outcomes.

This Benefits of Therapeutic Recreation Conference provided a wonderful starting point for researchers and clinicians seeking to substantiate claims of efficacy for therapeutic recreation. This is an effective approach because it provides guidance for future investigations and practice. It is, however, only a starting point and should be viewed as providing a general agreement. For evidence-based practice to develop, these general areas will need to be further defined using increasingly rigorous methods of evaluation.

For example, it is logical to assume that exercise (a component of many recreational activities) will produce some health benefits. The prescription of exercise, however, takes into account the conditions, frequency, duration, and intensity of the exercise which, when followed, increases the odds that exercise with the same prescription will produce the same results. Therapeutic recreation specialists (TRSs) often assume that recreational activities produce exercise benefits, but it is not known whether exercise prescriptions can be duplicated through TR interventions. Therefore, it is difficult to counsel people on proper use of recreational activity. Only recently has initial information on the appropriate activity prescription for maintaining or improving health been accepted. The Activity Pyramid (Figure 6.1) provides general recommendations for the frequency, duration and intensity of recreational activity (Corbin & Pangrazi, 1998), but specific prescriptions by TRSs to effect biopsychosocial change have yet to be developed.

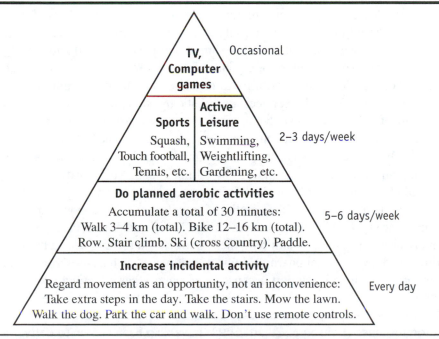

Figure 6.1 The Activity Pyramid (Rauramaa & Leon, 1996)

In addition to a lack of outcome data specific to TR interventions, there is a paucity of highly regarded, randomized, placebo-controlled studies. This need was identified by Shank, Kinney, and Coyle in their 1993 review of the state of the art in outcome research: "Tightly controlled experimental designs are needed to establish causal relations between TR interventions and outcomes/benefits" (p. 318). TRSs have not often used this type of rigorous test to determine intervention effectiveness but will have to if unspecified factors are to be separated from specified ones and prescription parameters developed. For example, in therapeutic recreation the perception of an activity is often touted as critical factor in determining the eventual benefit. But, how much of this is a placebo effect and how much is some other phenomenon? Before any benefit can be directly attributed to an intervention, this placebo factor needs to be teased out. In fact therapeutic recreation is well-positioned to take a lead in testing the placebo effect because recreational activity provides a natural venue. Placebo is a current topic of extreme interest to healthcare researchers and practitioners. Thus, controlled efficacy studies and those that look at patterns of activities in healthy individuals as well as those with dysfunctional conditions are sorely needed to help determine prescriptive parameters of recreational activities. In addition, there are few, if any, multicenter studies currently underway. Yet, these are the types of studies that carry the most weight because they help determine the specificity and generalizability of an intervention.

Another important factor to consider while developing criteria for evidence-based practice is the rapidly changing paradigm associated with healthcare. For instance, it is now assumed that psychological and social factors are inexorably intertwined with biological factors and have a major impact on a patient's susceptibility to illness and on treatment outcome (Shelton, 1999). Since TR services are holistic by nature their efficacy may be even greater than previously believed. There is no sense in wasting precious time studying outcomes that are not currently valued. The TR profession would be well-served by constant surveillance of the healthcare environment, anticipating and then participating (by taking a leadership position) in the agenda for change. Additionally, biological discoveries are beginning to further explain constructs like emotions, cognition, social support, and their importance in deriving treatment outcomes. This paradigm shift has provoked many disciplines into reexamining their theories and techniques. At the same time the delivery of nonpharmacological treatments, such as prescribed exercise, continue to gain support because basic science has effectively demonstrated how exercise can reverse dysfunctional health processes (Sallis & Owen, 1999). Other prescribed nonpharmacological treatments like the relaxation response (Benson & Stuart, 1992) have also been shown to deliver a consistent outcome (i.e., a relaxation of the autonomic nervous system).

These interventions and similar ones are being used by TRSs, yet discipline-specific efficacy has not been established.

Given the shift toward biopsychosocial interventions, TRSs must continually identify important outcomes and systematically study their applicability to the field. The rest of this chapter focuses on some physical, psychological, and social outcomes from related fields that support TR's efficacy. These contemporary outcome studies are representative of the changing healthcare paradigm and are directly related to therapeutic recreation (Russoniello, 2000). They provide fertile ground for future TR outcome studies and the basis for future evidence-based practices.

Future Outcomes

Outcomes established from studies conducted by related professions are important starting points for TRSs. The outcomes are categorized in three areas commonly addressed by healthcare practitioners using the biopsychosocial model: physical, psychological, and social. Whether these findings can be replicated when TRSs implement the techniques is still in question. Other areas not elaborated upon in this chapter but important components of evidence-based practice and areas for future outcome studies are cognitive and spiritual benefits of activity participation, compliance, and as mentioned earlier the placebo effect. For instance, a common belief among TRSs is that people will do more and get more benefit when they participate in recreational activities because they enjoy the activity. If this is true as verified through randomized control trials then therapeutic recreation offers a unique treatment advantage for patients. A comparative study with occupational and physical therapy in which therapeutic recreation demonstrates greater functional (i.e., physical, psychological, and social) outcomes and patient satisfaction would be a landmark study for therapeutic recreation. Individual experiences, personality, habits, and propensity to change also are related to treatment success (Shelton, 1999) and provide additional areas for future study.

Physical

The prescription of exercise has become a sophisticated science that requires specific training before one can become proficient. The use of exercise to obtain, maintain, and improve health is as old as recorded history (O'Morrow & Reynolds, 1989). Over the years exercise as a health intervention has become more and more accepted. Pollock and Wilmore (1990) provide an array of practices and procedures for treating cardiovascular disease, cardio-respiratory function, obesity, musculoskeletal function and prescriptions for prevention and rehabilitation. Sallis and Owen (1999) specifically address the use of physical activity to positively effect physical and psychological variables that contribute to medical and psychological disorders. A number of health outcomes obtained from prescribed exercise are illustrated in Table 6.1.

Clearly, there are numerous health benefits derived from exercise. There is this tendency, however, to generalize findings to other disciplines that use exercise. TRSs do not really know whether exercise experienced during a recreational activity has the same outcome as exercise conducted under different conditions. Putting a diverse group of individuals with varying goals into the same exercise group and without individualized (i.e., health outcome specific) treatment plans is no longer acceptable. Under the old method TRSs

Table 6.1 Summary of the effects of physical activity on health outcomes in adults (Sallis & Owen, 1999). Reprinted with permission of Sage Publications.

Health Outcome	Summary of Association
Longevity	⇧ ⇧ ⇧
Coronary heart disease	⇩ ⇩ ⇩
HDL cholesterol	⇧ ⇧
LDL cholesterol	0
Blood pressure	⇩ ⇩
Body fat	⇩ ⇩
Central body fat	⇩ ⇩
Noninsulin-dependent diabetes mellitus	⇩ ⇩ ⇩
Insulin sensitivity	⇧ ⇧
Colon cancer	⇩ ⇩
Breast cancer	⇩
Prostate cancer	⇦⇨
Bone mineral density	⇧ ⇧
Activities of daily living in the elderly	⇧ ⇧
Low-back pain	0
Osteoarthritis	⇩
Immune functioning	⇧ ⇧
Musculoskeletal injuries	⇧

Key:

0	no association
⇦⇨	inconsistent association, or very limited data
⇧	some evidence that physical activity increases this variable
⇧ ⇧	moderate evidence that physical activity increases this variable
⇧ ⇧ ⇧	strong evidence that physical activity increases this variable
⇩	some evidence that physical activity decreases this variable
⇩ ⇩	moderate evidence that physical activity decreases this variable
⇩ ⇩ ⇩	strong evidence that physical activity decreases this variable

often would measure success by attendance and participation only. This is a good example of Tukey's caveat in the opening quote as it is a lot easier to measure attendance than changes in maximum oxygen intake, resting heart rate, and/or blood pressure, pretreatment and posttreatment and over time. Yet, it is these latter outcomes that are patient-centered and directly related to improving health. In the future the prescriptive parameters of recreational activity need to be defined and standardized. Normative data on "normal" versus "abnormal" activity patterns following children and adults over extended periods of time would provide important references for clinicians and researchers.

Psychological

There is an established link between emotions and the onset and course of specific physical and psychological illnesses (Hafen, Frandsen, Karren & Hooker, 1992; Searight, 1999). Each affliction can cause or exacerbate the other. For instance a person with cancer may develop psychological problems. Similarly, fear, whether real or perceived, can cause or exacerbate physical illness such as cardiovascular disease (Sapolsky, 1998). Psychological illness as a result of unbalanced emotions includes an array of disorders such as depression, mania, and posttraumatic stress. Physical illnesses caused or exacerbated by psychological distress include cardiovascular disease, diabetes, and hypertension. For instance, Friedman and Ulmer (1984) found that hostility is a predictor of coronary heart disease. Remarkably, these authors also found that the condition could be treated using techniques similar to those used in therapeutic recreation like relaxation therapies and exercise. Depression and anxiety have also been linked to heart disease and other conditions including cancer (Hafen, Frandsen, Karren & Hooker, 1992).

Pert (1997) and others such as Ader, Felten, and Cohen (1991) have used basic science to illustrate a biological foundation to our emotional awareness that is facilitated through a direct link between the hormonal and nervous systems. These authors also demonstrated that molecules of emotion are shaped by our beliefs and expectations that in turn affect the way we experience our environment. Thus, techniques that help people reframe their experience from negative to positive, through cognitive therapy for example, also may change the molecules of emotion.

Counseling patients about the importance of emotional health and teaching techniques to change negative behaviors is an integral part of therapeutic recreation. Along with exercise it may be the most used TR technique. Counseling and psychotherapeutic techniques are efficacious and provide many benefits. The positive effects of counseling include changes in mood states as well as physical changes (e.g., positive immunological changes; Ornstein &

Sobel, 1989). The following list of patient outcomes compiled by Seligman (1994) was derived from psychotherapeutic processes. Seligman's work has demonstrated that cognitive therapy and interpersonal therapy provide moderate relief from unipolar depressive disorder and

- Cognitive therapy works very well in panic disorder.
- Systematic desensitization relieves specific phobias.
- Transcendental meditation relieves anxiety.
- Cognitive therapy provides significant relief of bulimia, outperforming medications alone. (pp. 965–966)

It is important to note the relevance of these outcomes because many TR practitioners currently employ some of these techniques and the opportunities for research are numerous.

To further substantiate the effectiveness of psychological techniques Seligman accepted a commission by *Consumer Reports Magazine* (1995) to study the long-term effects of psychotherapeutic interventions like counseling from the consumers perspective. The study (N=2,900) involved a survey to assess whether individuals who had received counseling services felt they were efficacious. Seligman would find that not only was psychotherapy effective, it was more effective than he thought because he believed, like many others, that greater outcome would occur under controlled conditions. Seligman therefore assumed there would be less of an effect demonstrated in the field due to the less controlled conditions, but the opposite was true. Additionally, the *Consumer Reports* study found that treatment by a mental health professional usually worked, and that there was no difference between psychotherapy alone and psychotherapy with medication. The study also found that long-term therapy was more effective than short-term therapy and that no specific modality did any better than any other for any problem. In conclusion the author asserts that the *Consumer Reports* study "has provided empirical validation of the effectiveness of psychotherapy" (Seligman, 1995, p. 974). In other words, the consumers felt that psychotherapeutic processes such as counseling produce positive health outcomes.

Outcomes derived from counseling by TRSs should be thoroughly explored in the future. Seligman's work provides a starting point. Other areas where established outcomes could improve services would be to determine whether people reveal more, are more relaxed, and comply better when counseling is done within a recreational activity. Different from leisure counseling where the focus is on increased awareness and participation in leisure, psychotherapy techniques used by therapeutic recreation may include cognitive restructuring, emotion identification and control, and relaxation techniques to decrease hyperarousal of the autonomic nervous system. While these results can be generalized, like the physical activity category (i.e., people who exercise more will have increased health benefits, people who use counseling and relaxation techniques will have less psychological distress), it is not known whether similar results would be found when the technique is applied by TRSs. Research that expands the knowledge of TR's contribution in counseling and psychotherapy is needed to support the development of evidence-based practice.

Social Support

Human beings are social animals and for good reason. Unlike any other animal, human infants are totally dependent on adult bonding and caring for survival. This same nurturing is needed throughout the lifespan as we depend on a cohesive society for food, shelter, production of goods, and information (Ornstein & Sobel, 1989). This need for social contact appears to include one-to-one relationships, group affiliations, and a sense of connectedness with humanity as a whole.

Two current theories address the concept of social support and its relationship to health. One theory posits that social support enhances health and well-being no matter how much stress a person experiences and may result from an overall positive feeling and sense of self-esteem, stability, and control over one's environment. The second theory says social support acts as a buffer against stress by protecting a person from the diseases that stress often causes (Hafen, Frandsen, Karren & Hooker, 1992). These theories provide guidance and support to practitioners and researchers seeking to understand the influence of social support on patient health and healing and support the notion that increases in social resources positively affect health. On the other hand, the effect of social isolation and/or abuse by "supporters" exacerbates physical and psychological problems (Sapolsky, 1998).

The impact of social contact can be both positive and negative. Lack of social support is experienced as loneliness. Strong social support evokes individual emotional and physical responses that are directly related to good health. For example, people with social support were shown to have lower risk for mortality than isolated counterparts (Hafen, Frandsen, Karren & Hooker, 1992; Sapolsky, 1998). Social support lowers mortality among those who are unhealthy and the strength of social networks was shown to predict mortality at two-, five-, ten-, and fifteen-year follow-ups. Moreover, social support has a direct impact on the homeostasis of the individual (Hafen, Frandsen, Karren & Hooker, 1992). Put another way, if we want to live longer and be happy we must continue to maintain social connections. Table 6.2 (p. 122) lists the negative impacts of poor social support on humans.

The quality of one's life is also greatly affected by these social connections as major surveys indicate "lonely people are dissatisfied with everything—living arrangements, number and quality of friends, work, and sex lives" (Ornstein & Sobel, 1989, p. 230). On the other hand, cancer support groups have improved participants' quality of life through social support. Astoundingly, the participants in the support group lived twice as long as those in the control group (Goleman & Gurin, 1993). Given these findings, it is important that TRSs study how they facilitate the improvement of an individual's social resources, and modify/develop programs to increase success in this area.

Table 6.2 The impact of social isolation on individual characteristics and susceptibility to illness (adapted from Pelletier, 1994)

Individual Characteristics	Susceptibility to Illness
Self-destructive lifestyle habits	Heart disease
More depression	Cancer
Greater incidence of suicide	Intestinal problems
Shorter life expectancy	Skin diseases
	Arthritis
	Headaches
	Pregnancy complications

Summary

This chapter provided an overview of some current outcome research methods being used to establish evidence-based practice in various healthcare professions. A brief review of TR's evolution toward this goal was presented. A method to help guide evaluators, researchers and practitioners in developing effective practice was explored. Outcomes important to TR's efficacy claims were presented to serve as additional guidance for the establishment of future outcomes and evidence-based practice.

Endnote

[1] In Chapter 2, Evidence-Based Practice, the criteria promoted by the Center for Evidence-Based Medicine is discussed.

Discussion Questions

1. Discuss techniques that TRSs currently use that have shown to be efficacious when studied by other professions.

2. Why is it important to develop a process to study the efficacy of therapeutic recreation?

3. What are some of the problems with measuring the efficacy of TR interventions?

4. Discuss the relationship between physical illness and psychological illness. Do these conditions coexist or are they separate?

5. Why is it important to establish that TR interventions are efficacious?

6. What recommendations would you give the TR profession for establishing treatment efficacy?

References

Ader, R., Felten, D., and Cohen, N. (1991). *Psychoneuroimmunology*. New York, NY: Academic Press.

American Psychiatric Association. (2000). *Diagnostic and statistical manual of mental disorders* (4th ed.). Washington, DC: Author.

Barkham, M., Evans, C., Margison, F., McGrath, G., Mellor-Clark, J., Milne, D., and Connell, J. (1998). The rationale for developing and implementing core outcome batteries for routine use in service settings and psychotherapy research. *Journal of Mental Health*, 7(1), 35–48.

Benson, H. and Stuart, E. (1992). *The wellness book*. New York, NY: Simon & Schuster.

Bergman, D.A. (1995). Thriving in the 21st century: Outcome assessment, practice parameters, and accountability. *Pediatrics*, 96(4), 831–836.

Corbin, C.B. and Pangrazi, R.P. (1998). Physical activity pyramid rebuffs peak experience. *American College of Sports Medicine's Health and Fitness Journal*, 2(1), 12–17.

Coyle, C.P., Kinney, W.B., Riley, B., and Shank, J.W. (Eds.). (1991). *Benefits of therapeutic recreation: A consensus view*. Philadelphia, PA: Temple University.

Dunn, J.K., Sneegas, J.J., and Carruthers, C. (1991). Outcome measures: Monitoring patient progress. In B. Riley (Ed.), *Quality management: Applications for therapeutic recreation* (pp. 107–115). State College, PA: Venture Publishing, Inc.

Friedman, M. and Ulmer, D. (1984). *Treating type A behavior and your heart*. New York, NY: Fawcett Crest.

Goleman, D. and Gurin, J. (1993). *Mind body medicine*. New York, NY: Consumer Reports Publishing.

Hafen, B.Q., Frandsen, K.J., Karren, K.J., and Hooker, K.R. (1992). *The health effects of attitudes, emotions, relationships*. Provo, UT: EMS Associates.

Huston, A.D. (1987). Clinical applications of quality assurance in evaluation of the therapeutic recreation setting. In B. Riley (Ed.), *Evaluation of therapeutic recreation through quality assurance* (pp. 67–75). State College, PA: Venture Publishing Inc.

Keith, R.A., Granger, C, Hamilton, B.B., and Sherwin, F.S. (1987). The Functional Independence Measure: A new tool for rehabilitation. *Advances in Clinical Rehabilitation*, 1, 6–18.

Long, A. and Fairfield, G. (1996). Confusion of levels in monitoring outcomes and/or process. *Lancet*, 347(9015), 1572.

Lyons, J.S. (1999). Tensions in the outcomes movement. *Outcomes and Accountability Alert*, 4(7), 12.

Moss, D. and Gunkelman, J. (2002). Task force report on methodology and empirically supported treatments: Introduction and summary. *Biofeedback, 30*(2), 19–20.

O'Morrow, G. and Reynolds, R.P. (1989). *Therapeutic recreation*. Englewood Cliffs, NJ: Prentice Hall.

Ornstein, R. and Sobel, D. (1989). *Healthy pleasures*. Reading, MA: Addison Wesley.

Pelletier, K.R. (1994) *Sound mind, sound body*. New York, NY: Simon & Schuster.

Pert, C.B. (1997). *Molecules of emotion*. New York, NY: Charles Scribner & Sons.

Philadelphia Panel. (2001). Philadelphia panel evidence-based clinical practice guidelines on selected rehabilitation intervention: Overview and methodology [Electronic version]. *Physical Therapy, 81*(10), 1629–1641.

Pollock, M.L. and Wilmore, J.H. (1990). *Exercise in health and disease*. Philadelphia, PA: W.B. Saunders.

Rauramaa, R. and Leon, A.S. (1996). Physical activity and risk of cardiovascular disease in middle aged individuals. *Sports Medicine, 22*(2), 65–69.

Riley, B. (1987). Conceptual basis of quality assurance: Application to therapeutic recreation. In B. Riley (Ed.), *Evaluation of therapeutic recreation through quality assurance* (pp. 7–24). State College, PA: Venture Publishing Inc.

Riley, B. (1991). Quality assessment: The use of outcome indicators. In B. Riley (Ed.), *Quality management: Applications for therapeutic recreation* (pp. 53–67). State College, PA: Venture Publishing, Inc.

Russoniello, C.V. (2000). Therapeutic recreation and behavioral medicine: Outcomes and cost effectiveness. *Annual in Therapeutic Recreation, 9*, 71–78.

Sallis, J.F. and Owen, N. (1999). *Physical activity and behavioral medicine*. Thousand Oaks, CA: Sage.

Sapolsky, R.M. (1998). *Why zebras don't get ulcers*. New York, NY: Barnes and Noble.

Searight, H.R. (1999). *Behavioral medicine: A primary care approach*. Philadelphia, PA: Brunner/Mazel.

Seligman, M.E.P. (1994). *What you can change and what you can't*. New York, NY: Knopf.

Seligman, M.E.P. (1995). The effectiveness of psychotherapy. The *Consumer Reports* study. *American Psychologist, 50*(12), 965–974.

Shank, J.W. and Kinney, W.B. (1991). Monitoring and measuring outcomes in therapeutic recreation. In B. Riley (Ed.), *Quality management: Applications for therapeutic recreation* (pp. 69–82). State College, PA: Venture Publishing, Inc.

Shank, J.W., Kinney, W.B., and Coyle, C. (1993). Efficacy studies in therapeutic recreation research: The need, the state of the art, and future implications.

In M.J. Malkin and C.Z. Howe (Eds.), *Research in therapeutic recreation: Concepts and methods* (pp. 301–335). State College, PA: Venture Publishing, Inc.

Shelton, S.B. (1999). The doctor-patient relationship. In A. Stoudemire (Ed.), *Human behavior* (pp. 3–33). Philadelphia, PA: Lippincott-Rave.

Stumbo, N.J. (2000). Outcome measurement in healthcare: Implications for therapeutic recreation. *Annual in Therapeutic Recreation, 9*, 1–8.

Tukey, J.W. (1979). Methodology and the statistician's responsibility for both accuracy and relevance. *Journal of the American Statistical Association, 74*, 786–793.

Wolski, C.A. (2002). Proof positive. *Rehab Management, 15*(7), 16–19, 66.

Selecting and Designing Intervention Programs for Outcomes

Jo-Ellen Ross, Ph.D., CTRS
Chicago State University

Candace Ashton-Shaeffer, Ph.D., CTRS/TRS
University of North Carolina at Wilmington

Outcomes, outcomes, outcomes...

These are at the forefront of most discussions today in healthcare and human services, but what about intervention programs and client needs—where do they fit? Outcomes focus on the product, but there is no product without programs. At the same time, if no outcomes are attached to a specific intervention program, then the value of the program is open to question. Outcomes provide a means for evaluating programs and holding agencies accountable for their services. Outcomes provide the foundation for program planning including selection of assessment instruments, selection of interventions and facilitation techniques, assignment of clients to programs, and development of program evaluation. This is true regardless of whether the intervention program is being delivered one-on-one or in a group. Consequently, outcomes must be identified *prior* to the selection and design of the intervention program.

This chapter focuses on the basics of designing effective intervention programs for outcomes. After defining outcomes, basic systems theory is explained and used as the model for designing outcome interventions. Then, the chapter focuses on the steps of designing intervention programs for outcomes by identifying the concepts and discussing the major components of programming for outcomes. Examples are provided along the way.

A Quick Look at Outcomes

Often the word "outcome" is used interchangeably with the word "benefit." For the purpose of this chapter, outcomes are defined as the immediate, specific results of an intervention program. Benefits are the more generic and long-term results of intervention programs. One might want to think of outcomes as similar to objectives and benefits as similar to goals. Both are important but each slightly different. Riley (1991) stated that "in direct application to therapeutic recreation, outcomes would be defined as the measurable change in clients' health status or well-being after receiving TR intervention" (p. 59). Shank and Kinney offered the following definition and discussion regarding outcomes:

> Outcomes are the observed changes in a client's status as a result of our interventions and interactions, whether intended or not. Outcomes…represent the end result of our care. Outcomes can be attributed to the process of providing care, and this should enable us to determine if we are doing for our clients that which we purport to do.…Outcomes represent those behaviors, attitudes, or knowledge that we can control and influence, and which, for the benefit of our clients, need to be changed in one direction or another. (1991, p. 76)

Stumbo (2000) identified the following five characteristics of outcomes: (a) measurable, (b) achievable, (c) demonstrable or documented, (d) predictable or causal, and (e) meaningful to the client. Outcomes can be divided into two categories: (a) functional—those that are instrumental for living, and (b) existential—those that provide meaning to life or enhance quality of life (Shank & Coyle, 2002). Functional outcomes are usually behavioral in nature, while existential outcomes are affective or spiritual. Healthcare and human service agencies traditionally have valued functional outcomes but are now beginning to also value existential ones (e.g., CARF, 2002a, 2002b; NIDRR, 2001).

Selecting Meaningful Outcomes

Before one can think of designing programs that produce outcomes, one must first select the desired outcomes. Too often therapeutic recreation specialists (TRSs) get caught up in the interventions and assessments and lose sight of the focus or the purpose of their intervention. Before one can select meaningful outcomes, one must understand the environment in which the client will be served and the intervention delivered. This includes (a) the setting where therapeutic recreation (TR) services are delivered and the target population, (b) relevant resources, (c) healthcare and disability paradigms, and (d) benefits categories.

Analysis of Setting and Population

The first step is to analyze the agency where TR services will be delivered by answering the following questions:

- What are the agency's mission, vision, and values?
- What external organizations influence what the agency does (i.e., funders, payers, regulatory and accrediting agencies)? What are these organizations' values, interests, and concerns?
- Who is the agency's target clientele (e.g., their illness(es) and/or disabling condition(s), functioning level, age, gender, ethnicity, living situation, tenure with agency, or length of stay at the facility)? What are their strengths, needs, and desires?
- What resources (e.g., number and expertise of staff and volunteers, supplies, equipment, time, funds) are available? (Stumbo & Peterson, 2004)

Then, the same questions need to be asked regarding the TR service. If the TR service is not its own department, then the department in which it is housed also needs to be examined.

Next, it is important to identify *and* understand which model and/or philosophy of therapeutic recreation the service aligns with as well as the service's scope of practice. For example, if the TR service aligns with the Leisure Ability Model (Stumbo & Peterson, 2004), then the scope of practice would include functional intervention, leisure education, and recreation participation; and outcomes should relate to leisure lifestyle and enhance quality of life. Such outcomes might include: ability to remain on task, ability to make decisions related to leisure participation, or ability to locate and use community leisure resources (Stumbo & Peterson, 2004). If, however, the TR service aligns with the Health Protection/Health Promotion Model (Austin, 1999), then the scope of practice would include prescriptive activities, recreation, and leisure; and outcomes should reflect health and wellness and promote optimal health. For example, the outcomes might include the ability to feel a sense of accomplishment or the ability to feel in control of one's life (Austin, 1999). Whichever model is selected, it is important to review the authors' writings for information that will be useful in identifying relevant outcomes associated with their model, and keep in mind the outcomes valued by the clients and agency.

Target Population's Characteristics

One needs to carefully examine the data the agency has regarding the TR service's target population. This includes exploring both diagnostic and demographic information, including age, sex, geographic locale, education level, race, ethnicity, religion, culture, and socioeconomic status; lifestyle, living situation, and family status; and numbers served and targeted to be served. If the agency lacks this information, then the TRS should seek it elsewhere (e.g., http://www.census.gov; http://govinfo.library.orst.edu/). It is extremely important to gain information about the targeted population's cultural background and affiliation as it is crucial that the outcomes be selected and stated in a way that is congruent with the client's cultural background and values. One example of this is the frequent citing of some form of independent functioning as an outcome. Yet in some cultures, for example Native Americans, independence is not valued; rather, Native Americans value communality. Another example would be that in the United States today our predominate culture tends to provide the same experiences for men and women, however, some cultures reject this notion. Additionally, it is important to consider the religious background, affiliation, and practices of the target population(s). For example, recognition of holidays, eating restrictions, dress, and engagement in certain leisure activities (e.g., cards, dancing, social interaction among males and females) varies across religions. Individuals who are Seventh Day Adventist, Jewish, or Seventh Day Baptist, among others, observe Saturday rather than Sunday as the Sabbath and therefore, may not participate in intervention programs on Saturday due to religious beliefs rather than dislike of program or behavior issue. The *Diagnostic and Statistical Manual of Mental Disorders, Fourth Edition Text Revision* (*DSM-IV-TR*; American Psychiatric Association, 2000) provides some guidelines about cultural influences related to treatment.

Relevant Resources

It is imperative that TRSs obtain background information on which to build a foundation for selecting meaningful outcomes. Consequently, prior to selecting outcomes, specialists need to consult the literature relevant to

- therapeutic recreation;
- health and human services;
- their agency's focus, consumers, and target population; and its accrediting, regulating, and funding organizations;
- legislation affecting their agency and target population; and
- consumer group(s) that represent their agency's target population(s).

To begin exploring the profession of therapeutic recreation, one should review the professional organizations' literature including standards of practice, codes of ethics, definitions, and scopes of practice (see the American Therapeutic

Recreation Association [ATRA] at http://www.atra-tr.org and the National Therapeutic Recreation Society [NTRS] at http://www.nrpa.org). It may also be useful to examine the knowledge and task areas for the practice of therapeutic recreation by Certified Therapeutic Recreation Specialists (CTRS) as identified by the National Council for Therapeutic Recreation Certification (NCTRC).

Next, the TRS should explore the external agencies and legislation relevant to their setting. For instance, if the TRS is working in a rehabilitation facility, regardless of whether it is a community or hospital-based facility, it is important to be familiar with the Rehabilitation Accreditation Commission (CARF) and its definition of outcomes. For example, in CARF's behavioral health standards, outcomes for people in community-based rehabilitation should address optimizing their personal, social, and vocational competency in order to live successfully in the community (CARF, 2002a). Additionally, CARF values consumers' satisfaction with the services they receive (CARF, 2002b).

If the TRS is working in the school system with students receiving special education services, then it is important for him or her to be familiar with the federal and state education legislation and regulations and the state education standards. For example, the North Carolina Department of Public Instruction (1999) states that students receiving special education should demonstrate competency in choosing and engaging in appropriate individual leisure/recreation activities.

TRSs working in long-term care facilities can locate potential outcomes to address in numerous sections of the Minimum Data Set (MDS; Centers for Medicare and Medicaid Services, 2002). Examples from MDS 2.0 include short-term memory problems (Section B. Cognitive Patterns), reduced social interaction (Section E. Mood and Behavior Patterns), expressed sadness/anger/empty feeling over lost roles/status (Section F. Psychosocial Well-Being), and limitations in range of motion (Section G. Physical Functioning and Structural Problems). TRSs should also consult Quality Indicators related to the MDS for additional ideas. Buettner (2000) provides a listing of the Quality Indicators and possible TR implications, many of which can be transformed into relevant TR outcomes and intervention programs.[1]

If the TRS is working in a nonprofit social service agency, then United Way of America might be a relevant resource. United Way of America (2002a) places a premium on outcomes and requires all funded programs to focus on, identify, measure, and report outcomes. Although United Way does not specify the outcomes per se, by reviewing its program foci the TRS can ascertain the outcomes it desires. For example, its "Mobilization for America's Children" (United Way, 2002b) includes school readiness for young children that could be translated into an outcome such as age-appropriate social and play skills.

It is also important to be aware of the national, state, and local consumer groups relevant to the target population(s) and their values. For example, if the TRS is working with individuals with cognitive disabilities, it would be useful to be aware of the national consumer group Self-Advocates Becoming Empowered (SABE USA; regional and state affiliates are frequently known as *People First*) and their strong emphasis on self-determination.

If the TR service is receiving funding from a grant, then the TRS needs to be aware of the basis on which the grant was awarded; that is, what the grant proposal stated as its intended outcomes. External funding agencies that award grants and contracts may require that certain outcomes be addressed, or they may leave the outcomes to the service or agency that received the funding. Regardless of who funds the TR services, which advocacy groups support the consumers receiving the services, what the scope of the TR services are and the legislation and regulations that apply, the outcomes should be desired by the consumers and their support networks.

Healthcare and Disability Paradigms

Another important area to explore prior to selecting outcomes is disability and healthcare paradigms. Both of these paradigms have been undergoing changes in recent years. Healthcare traditionally was based on the medical model paradigm, which focused on disease, cure, and illness management with the consumer (i.e., patient) in a passive role and the healthcare provider in control. Today, the medical paradigm is gradually being replaced by a holistic healthcare paradigm that focuses on health promotion, wellness, and quality of life and has the consumer and healthcare provider forming a partnership (Bandura, 1997, 2001). This enables TR interventions to focus more on wellness and quality of life rather than trying to fit into the medical model. Further, it provides the basis for TRSs to partner with clients in identifying outcomes and selecting interventions.

Concurrently, the disability paradigm has been undergoing a somewhat parallel shift from a medical-based paradigm to a social paradigm. Where previously the focus was on the individual and his or her disabling condition and remediating the condition, the upcoming paradigm acknowledges that disability results from the interaction "between characteristics of an individual (e.g., impairments and conditions, functional status, personal and socioeconomic qualities) and characteristics of the natural, built, cultural, and social environments" (National Institute on Disability and Rehabilitation Research, 2001, p. 1). This ecological and holistic approach to disability is not a new concept for therapeutic recreation (e.g., Howe-Murphy & Charboneau, 1987; Hutchison & Lord, 1979), but has not been voiced often enough in outcomes, intervention programs, or by agencies and other disciplines serving people with disabilities. In terms of outcomes, this new paradigm shift supports community-based interventions and ones focused on achieving outcomes related to learning real-life skills that are generalizable to the home and community (Shank & Coyle, 2002). It also supports outcomes related to changes in the physical and social environment or the addition of assistive technology rather than a change in the person.

In 2001, the World Health Organization (WHO) released its revised classification of disability, the *International Classification of Functioning, Disability and Health* (ICF), which replaces their previous classification entitled the *International Classification of Impairments, Disabilities, and Handicaps* (ICIDH). The ICF is an attempt to integrate the two disability paradigms; that is, the medical model of disability and the social model of disability. WHO identifies its classification system as a "biopsychosocial" approach and intends for this new classification to be used internationally for both research and clinical practice including as a basis for assessment, selecting treatment, and measuring outcomes (see Chapter 3 for more detailed information).

Benefits Categories

Once the TRS understands the system and climate within which therapeutic recreation will be delivered, examining some general categories of benefits of therapeutic recreation should help to target appropriate outcomes. Coyle, Kinney, and Shank (1991) identified the following six categories of benefits resulting from involvement in TR programs: (a) physical health and health maintenance, (b) cognitive functioning, (c) psychosocial health, (d) growth and personal development, (e) personal and life satisfaction, and (f) societal and healthcare system outcomes. Broida (2000) identified eight benefit categories: (a) physical benefits, (b) social benefits, (c) psychological/emotional benefits, (d) cognitive benefits, (e) expressive benefits, (f) benefits for recreation and leisure development, (g) benefits to the profession/staff, and (h) benefits to caregivers/parents/family. Driver and Bruns (1999) stated that in terms of leisure, benefits should relate to "improved condition," "prevention of a worse condition," or "realization of a specific satisfying psychological experience" (p. 354). Finally, Stumbo (2003) identified the following five categories of outcomes common to healthcare: (a) clinical status, (b) functional status, (c) well-being or quality of life, (d) satisfaction, and (e) cost or resource consumption. Research in the last two decades has documented that leisure, recreation, and TR interventions can indeed produce many specific outcomes in each area identified above. However, the TRS does not need to be concerned with trying to address *all* the various categories of outcomes. First and foremost, the consumers should drive the selection of outcomes.

In conclusion, the outcomes selected must fit the functioning, needs, and desires of the target population; the agency where the intervention program will be implemented; the scope of TR practice professionally and within the agency; available resources; and the current literature and trends. Outcomes are the answer to "why" the intervention is necessary.

Systems Approach

Carol A. Peterson first introduced TRSs to systems theory and how it can be used to design TR programs back in the 1970s (see Gunn & Peterson, 1978; Peterson, 1974, 1976). Subsequently, the systems approach to program planning has enjoyed widespread use in both therapeutic recreation and general recreation (e.g., Driver & Bruns, 1999). The majority of TRSs have been educated using some version of Peterson's systems approach to program design (i.e., Gunn & Peterson, 1978; Peterson & Gunn, 1984; Peterson & Stumbo, 2000; Stumbo & Peterson, 2004), which distinctly outlines the systems approach to program planning. Although this approach appears to be rather lengthy and cumbersome and is rarely followed precisely in practice, the overall premise of systems and the basic steps are the foundation for designing programs for outcomes.

The systems approach comes from management theory. Simply put, it involves an input, a process, and an output (see Figure 7.1). The input includes

- the clients, including their needs and preferences related to health and leisure, and their personal and cultural characteristics;
- the agency and its mission, values, standards, and resources;
- the TRS and his or her beliefs, values, skills, and knowledge related to therapeutic recreation; and
- the TR profession including scope of practice, standards of practice, and code of ethics.

This information forms the basis for the process, which in this case would be the TR intervention program and facilitation techniques used by the TRS. The output is the outcome(s) of the intervention. There is also a fourth component in systems theory which is an evaluation loop whereby changes in both the input and process can be made as a result of the feedback received from the output. For example, based on the client's assessment, the TRS designs a treatment plan for the client that includes an intervention. If the client takes part in the intervention but does not accomplish the expected outcomes of the intervention, the TRS reassesses the client and evaluates the intervention, and then

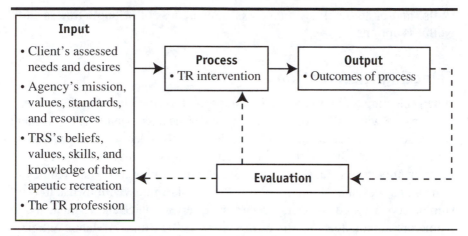

Figure 7.1 A schematic view of systems approach

makes adjustments to the client's treatment plan or the intervention accordingly so the client can succeed. Stumbo's Therapeutic Recreation Accountability Model (TRAM; 1996) is based on systems theory (see also Stumbo & Peterson, 2004). It provides a model for how TR services can be developed, delivered, and evaluated using systems theory.

Getting Started

The key to selecting and designing intervention programs for outcomes is contained in the word *congruency*. Congruency, according to the *Merriam-Webster Unabridged Dictionary* (2002), means "the quality or state of according or coinciding." This infers that all parts must be in agreement with each other; they must fit together. Consequently, the intervention must fit the outcome, resources, and client; the assessment must indicate the client's functioning in terms of the outcome; and the evaluation must determine if the client has reached the outcome.

The first stage of selecting and designing interventions for outcomes begins at the comprehensive planning stage. Once the TRS has all the input information gathered and identified, he or she is ready to (a) identify the outcomes to focus on, (b) select intervention programs to address those outcomes, (c) develop program goals for the interventions, and (d) develop the appropriate interventions including selecting suitable facilitation techniques. The program goals will provide direction for the intervention and link it to the outcome. For example, if the client's desired outcome is to increase fitness through engagement in in-home leisure, then the program goal might be "to facilitate the development of in-home fitness and wellness activity skills" and/or "to facilitate an increased awareness of in-home fitness and wellness options."

Selecting Interventions

When selecting an intervention, it is important to first identify which interventions are within the scope and resources of the agency and the department and/or service and skills of the staff. One does not select an intervention because it is appealing to the staff. A fairly comprehensive list of TR interventions/modalities can be found in Shank and Coyle (2002) and Kinney, Warren, Kinney, and Witman (1999). This pool of interventions has to be slimmed down based on agency, department, service, TRS, and client analysis. Numerous authors (e.g., Austin & Crawford, 2001; Bullock, Mahon & Selz, 1997; Shank & Coyle, 2002; Stumbo & Peterson, 2004) provide recommendations for selecting TR activities and interventions. They all agree that first and foremost, the client's needs and preferences should be considered. Shank and Coyle suggest that when choosing interventions, three primary areas should be considered: (a) the clients, (b) the intervention itself, and (c) the TRS. They provide a fairly comprehensive twelve-point checklist as a starting point for choosing an intervention (see Shank & Coyle, 2002, p. 160).

Review of Relevant Research

An underutilized but effective method of choosing an appropriate intervention for specific outcomes is through a review of relevant research. The TRS would search for an intervention that has been found to be effective in terms of the designated outcome for the specific population. Published research studies usually provide valuable information about which outcomes were achieved and which ones were not as a result of the intervention.

For example, a research study published in the *Therapeutic Recreation Journal (TRJ)* by Nour, Desrosiers, Gauthier, and Carbonneau (2002) showed that a home-based leisure education program focusing on empowerment and self-management of leisure was effective in increasing the total quality of life for older adults who had a stroke. The authors found, however, the intervention was not effective in reducing depression. Yet, they were unable to determine if it was the intervention, the assessment instrument (i.e., it may not have been sensitive enough), or the small sample size that caused the in-home leisure education program to be ineffective in reducing depression. Thus, if the outcome the TRS was interested in achieving for an older adult with a stroke was improved quality of life, an in-home leisure education intervention focusing on empowerment and self-management of leisure may be effective. But, if the TRS wanted to reduce depression, such an intervention may or may not be effective depending on the intervention or assessment tool used.

Another example, also from *TRJ*, is a study by Broach, Groff, and Dattilo (1997). They found that a therapeutic swimming program was effective in increasing cardiovascular endurance and decreasing body fat, but did not increase vital capacity. Journals from numerous disciplines such as gerontology, mental health and rehabilitation counseling, occupational and physical therapy, and adapted physical education, just to mention a few, include research that TRSs can use to justify using a specific intervention with a specific population to effect identified outcomes. One must be cautious, however, when interpreting and applying the results of published research.

When evaluating published research, the TRS should pay special attention to a number of issues:

1. the population studied;
2. the instrumentation used to measure the outcomes (e.g., Is it valid? reliable? adequate?);
3. the treatment(s) used (e.g., Is it described in sufficient detail? Were the people who administered it appropriately trained? Were the treatment protocols followed properly?);
4. any methodological limitations of the study; and
5. the results (e.g., Are they generalizable? Are they based on the data and not just speculation?). (Pyrczak, 1999)

If any of this information is unclear or missing, the author(s) should be contacted for clarification.

Activity Analysis

Another way to select an intervention, albeit not as reliable as using research, would be through activity analysis. If after conducting an activity analysis of a potential intervention it appears to support the designed outcome, then it may be an effective intervention. If the TRS wanted to choose an effective intervention for the outcome of development and maintenance of friendships, he or she would first have to identify what skills are needed. Activity analysis, where the TRS examines the activity in its purest form, would be helpful here (see Stumbo & Peterson, 2004). One major part of developing and maintaining friendships is social skills, such as initiating and maintaining conversations and listening skills. Once the TRS has determined what skills and resources are needed, the next step would be to brainstorm a list of potential activities or interventions that would involve the targeted behaviors.

Once the TRS has a list of potential activities, she or he should examine each activity by paying particular attention to the social interaction patterns and social skills needed to actually partake in the activity with the goal of identifying activities that inherently teach or use the skills the TRS seeks to develop. Once again, activity analysis will help with this step. Additionally, when selecting an activity to utilize for social skill intervention, it is important that the social skill be a dominant part of the activity and that the other domains (i.e., cognitive, physical, emotional) of the activity be within the abilities of the client. All too often, activities are chosen that may be done in a social setting but do not inherently require the social skills targeted for intervention.

For example, bingo is typically done in the company of others but does not require social interaction. Further, even when bingo is done in the company of others, its primary activity domains are cognitive and physical, not social or emotional. Therefore, if the skill to be developed is conversation then bingo would be a poor choice unless it is modified adequately to require these skills. A better activity for the development of social interaction skills revolving around conversation would be to engage the client in conversation on a particular topic that is familiar and comfortable for the client. Another option would be to develop or select a game that requires social interaction. For example, the TRS could develop a card game with discussion questions about friendship (e.g., "What do you think are the two most important qualities of a friend?" or "What are two leisure activities you would like to do with a friend? Why?"). The client would select a card, ask someone the question, and then once the person responded, the client (i.e., original asker) would respond to the question as well.

In addition to understanding the inherent skills and functioning necessary to successfully participate in and enjoy an activity, it is important to understand the steps needed to engage in the activity. Task analysis will help here (see Dattilo & Murphy, 1987).

Selecting or Designing the Assessment

Selecting or designing the assessment is a critical step in designing effective interventions. The assessment tool must be able to detect the client's functioning (i.e., strengths and needs) in terms of outcomes so the TRS knows if the client is in need of intervention, as well as if the client has benefited from the intervention. An example of an assessment instrument that was developed to specifically measure TR outcomes related to clients' leisure functioning is the Leisure Competency Measure (LCM; Kloseck & Crilly, 2002). Using the same measurement criteria as the Functional Independence Measure (FIM), it assesses the client's current level of functioning in eight areas related to leisure: (a) leisure awareness, (b) leisure attitude, (c) leisure skills, (d) cultural/social behavior, (e) interpersonal skills, (f) community integration skills, (g) social contact, and (h) community participation. It has been found to be useful, reliable, and valid with a number of populations including adult rehabilitation, geriatric, psychiatric, and adolescents (ages 13 and older). Thus, if an outcome for a resident in a long-term care facility was for the individual to participate appropriately in social situations with the other residents, the LCM may be an appropriate and effective tool for measuring the individual's level of functioning in a group before and after treatment (i.e., intervention). To learn more about the selection and design of assessments, see Chapter 9 as well as Shank and Coyle (2002) and Stumbo (2002a).

Planning the Intervention

When designing or choosing an intervention it is very important that the TRS identifies the goals of the intervention as well as defines its content and process or protocol. The program goals relate to the program's purpose and outcomes and provide the link between outcomes and performance objectives. For example, a program related to social skills development might have as a goal: "To facilitate the development of appropriate social skills in community leisure settings." The content and process of the intervention or the intervention's protocol is what activities, skills, knowledge, or topics the intervention will include (i.e., content) and how it will be delivered (i.e., process). This will help ensure that the intervention is implemented in a consistent manner to produce the desired outcomes. This is similar to baking a cake—one must use the right ingredients (i.e., content) and must follow the correct steps (i.e., process), otherwise one may not get the desired cake.

To identify the resources, skills, and processes needed, activity analysis and task analysis should be undertaken. Activity analysis provides the information regarding resources and skills needed to bake the cake. Task analysis helps the TRS identify the steps (i.e., process) needed to successfully complete the task; in this case, baking a cake. It is also important to explore if there is more than one way to do a task. For instance, returning to the cake, one could mix the batter by hand using a spoon, fork, or whisk, or by machine with an electric mixer or food processor. The method(s) chosen would depend on the resources available, the functioning of the client, the client's preferences, the client's goals, and what the environment supports. The methods used in specific interventions are also referred to as facilitation techniques (Kinney, Warren, Kinney & Witman, 1999).

When designing the intervention protocol, the TRS must keep in mind two things: (a) the desired outcomes, and (b) the clients' functioning levels. For example, the desired outcome for clients with traumatic brain injury and for clients with substance abuse problems may be community reintegration, and the intervention might be leisure education. Yet, the content of the leisure education intervention and how it is delivered would be quite different for each group because of the desired outcomes and functional levels of the clients. For instance, when working with clients with traumatic brain injury, the TRS might use cognitive retraining as a facilitation technique within the leisure education intervention, and when working with clients who have substance abuse problems, guided imagery may be used as a facilitation technique.

Evaluation

Finally, in order for an intervention program to be considered effective, no matter how well-planned it is to meet the clients' needs and desires, it must include an evaluation (see Chapter 11). The evaluation must be designed during the planning phase of the intervention program. TRSs will not know if a program truly produced the outcome they designed it for if they fail to evaluate it. Further, in order to monitor how effective the program is in enabling the client to reach the outcome, there needs to be ongoing or formative evaluation. Often the TRS can repeat the assessment he or she used to determine the client's needs as the evaluation or outcome measure and compare the results prior to and after the intervention. This is often referred to as pretesting and posttesting. This, however, is not sufficient to fully evaluate a program. In healthcare and human services today, one must consider the client's desires and satisfaction with services in addition to changes in their behavior or situation. Therefore, it is important at the start of the program or during the initial assessment to gather information about the client's desired outcomes. Then at the end of the program, and even periodically throughout the program, the TRS can ask the client if (a) she or he achieved or is making progress toward the desired outcomes, and (b) he or she is satisfied with the treatment (i.e., intervention program).

Matching Clients With Intervention Programs

Now that the outcomes are selected and tied to goals, intervention programs and facilitation techniques, and the client assessment and program evaluations are developed, it's time to focus on the individual clients and their strengths, needs, and desires. The first step here is to assess the client's functioning *and* desires utilizing the assessment tool(s) of the TR service. Then, the TRS can identify the appropriate outcomes and intervention program(s) for the client based on the assessment results. If the assessment indicates that the client needs to develop meaningful in-home leisure options and skills, then a treatment plan for the client would be developed to address this issue. The plan would include the appropriate intervention program(s) designed to focus on the issue. It would be important, however, before finalizing the treatment plan (i.e., the client's placement in particular intervention programs) to take a step back and question if the client really needs to change or if the environment needs to change. For instance, if the person had a high-level spinal cord injury maybe the problem area is that the home does not allow the person to move around so he or she can access leisure-related equipment and areas (e.g., computer, stereo, backyard), or maybe the individual lacks the skills to manipulate the leisure-related equipment, or maybe the person's attendant or family believes the individual is no longer capable of engaging in the activity or the activity is no longer appropriate for the individual. In the first instance, reorganization or modification of the home might be the appropriate intervention whereas in the second example, modification of the equipment, adaptation of the equipment with assistive technology, or replacement of the equipment with easier to use equipment might be the appropriate intervention. For the third example, leisure education involving the family/attendant might be the solution. Conceivably more than one intervention will be necessary. Consequently, different interventions would be selected based on the true problem. It is important that the client be involved whenever possible in the selection of the intervention(s).

Once the intervention program is selected, then performance objectives are written with the client to monitor and facilitate the client's movement toward attainment of the program's designated outcome (see Chapter 10). Periodically throughout the intervention program and at the end of the intervention program, the program would be evaluated to be sure it was supporting the client's attainment of the outcome. If not, the program might need to be modified or the TRS might need to reassess the client, discuss with the client her or his desired outcomes and satisfaction with the program, and/or consider changing the intervention program for the client.

Designing the Outcome-Based Intervention Program From Start to Finish

This section gives an example of designing a program for outcomes to provide TR services in a high school setting. The school and special education department have designated therapeutic recreation as the leader in providing transition services to community living. Students in the high school who receive special education services are the target population for the TR services. The students are males and females, ages 14 to 21 from a variety of ethnic and cultural groups, and have a wide range of cognitive, physical, social, and emotional functional skills and abilities. It is important to note that TR services within this setting will take place over an extended period of time—

that is, from the time that students are eligible for transition services between the ages of 14 and 16 to when they leave public school sometime prior to their 22nd birthday. The TRS has selected the Leisure Ability Model as the program's framework since the ultimate goal of the service is to facilitate independent living and community participation of which leisure is a vital part.

The next step is to identify the scope of TR services. Therapeutic recreation within this particular setting primarily will involve leisure education and participation in school and community recreation activities. Included within the federal scope of transition services for students with disabilities is independent living and community participation [Individulas with Disabilities Education Act (IDEA) of 1997, 20 U.S.C. Chapter 33(A) §1401(30)]. The school system, the director of special education, the special education teacher(s), and the TRS agree that (a) using public transportation for leisure, (b) managing money for basic leisure involvement, (c) leisure involvement in the community, (d) leisure involvement within one's own home, and (e) participating in lifelong leisure activity skills for overall wellness and health are the outcomes related to independent community participation that TR services should address. The TRS then develops intervention programs to address these outcomes using efficacy research studies or activity analysis and task analysis as the foundation. Next, the TRS develops and chooses assessments to measure the outcomes. For example, for an intervention program for independent use of community recreation activities or using public transportation, the TRS may use the Community Integration Program (Lauzen & Forbes, 2002). This program includes intervention protocols (including content and process, goals, and performance objectives) and offers measures that assess the student's functioning in the specific outcome both before and after the intervention.

Finally, the TRS would develop the evaluation for the intervention. The evaluation may consist of a method to record how well the student(s) did after each session, if the session was implemented as planned, and a reassessment of the student(s) at the end of the intervention.

When an individual student is referred to therapeutic recreation, the TRS would conduct an overall assessment of the student including his or her functioning level related to the service's scope of practice and his or her leisure-related preferences, participation patterns, strengths, and needs. If the student did indeed need to develop skills to use public transportation for leisure and the student and parent or guardian agreed this was an important and necessary skill, the TRS would develop goals and objectives related to this skill based on the student's functioning level for his or her Individualized Transition Plan (ITP) as part of his or her Individualized Education Program (IEP). After taking part in the designated intervention, the student would be reassessed to determine if his or her goals were achieved and this information would be included in the ITP.

Go Forth and Do It!

This chapter highlighted the basics for designing and selecting intervention programs for outcomes. The process of designing intervention programs consists of the following seven steps:

1. Analyze the environment in which TR services will be delivered and the potential recipients (i.e., target population),
2. Identify the outcomes for therapeutic recreation and analyze those outcomes,
3. Develop program goals,
4. Identify intervention programs,
5. Design the intervention programs including content and process,
6. Select or design a client assessment, and
7. Develop the evaluation plan.

Note that these steps take place *before* any client enters the program.

The process for selecting the intervention program for the individual client consists of five steps:

1. Assess the client's strengths, needs, desires, and resources;
2. Identify the client's outcomes;
3. Select the intervention program(s) and facilitation techniques, and develop individual performance measures;
4. Implement the intervention program; and
5. Evaluate the client's performance during the program and immediately on its conclusion.

These steps are only possible *after* the program has been fully designed.

The key to insuring that the intervention programs actually produce the targeted outcomes is congruency between and among the parts identified for both the client and the program. This requires much work and attention to detail by the TRS but results in effective intervention programs, meaningful outcomes for clients, and increased program quality. It also demonstrates the effectiveness of TR services, and consequently promotes the profession and gains support for it. For further assistance in this process, the reader is referred to the other chapters in this text as well as Stumbo and Peterson (2004), Shank and Coyle (2002), and Stumbo (2002a, 2002b, 2002c).

Endnote

[1] At the time of publication, the MDS 3.0 and the corresponding Quality Indicators were in draft form. The reader is advised to consult the latest version of the MDS and Quality Indicators. See http://csm.hhs.gov and search for MDS 3.0 for update information.

Discussion Questions

1. When planning an intervention program for outcomes, discuss the steps the TRS should follow *prior* to selecting the actual intervention activities.

2. What are the benefits to both the consumer and the TR profession of selecting and designing intervention programs for outcomes?

3. Discuss how the shifting disability and healthcare paradigms impact the design of intervention programs.

4. Identify a population and setting, and discuss what resources one should consult and why these resources could be used to assist in selecting outcomes for intervention programs. How would this be different if one was designing and intervention program for a different population and/or in a different setting?

5. Discuss how the characteristics of the target population impact selection of outcomes as well as selection and design of intervention. Provide examples for different populations.

6. What is the difference between the steps for designing intervention programs for outcomes, and selecting the appropriate intervention programs for specific clients? Why are these processes different?

7. What are two ways the TRS can determine if an intervention will have the desired outcomes? How would the TRS use each approach to develop an intervention?

References

American Psychiatric Association. (2000). *Diagnostic and statistical manual of mental disorders* (4th ed.; text revision). Washington, DC: Author.

Austin, D. (1999). *Therapeutic recreation: Processes and techniques* (4th ed.). Champaign, IL: Sagamore.

Austin, D. and Crawford, M. (2001). *Therapeutic recreation: An introduction* (2nd ed.). Needham Heights, MA: Allyn & Bacon.

Bandura, A. (1997). *Self-efficacy: The exercise of control*. New York, NY: Freeman.

Bandura, A. (2001). Social cognitive theory: An agentic perspective. *Annual Review of Psychology, 52*, 1–26.

Broach, E., Groff, D., and Dattilo, J. (1997). Effects of an aquatic therapy swimming program with adults with spinal cord injuries. *Therapeutic Recreation Journal, 31*, 160–173.

Broida, J.K. and National Therapeutic Recreation Society (2000). *Therapeutic recreation—The benefits are endless… Training program and resource guide*. Ashburn, VA: National Recreation and Park Association.

Buettner, L.L. (2000). Gerontological recreation therapy: Examining the trends and making a forecast. *Annual in Therapeutic Recreation, 9*, 35–46.

Bullock, C., Mahon, M., and Selz, L. (1997). Introduction to therapeutic recreation: An evolving profession. In C. Bullock and M. Mahon (Eds.), *Introduction to recreation services for people with disabilities: A person-centered approach* (pp. 299–344). Champaign, IL: Sagamore.

CARF (2002a). What is behavioral health? Retrieved November 18, 2002, from http://www.carf.org/BehavioralHealth/BHProg.htm

CARF (2002b). What is quality? Retrieved November 17, 2002, from http://www.carf.org/AboutCARF/Quality.htm

Centers for Medicare and Medicaid Services (2002). *Revised long-term care resident assessment instrument user's manual, version 2.0*. Baltimore, MD: Author.

Coyle, C.P., Kinney, W.B., and Shank, J.W. (1991). A summary of benefits common to therapeutic recreation. In C.P. Coyle, W.B. Kinney, B. Riley, and J.W. Shank (Eds.), *Benefits of therapeutic recreation: A consensus view* (pp. 353–385). Philadelphia, PA: Temple University.

Dattilo, J. and Murphy, W.D. (1987). *Behavior modification in therapeutic recreation*. State College, PA: Venture Publishing, Inc.

Driver, B.L. and Bruns, D.H. (1999). Concepts and uses of the benefits approach to leisure. In E.L. Jackson and T.L. Burton (Eds.), *Leisure studies: Prospects for the twenty-first century* (pp. 349–369). State College, PA: Venture Publishing, Inc.

Gunn, S.L. and Peterson, C.A. (1978). *Therapeutic recreation program design: Principles and procedures.* Englewood Cliffs, NJ: Prentice Hall.

Howe-Murphy, R. and Charboneau, B.G. (1987). *Therapeutic recreation intervention: An ecological perspective.* Englewood Cliffs, NJ: Prentice Hall.

Hutchison, P. and Lord, J. (1979). *Recreation integration: Issues and alternatives in leisure services and community involvement.* Ottawa, ON: Leisurability.

Kinney, J.S., Warren, L., Kinney, T., and Witman, J. (1999). Use of therapeutic recreation modalities and facilitation techniques by therapeutic recreation specialists in the northeastern United States. *Annual in Therapeutic Recreation, 8,* 1–11.

Kloseck, M. and Crilly, R. (2002). Leisure Competency Measure. In J. Burlingame and T.M. Blaschko (Eds.), *Assessment tools for recreational therapy and related fields* (3rd ed.; pp. 629–637). Ravensdale, WA: Idyll Arbor.

Lauzen, S. and Forbes, J. (2002). Community Integration Program. In J. Burlingame and T.M. Blaschko (Eds.), *Assessment tools for recreational therapy and related fields* (3rd ed.; pp. 581–603). Ravensdale, WA: Idyll Arbor.

Merriam-Webster Unabridged Dictionary. (2002). Retrieved November 10, 2002, from http://unabridged.merriam-webster.com/cgi-bin/unabridged?va=congruency

National Institute on Disability and Rehabilitation Research (NIDRR). (2001). *National Institute on Disability and Rehabilitation Research long-range plan for the fiscal years 1999–2003.* Retrieved November 18, 2002, from http://www.ncddr.org/new/announcements/nidrr_lrp/execsum/newp.html

North Carolina Department of Public Instruction (1999). *North Carolina alternative assessment for students with disabilities.* Raleigh, NC: Author.

Nour, K., Desrosiers, J., Gauthier, P., and Carbonneau, H. (2002). Impact of a home leisure education program for older adults who have had a stroke. *Therapeutic Recreation Journal, 36,* 35–47.

Peterson, C.A. (1974). Applications of systems analysis procedures to program planning in therapeutic recreation service. In E.M. Avedon (Ed.), *Therapeutic recreation service: An applied behavioral science approach* (pp. 128–155). Englewood Cliffs, NJ: Prentice Hall.

Peterson, C.A. (1976). *A systems approach to therapeutic recreation program planning.* Champaign, IL: Stipes.

Peterson, C.A. and Gunn, S.L. (1984). *Therapeutic recreation program design: Principles and practices* (2nd ed.). Englewood Cliffs, NJ: Prentice Hall.

Peterson, C.A. and Stumbo, N.J. (2000). *Therapeutic recreation design: Principles and procedures* (3rd ed.). Needham Heights, MA: Allyn & Bacon.

Pyrczak, F. (1999). *Evaluating research in academic journals: A practical guide to realistic evaluation.* Los Angeles, CA: Pyrczak Publishing.

Riley, B. (1991). Quality assessment: The use of outcome indicators. In B. Riley (Ed.), *Quality management: Applications for therapeutic recreation* (pp. 54–67). State College, PA: Venture Publishing, Inc.

Shank, J. and Coyle, C. (2002). *Therapeutic recreation in health promotion and rehabilitation.* State College, PA: Venture Publishing, Inc.

Shank, J. and Kinney, W.B. (1991). Monitoring and measuring outcomes in therapeutic recreation. In B. Riley (Ed.), *Quality management: Applications for therapeutic recreation* (pp. 69–82). State College, PA: Venture Publishing, Inc.

Stumbo, N.J. (1996). A proposed therapeutic recreation accountability model. *Therapeutic Recreation Journal, 30,* 246–259.

Stumbo, N.J. (2000). Outcome measurement in healthcare: Implications for therapeutic recreation. *Annual in Therapeutic Recreation, 9,* 1–8.

Stumbo, N.J. (2002a). *Client assessment in therapeutic recreation services.* State College, PA: Venture Publishing, Inc.

Stumbo, N.J. (Ed.). (2002b). *Leisure education I: A manual of activities and resources* (2nd ed.). State College, PA: Venture Publishing, Inc.

Stumbo, N.J. (Ed.). (2002c). *Leisure education II: More activities and resources* (2nd ed.). State College, PA: Venture Publishing, Inc.

Stumbo, N.J. (2003). Outcomes, accountability, and therapeutic recreation. In N.J. Stumbo (Ed.), *Client outcomes in therapeutic recreation services* (pp. 1–24). State College, PA: Venture Publishing, Inc.

Stumbo, N.J. and Peterson, C.A. (2004). *Therapeutic recreation program design: Principles and procedures* (4th ed.). San Francisco, CA: Benjamin Cummings.

United Way of America. (2002a). Outcome measurement resources network. Retrieved November 19, 2002, from http://national.unitedway.org/

United Way of America. (2002b). Mobilization for America's children. Retrieved November 19, 2002, from http://national.unitedway.org/mobilization/

World Health Organization. (2001). *International classification of functioning, disability and health.* Geneva, Switzerland: Author.

Standardizing Practice and Outcomes Through Clinical Practice Guidelines: Recommendations for Therapeutic Recreation

Chapter

8

Colleen Deyell Hood, Ph.D., CTRS
Oklahoma State University

Standards of care, clinical practice guidelines, and evidence-based medicine have received a tremendous amount of attention in the healthcare community over the past twenty years. Standards of care are detailed models of intervention processes "that enumerate the goals, objectives, settings, processes, procedures, and interactions of [an] intervention" (Callahan, 1996, p. 287). Clinical practice guidelines are defined as "systematically developed statements to assist practitioners and patient decisions about appropriate healthcare for specific clinical circumstances" (Institute of Medicine, 1990, p. 27). As presented in Chapter 2, evidence-based medicine is the "conscientious, explicit and judicious use of current best evidence in making decisions about individualized patient care" (Sackett, Rosenberg, Gray, Haynes & Richardson, 1996, p. 71). Standards of care are the most explicit description of practice; clinical practice guidelines establish parameters for treatment by providing general decision-making directions for practitioners; and evidence-based medicine makes clinical recommendations on thorough systematic reviews of the research literature. The terms clinical practice guidelines and evidence-based medicine have been used somewhat synonymously, however, evidence-based medicine tends to be more heavily reliant on randomized controlled research programs. Clinical practice guidelines, while utilizing research findings, tend to be based on a combination of research findings *and* expert consensus (Ewalt, 1995; Howard & Jenson, 1999; Patil, 1999).

Clinical practice guidelines have been said to reduce healthcare costs, to improve the quality of care delivered to patients, to reduce the variability of services received by patients, and to increase the skills and knowledge of healthcare providers (Woolf, Grol, Hutchinson, Eccles & Grimshaw, 1999). Perhaps one of the greatest contributions of clinical practice guidelines to healthcare is the potential standardization of practice (Clinton, McCormick & Besteman, 1994) and the production of desired client outcomes (Howard & Jenson, 1999; Woolf, Grol, Hutchinson, Eccles & Grimshaw, 1999). As Weingarten (2000) stated, "practice guidelines have been developed by a myriad [sic] of government, subspecialty, and local organizations in an attempt to reduce undesirable variations in care and to improve the quality of care" (p. 4S). Scalzitti stated that

> The consolidation and gauging of recent evidence from the litera-ture about the relative effectiveness of various treatment strategies should result in clinicians changing their attitudes about treatment choices, which will lead to behavior changes (e.g., greater use of treatment with known effectiveness) and ultimately improve patient outcomes. (2001, p. 1622)

Practice guidelines should provide healthcare professionals with a decision-making tool to guide the assessment of clients and the resultant treat-ment interventions (Hood, 2001). Furthermore, through the use of evidence-based practice guidelines, practitioners can utilize the results of a variety of research studies that examine the effectiveness of various treatment interven-tions. Ideally the use of practice guidelines should result in similar treatment interventions for similar patients regardless of geographic location or treat-ment network. However, the reality of practice guideline development and use does not always match the idealistic view of the impact of practice guide-lines on healthcare delivery.

The field of medicine, which has the longest history of practice guide-line development and use, has shown great variability in the actual use of practice guidelines in day-to-day practice. There have been a number of studies and commentaries discussing the problems associated with physicians' lack of use of published guidelines (Cabana et al., 1999; Rich, 2002). Cabana and associates conducted a meta-analysis of barriers to guideline use by physicians and identified several major barriers to practice guideline use. Two major barriers identified were lack of awareness of the various practice guidelines, and lack of familiarity with the guidelines that do exist. One major challenge facing physicians and allied health professionals is the vast number of practice guidelines currently available (Rich, 2002). The *People's Medical Society Newsletter* (1999) indicated that in 1994, there were more than 1,600 different practice guidelines issued by 60 different organizations, and as of 1997, the American Medical Association identified 2,200 practice guidelines. Kendrick (2000), in his discussion of the use of clinical practice guidelines in general practice, identified that there were over 45 different guidelines related to diagnosing and treating major depression. For many individuals, the shear number of practice guidelines available and the often contradictory information (People's Medical Society, 1999) contained in them results in lack of use and skepticism as to their credibility. Moreover, Cabana and associates indicated that even if a health professional can sort through the vast number of guidelines, the time required to become familiar with a particular guideline and to understand the recommendations contained within the guidelines might be unavailable to the typical practicing physician.

Cabana and associates (1999) also suggested that there are a number of barriers related to beliefs about the worth of practice guidelines in general and of specific guidelines in particular. They found that at least 10% of study respondents disagreed with the ideas of practice guidelines in general. These physicians thought that the guidelines available were too rigid, were not practical, were oversimplified, were not applicable to their practice and patients, and so forth.

Carnett (2002) reported the statements of medical quality scientist David Eddy who stated that "approximately 19% of what is practiced in medicine is based on science, and the rest is based on soft-science" (p. 61). This represents the fundamental dilemma in healthcare between the art and science of practice. Healthcare professionals who believe more in the art of practice will be less likely to use practice guidelines (see Chapter 2). Moreover, Carnett also suggested that "physicians resent, if not resist, outside influence on their practice style" (p. 61). Harding (1994) indicated physicians might not believe in the value of practice guidelines because they realize that many patients do not want their physician to follow practice guidelines—patients expect individualized care. Clearly, if the users and recipients of clinical practice guidelines question their utility in general, the quality of a particular guideline will have little impact on whether a physician uses the guideline or not.

Oftentimes specific practice guidelines are not put in use because the healthcare provider does not believe in the value of a particular guideline. This may occur if the provider finds the recommendations included in the guideline to be contradictory to current practice or educational preparation (Kendrick, 2000). Guidelines that include practice recommendations outside of the typical scope of practice for a particular provider will be much less likely to be adopted (Grol et al., 1998).

Kendrick (2000) also suggested that some general medicine physicians do not use clinical practice guidelines because the guidelines make recommendations that contradict their intuition and standard practice. For example, in a study examining the use of practice guidelines in teaching general medicine practitioners about depression in Great Britain, the results showed no improvement in diagnosis or treatment after the educational programs. One of the conclusions was that, while antidepressant medications were recommended for all diagnosed cases of depression, most general practitioners felt that antidepressants were not warranted when they knew the depression to be caused by social problems. As such, many general practitioners did not prescribe antidepressants for what they viewed as minor situational depression (Kendrick, 2002). This barrier is related to Strumberg's (1999) findings that physicians do not use guidelines because of (a) habit and routine; (b) lack of belief that she or he can perform the guideline recommendations; and/or (c) lack of belief that the guideline will lead to improved client outcomes. Interestingly, Weingarten (2000) cited several studies that demonstrated the effectiveness of guidelines in improving both the process and outcome of care. He indicated that "55 of 59 guideline studies demonstrated at least one beneficial change in the process of care, and 9 of 11 studies that examined patient outcomes showed improved care" (p. 4S). However, Weingarten also stated that improved client outcomes were dependent to a large degree on the type of guideline implementation strategies or training programs.

An important issue related to the use of specific guidelines is the source and quality of the practice guidelines published. Some guidelines are developed at the national level through the Agency for Healthcare Research and Quality (AHRQ; formerly the Agency for Healthcare Policy and Research [AHCPR], an organization created and funded by the Department of Health and Human Services in 1989 to assist in the development of guidelines by private organizations), or through national professional organizations. Some guidelines are developed locally through a hospital system or through state organizations. Some of the state guidelines actually restate standards developed by others (Moskowitz, 1999), while some contradict national guidelines. The issue of credibility is very important in usage patterns. Many physicians indicated that they do not use practice guidelines because they are not credible or because the physicians do not have the skills to assess credibility (Cabana et al., 1999).

One of the greatest difficulties for most practitioners is assessing the credibility of the various available practice guidelines. Grol and associates (1998) found that "recommendations were more adhered to when an explicit description of the scientific evidence was available and the evidence was straightforward and not conflicting" (p. 860). The most highly regarded guidelines tend to be based on a systematic review of existing evidence; however, many guidelines published are based on consensus- or expert-based models (Browman, 2001). In particular, guidelines published in allied health fields tend to be based on a combination of expert consensus and research findings.

Therapeutic recreation specialists (TRSs) examining existing practice guidelines for practice implications and developing therapeutic recreation (TR) specific guidelines should be familiar with the various rating scales used to evaluate the supporting evidence for guidelines. Shekelle, Woolf, Eccles, and Grimshaw (1999) provide an overview of one of the most widely accepted rating scales of recommendations, first developed by the Canadian Medical Association:

Category A Recommendation: Based on randomized control studies.

Category B Recommendation: Based on nonrandomized studies, quasi-experimental designs.

Category C Recommendation: Based on nonexperimental descriptive studies, such as comparative studies, correlational studies, case-control studies.

Category D Recommendation: Based on evidence from expert committee reports or opinion, or clinical experience of respected authorities, or both. (p. 595)

It is interesting to note that these categories of recommendations are based on study design, rather than on consistency of findings across studies, or some other measure of the quality of the study results. It is also likely that this classification scheme arises historically from standard drug trials since drug therapy interventions are common components of practice guidelines in medicine and psychiatry. Focusing primarily on study design can lead to problems of credibility, and as such a number of other rating schemes have been proposed (Liberati, Buzzetti, Grilli, Magrini & Minozzi, 2001). Given that most allied health professions tend to focus more on related psychosocial issues, these types of rating schemes may be less helpful in assessing the strength of the recommendations. Typically, allied health professions rely to a larger degree on consensus- or expert-based guidelines which in many ways are more pragmatic than the typical medical guidelines which have extensive, expensive, and time-consuming systematic reviews of research (Browman, 2001).

Credibility is clearly viewed as one of the most important concerns with clinical practice guidelines identified by physicians. Credibility of practice guidelines is also a huge issue for allied health professions. The general belief is that guidelines must be based on empirical, randomized research studies in order to contain valuable recommendations, and this belief may give rise to difficulties. Interestingly, Lohr (1995) indicated that even in medicine, many practices are not supported by empirical evidence. She stated in an Institute of Medicine report that

For perhaps 4% of all health services, the scientific evidence is strong; for perhaps 45% of patient care, the evidence is at best modest (although the level of consensus among clinicians may be fairly robust); and for the other 51%, the evidence is very weak or nonexistent (although, again agreement among physicians or others may be considerable). (1995, p. 53)

Geddes and Carney (2001) discussed the place of clinical practice guidelines in psychiatry. They suggested that guidelines based on empirical evidence-based approaches are fundamentally in conflict with the philosophy and beliefs of many practicing psychiatrists. Psychiatrists often place as much or more value on theory-driven interventions or interventions developed in the course of their practice. They stated that "the acceptance of the need for evidence-based practice, requires acceptance that research findings should inform practice, rather than viewing research as a separate activity" (p. 403).

Peebles (2000) also discussed the gap between typical research endeavors designed to produce evidence of effectiveness and the realities of psychological practice. He indicated that the types of research projects most highly valued in developing guidelines are those that cannot capture the complexity of working with clients in the context of their lives and addressing psychosocial issues. "The belief [that there is] a single reality that can be consistently perceived by numerous individuals" (p. 663) is fundamental to evidence-based practice and antithetical to the reality of working with human beings. As such, Peebles believes that there is a fundamental gap between the evidence used to support practice and the information needed to fundamentally improve practice.

Epstein (1996), a researcher in social work, also discussed the philosophical difficulty inherent in applying evidence-based guidelines to real-life situations. He contrasts research-based practice with practice-based research. Research-based practice "uses social science research methods, designs, and instruments deductively in search of cause-effect knowledge about practice" (p. 98). Practice-based research, on the other hand, "uses research concepts, techniques, and analogs reflectively and inductively as adjuncts to practice (in other words, research on treatment versus research in treatment)" (p. 98).

The final set of barriers to guidelines use identified by Cabana and associates (1999) are related to external factors such as complexity of the guidelines published, the presence of contradictory guidelines, lack of time and resources, and so forth. Developers of guidelines should examine these external barriers carefully before presenting the guidelines to practitioners, which assures that the published guidelines are user friendly.

Clearly there are a number of challenges associated with developing and using clinical practice guidelines to standardize practice and improve client outcomes. The challenges faced by the medical community are magnified in allied health professions due to a number of factors. First, many of the most credible clinical practice guidelines in medicine arise from randomized drug trials; generally allied health professions do not have drug therapy as part of their practice, thus existing guidelines may not provide much guidance. In addition, this type of research (i.e., randomized control studies) may not be the most valued, relevant source of information for allied health professions. Second, the issues that allied health professions address are often multifaceted and difficult to measure; hence, the added difficulty in obtaining evidence (as it is currently defined) to support various interventions. Third, there is some debate about the relevance of traditional medical research and philosophies to practice in the allied health professions.

Recommendations for the Development and Use of Clinical Guidelines in Therapeutic Recreation

(1) Create a profession-wide mechanism for guideline development and use. One of the identified barriers to guideline use is the vast number of guidelines available to physicians. Clearly this is not a problem for the profession of therapeutic recreation or any other allied health profession for that matter (Dracup, 1996; Ewalt, 1995; Howard & Jensen, 1999; Jackson, 1999; Kirk, 1999; Nickelson, 1995). However, this problem should suggest caution to the field of therapeutic recreation in terms of proceeding with guideline development. The process of guideline development and use should be a national endeavor and should proceed systematically. In addition, there is some evidence that guideline development benefits from interdisciplinary input (Miller & Petrie, 2000). In fact, the Agency for Healthcare Research and Quality (AHRQ) uses interdisciplinary teams in the development of their practice guidelines. Weinstein, McCormack, Brown, and Rosenthal (1998) discussed the merits of collaborative guideline development. They suggested that health professions that work together as part of a treatment team may benefit from collaborative guideline development. The benefits of such a process at the Harvard University Health Services were greater clarity of scope of practice and increased effectiveness of services delivered (Weinstein, McCormack, Brown & Rosenthal, 1998).

(2) Examine existing practice guidelines used in treating client groups of interest to determine the potential role of therapeutic recreation. Some of the most highly regarded guidelines within the field of medicine are those that are developed by the AHRQ. While therapeutic recreation is not likely to be mentioned specifically in any guidelines developed by the AHRQ, it would be of great benefit to examine existing guidelines to determine if there are possible connections to TR practice. In fact, in many ways, all TR practitioners could benefit from examining the guidelines that are used in their respective healthcare settings. For example, several existing guidelines for mental illness and substance abuse specifically identified recreation involvement, peer relationships, family communication and connections, coping skills, and stress management as targeted areas for treatment (American Academy of Child and Adolescent Psychiatry, 1997a, 1997b; American

Psychiatric Association, 1998). All of these are commonly addressed in TR interventions, and as such would be excellent issues on which to develop TR specific guidelines. In the quick reference guide to a guideline developed for poststroke rehabilitation, community reintegration is identified as a major focus of intervention (AHRQ, 1995). Table 8.1 provides an overview of electronic avenues through which to access existing clinical practice guidelines. Any TR guideline that specifically addresses issues identified in AHRQ guidelines would likely be well-received in the healthcare environment.

(3) **Through collaborative efforts, develop descriptions of best practice or standards of care.** Westmoreland, Wesorick, Hanson, and Wyndarden (2000) described a process used in nursing to develop the preliminary stage of guideline development—referred to as Clinical Practice Model Practice Guidelines (CPMPGs). These CPMPGs are "clinical tools used to delineate the scope of practice and facilitate the delivery of high-quality, effective patient care" (p. 16). These guidelines are based on consensual validation, which is the process of achieving agreement between authors and multiple practitioners on the content of the guideline. CPMPGs are clinical tools related to scope of practice. "They delineate the professional services of nurses [or other health professionals] and the current research and practice-based knowledge related to those services" (p. 17).

In reality, before therapeutic recreation can begin to compile evidence from rigorous research studies as to the effectiveness of interventions, these intervention practices must be described clearly, consensus must be reached within the field, and the practices must be implemented across the field and the country. Once TRSs have some standardized practice, they can then begin to collect efficacy data to support these practices.

(4) **Gather evidence to support best practices**—both expert clinical consensus and scientific evidence. "Guidelines that are based on a combination of sound scientific research and expert clinical consensus have been shown to result in more efficient and effective process and outcomes of care" (Carnett, 2002, p. 67). Westmoreland and colleagues (2000) indicated that CPMPGs are generally based on professional literature, published research, and clinical expertise. After the guidelines are developed, they are peer reviewed prior to dissemination and implementation. While results from randomized research studies are more highly valued, many professions recognize the value of consensus-based guidelines. "The best practice guidelines are accompanied by systematic reviews of the literature, although if the evidence is insufficient a consensus can be reached based on pathophysiologic rationale, clinical judgment, and expert opinion" (Fields, 2000, p. 59).

(5) **Disseminate guidelines and train practitioners in implementation.** A number of studies indicate that merely making practice guidelines available to healthcare professionals does not result in changes in practice or

in using the guideline recommendations (Medeiros, 2002). In order to improve quality of care and to standardize practice, practitioners must be trained in using the practice guidelines (Goode et al., 2000). Weingarten (2000) stated that "certain guideline implementation strategies have been found to consistently improve patient care, while other strategies have been shown to result in minimal impact" (p. 5S). He also suggested that most of the efforts toward

---

Table 8.1 Where to find clinical practice guidelines (adapted from McSweeney, Spies & Cann, 2001)

Archives of Clinical Practice Guidelines and Systematic Reviews

The National Guideline Clearinghouse (NGC): A public resource for evidence-based clinical practice guidelines, sponsored by the Agency for Healthcare Research and Quality in partnership with the American Medical Association and the American Association of Health Plans.
  http://www.guideline.gov

Primary Care Practice Guidelines: Clinical practice guidelines for primary care; meta-archive of clinical practice guidelines.
  http://www.medicine.ucsf.edu/resources/guidelines/guide.html

The Canadian Medical Association Infobase: Includes clinical practice guidelines and abstracts.
  http://www.cma.ca

Alberta Clinical Practice Guidelines
  http://www.albertadoctors.org/resources/guideline.html

St. Michael's Hospital Health Science Library: Excellent source of links to other clinical practice guidelines sources.
  http://www.stmichaelshospital.com/content/programs/hslibrary/index.asp

Bandolier: Evidence-based medicine topics presented in bullet form.
  http://www.jr2.ox.ac.uk/bandolier

Cochrane Database of Systematic Reviews: Complete clinical practice guidelines are restricted to paid members; topics and abstracts are free.
  http://cochrane.org

Medical Matrix: Meta-archive of clinical practice guidelines. Requires subscription.
  http://www.medmatrix.org/_Spages/Practice_Guidelines.asp

Medscape Multispecialty Practice Guidelines: Clinical practice guidelines for various specialties; requires free registration.
  http://www.medscape.com

Scottish Intercollegiate Guidelines Network: Clinical practice guidelines for primary care; emphasis on cardiovascular disease, cancer, and mental health.
  http://www.sign.ac.uk/guidelines/published/index.html

(continued on p. 158)

Table 8.1 Where to find clinical practice guidelines (continued; adapted from McSweeney, Spies & Cann, 2001)

Electronic and Citation Databases

National Library of Medicine
http://www.nlm.nih.gov

Cumulative Index to Nursing and Allied Health Literature (CINAHL): Subscription required. Can limit search to practice guidelines. Comprehensive coverage of nursing and allied health literature.
http://www.cinahl.com

HealthWeb: Health resources that are evaluated by librarians at academic health centers. Comprehensive list of clinical categories. Extensive user guides.
http://healthweb.org/userguides.cfm or http://healthweb.org

Medline: Covers a broad range of medical and nursing literature.
http://www.ncbi.nlm.nih.gov/entrez/query.fcgi

Other Searchable Resources

Centre for Evidence-Based Medicine: Web pages of organizations that provide evidence-based practice information.
http://cebm.net/index.asp

Evidence-Based Medicine: Extensive list of evidence-based practice resources.
http://www.herts.ac.uk/lis/subjects/health/ebm.htm

Health Services/Technology Assessment Tests (HSTAT): Provides search of many government guidelines. protocols, consensus statements, and reports.
http://hstat.nlm.nih.gov

MDChoice: Provides clinical practice guidelines and links related to evidence; free subscription required to access search results.
http://mdchoice.com/index.asp

MedWeb at Emory University: Biomedical and health sites classified by clinical practice, specialty, disease, drugs, and so forth.
http://www.medweb.emory.edu/MedWeb

MedWeb Plus: Provides direct links. Under "Clinical Practice," search by "evidence-based medicine" or "practice guidelines."
http://www.medwebplus.com/

New York Academy of Medicine, Evidence-Based Medicine Resource Center: Resources related to evidence-based practice and methods of establishing evidence base.
http://www.ebmny.org

increasing guideline usage are through continuing education and training interventions, which have not historically proven to be successful in creating long-term changes in practice. Weingarten cited several studies that suggested that education interventions coupled with endorsement by leaders in the field have a much better rate of success at guideline adoption. In addition, one-to-one training and consumer awareness programs have been found to have a positive impact on guideline use (Weingarten, 2002).

As the field of therapeutic recreation moves forward in practice guideline development, it will be very important that practitioners are trained in the use of the various guidelines. Without this training, it seems apparent that practitioners will either not use the guideline or will implement it less effectively, thus negatively impacting client outcomes. In fact, it may be necessary to make access to published TR guidelines dependent upon the completion of competency-based continuing education.

(6) **Collect program evaluation data**. The goal of program evaluation is to "describe and assess the worth of a service or resource in order to facilitate decisions regarding it" (Peebles, 2000, p. 665). Several levels of program evaluation/evaluation research/efficacy research must occur prior to the initiation of broad efficacy research projects. First, the process and techniques used in various program intervention sessions must be evaluated to determine if they bring about the desired client outcomes (i.e., program evaluation). Second, the combination of various program intervention sessions must be evaluated to determine if they add up to the desired change in target area (i.e., program evaluation research). Finally, the totality of all the program intervention areas should be evaluated to determine if they result in the broad goals of TR intervention (i.e., efficacy research).

An example will help clarify this process. In the coping skills clinical practice guidelines under development for ATRA, several areas have been targeted as being essential intervention areas to improve coping for individuals in recovery from alcohol abuse. These broad areas are social and relational competence, stress and coping techniques, cognitive coping skills, and lifestyle management. In a program evaluation model, the first step would be to determine if each session brings about the desired changes. For example, is the session focusing on teaching breathing techniques that are effective in helping clients to use those techniques in stressful situations? The second step would be to determine if the six sessions focusing on stress management techniques result in a better ability to handle stress on a daily basis. For example, the six sessions are: (a) breathing techniques, (b) recognizing stressful situations and responses, (c) the role of exercise in stress management, (d) modifying the environment to reduce stress, (e) using leisure as a tool for stress management, and (f) understanding the role of stress management in the maintenance of recovery. Do these six sessions improve client commitment to and ability to use stress management strategies in order to maintain recovery? The final step is to determine if the four broad areas identified above (i.e., social and relational competence, stress and coping techniques, cognitive coping skills, and lifestyle management) result in better long-term coping for clients.

(7) **Use program evaluation data to support the design and implementation of efficacy research** projects leading to evidence on which to base practice. Peebles described the purpose of research as "efforts to describe, predict and understand phenomena and their interrelationships in order to contribute to a body of empirical knowledge" (2000, p. 665). Once the field of therapeutic recreation has reached consensus on scope of practice and best practice, collaborative research teams can be formed to conduct more stringent research projects that more closely meet the criteria for credibility necessary for evidence-based practice. However, a caution must be raised, in that traditional randomized experimental designs may not be effective in assessing psychosocial interventions and/or complex client issues. In addition, these designs may not reflect the paradigm of practice in allied health professions such as therapeutic recreation. As such, therapeutic recreation must also be willing to use others forms of "knowing" in developing evidence for practice, such as case studies, qualitative studies, and clinical experience. As Patil (1999) indicated, all clinical decisions are based on a combination of clinical experience, scientific evidence, and guidelines. It makes sense that the evidence we use to support guidelines also consist of those elements.

Summary

As TRSs begin to develop standards of care and clinical practice guidelines, it is recommended that they review existing guidelines to avoid duplication. From there, therapeutic recreation can initiate descriptions of best practice (i.e., standards of care) and guideline development by soliciting consensus and expert opinion from practitioners and researchers through a national and international effort. This would, in turn, lead to continuing education efforts directed specifically at training for effective guideline use. Once descriptions of best practice and guidelines are disseminated widely and are being used effectively, national research programs can be initiated to determine the effectiveness of the guidelines.

Discussion Questions

1. How are the definitions of clinical practice guidelines and evidence-based medicine similar? How are they different? Describe which term has the most relevance for your practice as a TRS.

2. Identify potential steps to standardize practice in therapeutic recreation and your role as a TRS in this process.

3. Describe the "problem" of relying on randomized control studies for allied health professions. Describe the benefits of this type of research evidence.

4. Identify a client outcome you are interested in attaining. Describe how you would formulate a plan to collect program evaluation information, to conduct evaluation research, and to participate in efficacy research related to the desired client outcome.

5. There are a number of existing practice guidelines available to the public. Using the web resources included in Table 8.1, locate and examine an existing clinical practice guideline. Evaluate the degree to which the guideline overlaps with TR practice and/or the degree to which the guideline provides direction for TR practice.

6. The implementation of clinical practice guidelines is a challenging issue. Describe the reasons why clinical practice guidelines are not used more uniformly in medicine. Formulate a plan for the systematic implementation of a TR clinical practice guideline.

7. If you were designated to develop a national strategy for clinical practice guideline development, what would your plan be and how would you implement the plan?

References

Agency for Healthcare Policy and Research. (1995). *Post-stroke rehabilitation clinical guideline number 16* (AHCPR Publication No. 95-0062). Retrieved October 24, 2002, from http://hstat.nlm.nih.gov/hq/Hquest/db/local.arahcpr.arquick.psrq/screen/

American Academy of Child and Adolescent Psychiatry. (1997a). *Practice parameters for the assessment and treatment of children and adolescents with substance use disorders*. Retrieved October 24, 2002, from http://www.guideline.gov/VIEWS/summary.asp?guideline=316&

American Academy of Child and Adolescent Psychiatry. (1997b). *Practice parameters for the psychiatric assessment of children and adolescents*. Retrieved October 24, 2002, from http://www.guideline.gov/VIEWS/summary.asp?guideline=313&

American Psychiatric Association. (1998). *Practice guideline for the treatment of patients with panic disorder*. Retrieved October 24, 2002, from http://www.guideline.gov/VIEWS/summary.asp?guideline=669&

Browman, G.P. (2001). Development and aftercare of clinical guidelines: The balance between rigor and pragmatism. *Journal of the American Medical Association, 286*, 1509–1511.

Cabana, M.D., Rand, C.S., Powe, N.R., Wu, A.W., Wilson, M.H., Abboud, P.C., and Rubin, H.R. (1999). Why don't physicians follow clinical practice guidelines? A framework for improvement. *Journal of the American Medical Association, 282*, 1458–1465.

Callahan, J. (1996). Social work with suicidal clients: Challenges of implementing practice guidelines and standards of care. *Health and Social Work, 21*, 287–291.

Carnett, W.G. (2002). Clinical practice guidelines: A tool to improve care. *Journal of Nursing Care Quality, 16*, 60–70.

Clinton, J.J., McCormick, K., and Besteman, J. (1994). Enhancing clinical practice: The role of practice guidelines. *American Psychologist, 49*(1), 30–33.

Dracup, K. (1996). Putting clinical practice guidelines to work. *Nursing, 26*(2), 41–48.

Epstein, I. (1996). In quest of a research-based model for clinical practice: Or, why can't a social worker be more like a researcher? *Social Work Research, 20*, 97–100.

Ewalt, P. (1995). Clinical practice guidelines: Their impact on social work in health. *Social Work, 40*(3), 293–294.

Fields, S.D. (2000). Clinical practice guidelines: Finding and appraising useful, relevant recommendations for geriatric care. *Geriatrics, 55*, 59–63.

Geddes, J. and Carney, S. (2001). Recent advances in evidence-based psychiatry. *Canadian Journal of Psychiatry, 46*, 403–406.

Goode, C.J., Tanaka, D.J., Krugman, M., O'Connor, P., Bailey, C., Deutchman, M., and Stolpman, N.M. (2000). Outcomes from use of an evidence-based practice guideline. *Nursing Economics, 18*, 202–207.

Grol, R., Dalhuijsen, J., Thomas, S., Veld, C., Rutten, G., and Mokkink, G. (1998). Attributes of clinical guidelines that influence the use of guidelines in general practice: Observational study. *British Medical Journal, 317*, 858–861.

Harding, J. (1994). Cookbook medicine. *Physician Executive, 20*, 3–6.

Hood, C. (2001). Clinical practice guidelines—A decision-making tool for best practice? In N. Stumbo (Ed.), *Professional issues in therapeutic recreation: On competence and outcomes* (pp. 189–213). Champaign, IL: Sagamore.

Howard, M. and Jenson, J. (1999). Clinical practice guidelines: Should social work develop them? *Research on Social Work Practice, 9*(3), 283–301.

Institute of Medicine, Committee on Clinical Practice Guidelines. (1990). *Guidelines for clinical practice: Directions for a new program.* Washington, DC: National Academy Press.

Jackson, V. (1999). Clinical practice guidelines: Should social work develop them? *Research on Social Work Practice, 9*(3), 331–337.

Kendrick, T. (2000). Why can't GPs follow guidelines on depression? *British Medical Journal, 320*, 200–201.

Kirk, S.A. (1999). Good intentions are not enough: Practice guidelines for social work. *Research on Social Work Practice, 9*(3), 302–310.

Liberati, A., Buzzetti, R., Grilli, R., Magrini, N., and Minozzi, S. (2001). Which guidelines can we trust? Assessing the strength of evidence behind recommendations for clinical practice. *Western Journal of Medicine, 174*, 262–265.

Lohr, K.N. (1995). Guidelines for clinical practice: What they are and why they count. *Journal of Law, Medicine & Ethics, 23*, 49–56.

McSweeney, M., Spies, M., and Cann, C.J. (2001). Finding and evaluating clinical practice guidelines. *The Nurse Practitioner, 26*(9), 30–49.

Medeiros, J.M. (2002). Barriers to compliance with evidence-based clinical practice guidelines. *Journal of Manual and Manipulative Therapy, 10*, 7–9.

Miller, J. and Petrie, J. (2000). Development of practice guidelines. *The Lancet, 355*, 82–83.

Moskowitz, D.B. (1999, September). Treatment guidelines: Who's paying attention? *Business and Health*, 47–48.

Nickelson, D.W. (1995). The future of professional psychology in a changing healthcare marketplace: A conversation with Russ Newman. *Professional Psychology, 26*, 366–370.

Patil, J.J.P. (1999). Evidence-based medicine and clinical experience. *Journal of Evaluation of Clinical Practice, 4*, 423–425.

Peebles, J. (2000). The future of psychotherapy outcome research: Science or political rhetoric? *Journal of Psychology, 134*, 659–669.

People's Medical Society. (1999, February). Why don't doctors follow clinical practice guidelines? *People's Medical Society Newsletter*, 4–5.

Rich, M.W. (2002). From clinical trials to clinical practice: Bridging the gap. *Journal of the American Medical Association, 287*, 1321–1323.

Sackett, D.L., Rosenberg, W.M.C., Gray, J.A.M., Haynes, R.B., and Richardson, W.S. (1996) Evidence-based medicine: What it is and what it isn't. *British Medical Journal, 213*, 71–72.

Scalzitti, D.A. (2001). Evidence-based guidelines: Application to clinical practice. *Physical Therapy, 81*, 1622–1628.

Shekelle, P., Woolf, S.H., Eccles, M., and Grimshaw, J. (1999). Developing guidelines. *British Medical Journal, 318*, 593–596.

Strumberg, J.P. (1999). Implementing best practice guidelines: The influence of personal characteristics. *Journal of Evaluation in Clinical Practice, 5*, 223–226.

Weingarten, S. (2000). Translating practice guidelines into patient care: Guidelines at the bedside. *Chest, 118*, 4S–7S.

Weinstein, M.E., McCormack, B., Brown, M.E., and Rosenthal, D.S. (1998). Build consensus and develop collaborative practice guidelines. *Nursing Management, 29*, 48–52.

Westmoreland, D., Wesorick, B., Hanson, D., and Wyndarden, K. (2000). Consensual validation of clinical practice model practice guidelines. *Journal of Nursing Care Quality, 14*(4), 16–27.

Woolf, S., Grol, R., Hutchinson, A., Eccles, M., and Grimshaw, J. (1999). Potential benefits, limitations, and harms of clinical guidelines. *British Medical Journal, 318*, 527–530.

Assessment:
The Key to Outcomes and Evidence-Based Practice

Norma J. Stumbo, Ph.D., CTRS
Illinois State University

What do we know for sure about healthcare in 2003? We know that diagnostic-related groups (DRGs) do not work well because people are more than the sum of their diagnostic test results, and individuals with some chronic illnesses may require a full range of services over an extended period of time (Durbin, Cochrane, Goering & Macfarlane, 2001). On the other hand, we know that managed care has promoted the use of clinical practice guidelines but their development requires the ability to delineate who benefits from the practice and in what ways they benefit, as well as research on cost, effectiveness, and client satisfaction (Mordock, 2000). So while healthcare professionals recognize that individuals are more than their illnesses, they are presented with the challenge to standardize treatment and measure its outcomes on those individuals. No easy task, you say?

This chapter, on the relationships between client assessment, outcomes, and evidence-based practice, will address these dilemmas and also provide insight into their solutions. This chapter will explain that, based on the types of outcomes selected to be studied, client assessment might be the same instrument as the outcome measure—or may not. It depends on what outcomes are targeted for measurement, what client assessment is used, and the aim of the outcome measurement. The first section will clarify terminology related to assessment and outcomes, while the second section will review the categories of healthcare outcomes presented in Chapters 1 and 2. The third section discusses the relationship between client assessment and outcome measures. Measurement characteristics then are covered before the final discussion of clinical decisions and patient management.

Important Terminology

Because the outcomes literature is replete with sometimes conflicting definitions of terms, clarification of the most important ones to this discussion will be presented. According to Peterson and Stumbo

> *Client assessment* is the systematic process of gathering and analyzing selected information about an individual client, and using the results for placement into a program(s) that is designed to reduce or eliminate the individual's problems or deficits with his or her leisure, and that enhance the individual's ability to independently function in leisure pursuits. (2000, p. 200)

According to these authors, assessment involves

- gathering selected pieces of data
- about an individual, involving a
- systematic process of collecting, analyzing and reporting which
- results in the ability to make decisions for placement into therapeutic recreation (TR) programs that
- have been designed to reduce or eliminate problems so that the
- individual can independently function in his or her leisure. (Peterson & Stumbo, 2000, p. 200–201)

Among the primary reasons for client assessment is to place the right clients within the right interventions. Assessments results should "indicate that a particular intervention will be most effective in maximizing the patient's outcome" (Fritz & Wainner, 2001, p. 1547). Stumbo and Peterson (2004) and Stumbo (2002) noted that there are multiple purposes of client assessment in addition to placement into intervention programs. One of these purposes is the measurement of outcomes. Assessment is "a keystone in the process of maximizing patient outcomes, representing culmination of the examination and evaluation process and directing subsequent decisions related to prognosis and interventions" (Fritz & Wainner, 2001, p. 1546).

Client outcomes are those events or changes that occur in a client as the result of involvement in an intervention process (McCormick & Funderburk, 2000; Wade, 1999). In an earlier chapter, Table 1.1 (p. 5) provided a list of outcomes definitions and Figure 1.1 (p. 5) illustrated that outcomes are the changes that occur in a client between entry point A and exit (discharge) point B. Client outcomes and their measurement is an important part of evidence-based practice; that is, supplying clients with interventions that have been demonstrated through research to be efficacious or effective.

According to Belsey and Snell (2001) *evidence-based practice* involves four distinct actions of the part of the healthcare professional:

1. production of evidence through research and scientific review;
2. production and dissemination of evidence-based clinical guidelines;
3. implementation of evidence-based, cost-effective practice through education and management of change; and
4. evaluation of compliance with agreed practice guidance and patient outcomes.

As mentioned in Chapter 2, evidence-based practice ideally increases the "proof" that certain interventions produce certain outcomes, and thus provides a sense of efficacy and standardization of patient care and quality. When professionals are delivering evidence-based practice, they (and their clients) can be confident that the best possible care is being provided and will produce the most desirable, intended, and meaningful outcomes.

What Are Categories of Healthcare Outcomes?

As mentioned in the first chapter of this text, many healthcare authors have provided categories of service outcomes. There are five categories of health-care outcomes mentioned in the literature: (a) clinical status, (b) functional status, (c) well-being or quality of life, (d) satisfaction (Blankertz & Cook, 1998; Hendryx, Dyck & Srebnik, 1999; Leiter, 1995; McGlynn, 1995; Tully & Cantrill, 1999; Wetzler, 1992), and (e) cost and resource consumption (Brailer & Kim, 1996; Johnson, 1993; Tramm, 1995).

Clinical status may include measurements of psychopathology, symptomatology, short-term changes in symptoms or severity of problems or syndromes targeted by services (Hendryx, Dyck & Srebnik, 1999; Mason, 2000). McCormick and Funderburk (2000) cited Granger (1984) and Ware (1997) to describe clinical status as changes that are measured at the organ level, such as blood pressure, temperature, white blood cell count, respiration, fitness, and so forth.

Functional status includes ability to fulfill social and role functions that reflect broad long-term effects after services have ended and which tend to reflect a person or family's ability to lead a successful, productive, satisfying life. Examples include ADLs; life and self-care skills; safety; stability of living environment; relationship abilities such as marriage, parenting, and sibling interactions; school or employment status; and display of at-risk behaviors (Granger, 1984; Hendryx, Dyck & Srebnik, 1999; Mason, 2000; McCormick & Funderburk, 2000; Tully & Cantrill, 1999; Ware, 1997).

Well-being or *quality of life* includes the personal or subjective definition of well-being for the individual. It may involve relative assessment of satisfaction with living conditions, work or school, leisure, finances, and whether basic and fundamental needs are met (Hendryx, Dyck & Srebnik, 1999; Mason, 2000; McCormick & Funderburk, 2000; Russo, Roy-Byrne, Jaffe & Ries, 1997).

Satisfaction measures usually target satisfaction with services received. These assessments may help to determine the patients' opinions about whether care is accessible, affordable, effective, and professional (Hendryx, Dyck & Srebnik, 1999; Mason, 2000; McCormick & Funderburk, 2000; Mordock, 2000).

Costs and resource consumption balance the need to reduce costs with unfavorable impacts on the quality of care (Brailer & Kim, 1996; Johnson, 1993).

Tully and Cantrill (1999) noted that these five categories are only one way to discuss outcome measures. A second way is by breadth of coverage. They include four categories of outcome measurement coverage: (a) generic, (b) disease-specific, (c) domain or dimension specific, and (d) patient centered.

Generic outcome measures are those that "tap into a broad range of aspects of a respondent's life and, therefore, are often described as 'health status' or 'health-related quality-of-life' instruments by their developers" (Tully & Cantrill, 1999, p. 103). Tully and Cantrill (1999) noted that these instruments may be used with a wide range of conditions and many types of subjects, which allow for comparisons between groups. However, because of their elasticity, it is recommended that they be used in conjunction with more specific outcome measures. Mordock (2000) argued that global measures are not recommended for assessing the effects of interventions targeting specific behaviors as they are relatively insensitive to changes resulting from such interventions.

Disease-specific outcome measures are those that "tap into the relevant areas of the respondent's life that may be affected by the disease in question, such as dexterity problems with rheumatoid arthritis, that are usually excluded from the wider scope of the generic instruments" (Tully & Cantrill, 1999, p. 104). They have the converse problems to generic measures—they may be too narrow and miss important outcomes for larger issues.

Domain or *dimension-specific* measures concentrate on specific areas of health, such as psychological well-being, activities of daily living, or pain (Tully & Cantrill, 1999). Sometimes these instruments are used to fill in the blanks left by broader, more generic outcome measures.

Patient-centered outcome measures focus on the outcomes perceived by the client himself or herself (Tully & Cantrill, 1999). While this seems to be quite sensible, the patient's perspective has often been ignored (Fischer, 2000; Jinnett, Alexander & Ullman, 2001; Kressel, DeLeon, Palij & Rubin, 2000; Mordock, 2000; Russo, Roy-Byrne, Jaffe & Ries, 1997). This notion will be explored later in this chapter.

Fritz and Wainner (2001) noted the following about assessment or diagnostic tools in physical therapy:

> Diagnosis is an important aspect of physical therapist practice. Selecting tests that will provide the most accurate information and evaluating the results appropriately are important clinical skills.... Determining the best diagnostic tests for use in clinical situations requires an ability to appraise evidence in the literature that describes the accuracy and interpretation of the results of testing. Lack of awareness of these issues may lead to misinterpretation of results. The application of evidence to clinical practice also requires an understanding of evidence and its use in decision making. (p. 1546)

Fritz and Wainner (2001), among other authors, noted that the purpose of the assessment tool has important implications for reviewing the evidence and making decisions for clinical practice. The full process must be understood prior to selecting and implementing client assessment and outcome measures. "When clinicians do not consider the purpose of diagnostic tests used in practice, they are susceptible to viewing tests as either good or bad, without recognizing that a test may be useful for one purpose, but inappropriate for another purpose" (Fritz & Wainner, 2001, p. 1549).

The Relationship Between Assessment and Outcome Measures

There are three broad ways to view the relationships between client assessment and outcome measurement. The first is a direct, one-to-one relationship in which outcome measurement tests whether each problem or deficit targeted in the assessment has improved (Elliott, 1992; Parsons, Bruce Higley, Wallock Okerlund, Thorstensen & Gray, 1995). This is most likely to be used in individual services, such as therapeutic recreation, when outcomes directly attributable to service provision are of interest. On an individual client basis the question might be: Was the *x* intervention successful in improving this patient's deficit *a*? This is depicted in Figure 9.1 (p. 170). A

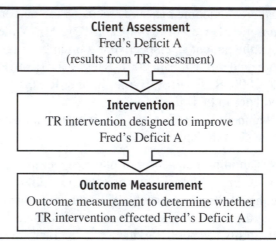

Figure 9.1 Relationship between client assessment and outcome measurement for Fred (Individual Client)

second case may be measurement of a service such as therapeutic recreation. Were TR services successful in improving this group of clients' deficits *a*, *b*, and *c*? This relationship is shown in Figure 9.2. A third way they are related is when all services are expected to improve or change a client's deficit. For example, did all the rehabilitation services improve this individual's (or group of individuals') quality of life? This relationship is illustrated in Figure 9.3.

The following lengthy quote from Fritz and Wainner (2001) speaks to the relationship between assessment and outcomes:

> Although it may not be viewed in this manner by all therapists, the diagnostic process is essentially an exercise in probability revision. Prior to performing a test, a therapist has some idea of the likelihood that the patient has the condition of interest. The likelihood may be most readily expressed in qualitative terms such as "highly likely," "very likely," and so forth. These terms, however, can be made more quantitative by speaking in terms of probabilities....The therapist can also have in mind a treatment threshold level of certainty at which he or she is will be "sure enough" and ready to act...treatment threshold may not be explicitly stated, but we believe that all therapists reach a point when the examination and evaluation process stops and intervention begins....The amount of data required to move beyond the treatment threshold is partly determined by the pretest probability that the condition of interest is present. The pretest probability is an important consideration for examining the diagnostic process because it determines

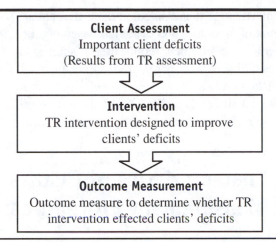

Figure 9.2 Relationship between client assessment and outcome measurement for TR services (Individual Service)

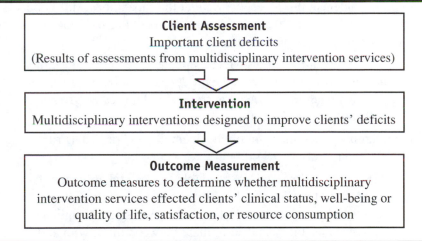

Figure 9.3 Relationship between client assessment and outcome measurement for multidisciplinary services (All Services)

how much data will be required to reach a treatment threshold. (p. 1560)

These three figures demonstrate that client assessment, outcomes measurement, and evidence-based practice are related tasks in quality healthcare (Coye, 2001; Mason, 2000). Client assessment provides the baseline and potential outcome measure to demonstrate the results of clinical practice, and this information is cumulated through outcome measures and translated eventually into evidence-based practice.

Since client assessment and outcome measurement are so crucial to both the demonstration of outcomes and evidence-based practice, these processes need to meet certain measurement requirements, such as validity, reliability, practicality or usability, as well as sensitivity to change and patient-centered measurement (Blankertz & Cook, 1998; Granello, Granello & Lee, 1999; Richardson, 1997; Tully & Cantrill, 1999). The next section of this chapter will discuss these necessary characteristics of measurement procedures.

Characteristics of Quality Measurement Procedures

The "goodness" of the assessment procedure will directly affect the "goodness" of the results that can be used for client placement into programs and the measurement of outcomes. Sometimes, there are major assumptions made by the stakeholders or misconceptions about the capabilities and "goodness" of outcome measurement that are not true. Some of these mistaken assumptions or misconceptions include that

- Many standardized tools with acceptable reliability and validity are already available or can be produced quickly, and agencies can easily administer them to treated and untreated groups. (Mordock, 2000, p. 690)

- Diagnostic tests can simply be deemed good or bad. (Fritz & Wainner, 2001, p. 1548)

- Measuring instruments are available that can reliably identify children or families as falling into either a dysfunctional or functional group, current instruments have high discriminant validity (the ability to discriminate between those with and without a disorder), or the number of false positives (clients who score above a critical cut-off score for dysfunction who actually are not dysfunctional) and false negatives (clients who score below a critical cut-off score but who actually are dysfunctional) will be low. (Mordock, 2000, p. 690)

- A number of studies have been completed with measurement procedures that produce valid, reliable, and significant results, and a significant number of outcome studies have produced change scores that show the effects of intervention have been proven. (Mordock, 2000)

- The results of outcome measurement are the result of efficacious interventions. (Fritz & Wainner, 2001)

It is clear that many incorrect assumptions and misconceptions abound about the relationship between client assessment, intervention, and outcome measurement. It becomes mandatory that each individual professional be responsible for comprehending measurement properties and for using them to understand, develop, and use the best possible procedures.

Blankertz and Cook (1998) presented a number of considerations for selecting healthcare measurement tools, such as

(a) unit of analysis (i.e., person centered),

(b) focus or domains covered by of the instrument (e.g., deficits, quality of life, clinical status),

(c) sources of data (e.g., client, family, caregivers, employers, medical records, survey instruments),

(d) timing of data collection, and

(e) target audience of gathered information (e.g., stakeholders).

The following measurement characteristics will be presented: validity, reliability, practicality/usability, sensitivity to change, and perspective.

Validity

Assessment, though a conceptually and methodologically complex task, is at the heart of matching clients to appropriate treatments, and monitoring client outcomes (Connors et al., 1994; Mason, 2000; Riehman, Wolford, Knapp, MacCallum & Murray, 1983). One of the requisite characteristics is that the results of the measurement process yield information that is reflective of the actual individual, situation, or circumstance. Assessment should

> respect the complex interrelations of our lives; they do not reduce lives to a variable or to any system of explanation. The goal is understanding rather than explanation. Although never complete, understanding via an assessment is adequate when it assists interested parties to similarly comprehend a situation, and when specific, viable individualized suggestions for change have been developed. (Fischer, 2000, pp. 6–7)

According to Peterson and Stumbo, "*Validity* of an assessment refers to the extent to which it meets its intended purpose. It concerns what the test measures and how well it does so" (2000, p. 207). Validity refers to the extent to which the results of an evaluation procedure serve the particular use(s) for which it was intended. That is, does the instrument measure what it is intended to measure? Validity is always concerned with the specific use to be made of the results, and with the soundness of the interpretations. Tests or instruments are used for several types of judgment, and for each type of judgment, a different type of investigation is required to infer validity.

Evidence to support validity of a measurement tool's results can be gathered in a variety of ways. Stumbo and Peterson (2004) and Stumbo (2002) have discussed content validity, construct validity and criterion-related validity, therefore, the following discussion will be brief.

Evidence of content validity shows the degree to which assessment content covers a representative sample of the domain in question (Stumbo & Peterson, 2004). Evidence of content-related validity is the extent to which a test or instrument measures a representative sample of the domain of tasks or content under consideration. Content validity is important when the user wishes to describe how an individual performs on a domain of tasks that the instrument is supposed to represent. Content validity should answer the question: "How well does the content of this procedure constitute an adequate sample of the subject matter?" (Stumbo, 2002).

Evidence of criterion-related validity concerns the inferences or predictions made from a person's assessment results in relation to another variable called an independent criterion. Criterion-related validity describes the extent to which the test's performance is related to another valued measure of performance. It is used when one score (i.e., predictor) is used to estimate another score (i.e., criterion). Most individuals have experience with tests such as the ACT or the SAT (i.e., predictor) to predict success in college (i.e., criterion). There are two types of criterion-related validity: *concurrent* and *predictive* validity (Stumbo, 2002).

Evidence of construct validity is present when an unobservable trait is being measured to assure that it is being measured adequately (Stumbo & Peterson, 2004). Familiar sychological constructs include self-esteem, anxiety, locus of control, extroversion, depression, and intelligence. Constructs in therapeutic recreation may include leisure lifestyle, wellness, leisure satisfaction, perceived freedom, leisure motivation, and quality of life. It is believed that these constructs exist, but they exist only to the degree that they can be described, organized, and tested.

Two other types of validity—internal and external—also are important to the notion of measuring outcomes. *Internal validity* is the ability of the measurement collection system to accurately answer the clinical question (DePoy & Gitlin, 1998). If the measurement process has internal validity, there is a considerable degree of confidence that the reported outcome was the result of the intervention and not some extraneous factor (DePoy & Gitlin, 1998; Granello, Granello & Lee, 1999; King & Teo, 2000). The question examined for internal validity is: "To what extent do the outcomes result directly from the intervention (rather than some other factor)?"

External validity refers to the capacity to generalize findings and develop inferences from the sample (i.e., groups of clients studied) to a larger population (i.e., most clients with those conditions; Depoy & Gitlin, 1998; Granello, Granello & Lee, 1999; King & Teo, 2000). The question examined for external validity is: "To what extent can these findings be globalized to others in this situation or with these conditions?"

External validity has also been called *ecological validity*—the extent to which the measurement process emulates the real world in which it is conducted (Thomas & Nelson, 2001). Mason (2000) suggested that ecological validity be determined by how the measurement procedures "fit" into the agency's existing operations:

> It is also important that these indicators [outcome measures] have ecological validity; that is, these indicators must be supported, to some degree, by existing work activities, guidelines, or regulations. Indicators that lack ecological validity are typically viewed as artificial, are poorly utilized, or are measured inconsistently because of the perceived lack of relevance or because measuring requires significant amounts of activity that are not directly related to the delivery of services. It is also a good idea to maintain a healthy mixture of different types of indicators (e.g., process, clinical, functional, and satisfaction). (Mason, 2000, p. 83)

Reliability

Reliability is another concept important to measurement tools. *Reliability* "refers to the estimate of the consistency of measurement" (Peterson & Stumbo, 2000, p. 210). Reliability of assessment results means that a sample of persons would receive relatively the same scores when reexamined on different occasions, with a different set of equal items, or under specific conditions. Reliability estimates essentially ask: "How accurately and consistently does the instrument measure what it is intended to measure?" or "To what degree are the assessment scores free from errors of measurement?" (Stumbo, 2002).

Since a person's absolute true score is difficult to determine, reliability actually presents an estimate of the effects of changing conditions on the person's score. Reliability of assessment scores can be estimated in three ways:

1. *stability measures* (i.e., how stable is the instrument over time?),
2. *equivalency measures* (i.e., how closely related are two or more forms of the same assessment?), and
3. *internal consistency measures* (i.e., how closely are items on the assessment related?). (Stumbo, 2002, p. 42)

The professional may be interested in multiple types of reliability, depending on the nature and purpose of the measurement tool. Methods of determining reliability are essentially means of determining how much error is present under different conditions (Stumbo, 2002).

Beyond validity and reliability, there are several measurement characteristics that may be important to consider when selecting standardized or developing "homegrown" instruments. Among these are practicality and usability, sensitivity to change, and patient perspective.

Practicality and Usability

Practicality and usability are concerned with the staff, time, and resource costs associated with the measurement process.

> The practicality of outcome instruments depends upon the situations in which they are completed, and this needs to be borne in mind during development. The best instrument for the particular instance will inevitably be a compromise between scientific rigour and practical constraints. (Tully & Cantrill, 1999, p. 107)

Such considerations might include the amount of training need to successfully implement the process, affordability to clients and the agency, timing of data collection, ability to use the outcome information to improve the care system, incentives to improve the quality of care, and ability to meet the needs of stakeholders and interested others (Granello, Granello & Lee, 1999; Hendryx, Dyck & Srebnik, 1999; Kennedy & Barter, 1995; Mordock, 2000; Tully & Cantrill, 1999).

Two Additional Characteristics: Sensitivity and Perspective

Two other measurement characteristics are mentioned frequently in the healthcare outcomes literature: sensitivity to change and patient perspective. *Sensitivity to change* includes the instrument's ability to detect subtle changes in the dimension(s) under consideration (Arrowsmith, 1999; Granello, Granello & Lee, 1999; Tully & Cantrill, 1999; Whitty et al., 1997). Sensitivity is usually measured by the calculation of a statistical effect size or the intuitive judgment of the clinical importance of difference in scores (Tully & Cantrill, 1999). Hatala, Holbrook, and Goldsmith (1999) defined clinical importance as the smallest difference in patient outcome that would lead to an important difference in patient health status (or other valued outcome).

Another recent thrust in outcome measurement literature is the notion of a *patient-centered perspective*. All too often, clinical measures have been based on the observations of clinicians at the expense of the client's perspective (see Chapter 5 for a fuller discussion). However, there is now impetus to include the client as a major source of outcome information (Fischer, 2000; Jinnett, Alexander & Ullman, 2001; Kressel, DeLeon, Palij & Rubin, 2000; Mordock, 2000; Tully & Cantrill, 1999; Whitty et al., 1997). "Patient-centred instruments are one of the most encouraging areas of research…incorporating the individual's viewpoint into routine healthcare assessment" (Tully & Cantrill, 1999, p. 108). Russo, Roy-Byrne, Jaffe, and Ries (1997) noted that "both self- and clinician-rated measures should be used to give a fuller description of patient outcome…self-ratings provide a unique perspective on severely ill patients as do clinician ratings" (pp. 213–214). On one hand, clients' views on outcomes often can counterbalance and address the short-comings of clinicians' views (Tully & Cantrill, 1999), but on the other hand, because clients typically experience multiple and complicated problems, it also can make the measurement process much more complex (Proctor, 2001).

Clinical Decisions and Patient Management

Client assessment and outcome measurement assist the professional in clinical decision making and patient management. Numerous decisions must be made that incorporate data from assessment and outcome tools into clinical practice:

> Central to the concept of evidence-based practice is the integration of evidence into the management of patients…[this] involves a complex interaction between the strength of the evidence offered through the use of a test and the unique presentation of an individual patient. (Fritz & Wainner, 2001, p. 1547)

Mason (2000) noted that outcome measurement evidence might not always be as stringent as the "gold standard" of randomized control trials:

> Empirical research typically involves the strongest control or manipulation of variables in order to produce data that are as unbiased as possible. Outcome evaluation typically lacks such rigourous control, and actually may be more interested in producing biased results. That is, an agency or program often engages in outcomes evaluation for a specific purpose (e.g., to provide evidence that a program is successful) rather than as an exploratory exercise. (Mason, 2000, p. 85)

Rigor (i.e., use of accepted scientific methods) must be balanced with intended use within the real world. This requires a great deal of clinical expertise and judgment on the part of the professional. For example, the specialist must make decisions about what information is important, what data collection techniques to use, how data will be interpreted, and how that information can be used to evaluate client outcomes (Fritz & Wainner, 2001; Mordock,

2000; Stumbo, 2002). Evidence-based practice does not eliminate the need for stringent controls, yet also demands significant expertise (not individual opinion or tradition) to translate that data into meaningful outcome information (Fritz & Wainner, 2001).

Richardson (1997) noted that at least five measurement decisions require the infusion of clinical expertise and judgment: (a) when gathering clinical findings from the interview and examination, (b) when formulating a synthesis of framing a clinical problem, (c) when working through differential diagnosis for that clinical problem with a patient, (d) when selecting diagnostic tests and test strategies, and (e) when interpreting the test results for that patient.

Fritz and Wainner documented this need in physical therapy:

Diagnostic tests play a critical role in the management of patients in physical therapy. The results of individual tests are evaluated... ultimately leading to a decision to use a certain intervention that is believed to provide optimal outcomes for the patient. The ability to judge evidence for diagnostic tests, select the most appropriate test for an individual patient, and interpret the results will need to become familiar skills if physical therapy diagnosis is to become a more evidence-based practice....Reliance on patient management systems that are not evidence-based...has negative consequences not only for practitioners, but also for the profession of physical therapy as a whole. Without evidence-based diagnosis, interventions will continue to be based on observation that may not even be systematic...[T]he solution is not only to explore new and innovative interventions, but [also] to refine the process by which interventions are linked to examination findings by studying evidence-based diagnosis. (2001, p. 1562)

So once again we arrive at the junction of science and art. As Rosoff (2001) and Nichols (2001) noted in their work, clinical services that attempt to embrace evidence-based practice are required to balance the "art" of patient care with the "science" of outcome measurement. As mentioned before, when "healthcare professionals use the findings of sound research to help guide their clinical decision making, the outcomes for those for whom they are caring ought to be optimized" (King & Teo, 2000, p. 608). Mason (2000) echoed these sentiments with this warning:

Measurement systems often collect massive amounts of data, but produce relatively little information. Information is derived from data....At the outset of establishing a system that collects and produces data, it is necessary to identify clear boundaries for what will be collected and how the data will be used....The whole purpose of developing an outcome measurement system is not to measure outcomes, but rather to evaluate services and make changes based on the results. (Mason, 2000, p. 87–88)

As Wade (1999) so eloquently reminds all healthcare professionals "outcome measures are only tools, not solutions" (p. 95).

Summary

This chapter has attempted to make the connection between client assessment, intervention, outcome measurement, and evidence-based practice. It began with a review of the terms client assessment, outcomes, and evidence-based practice, as well as the five categories of healthcare outcomes as discussed in Chapter 2. Measurement characteristics, including validity, reliability and practicality, were discussed, in addition to internal and external validity, sensitivity to change, and patient-centered perspective. The chapter closed with a discussion about the role of assessment and outcome measurement in clinical decisions and patient management.

Discussion Questions

1. From your prior experience and readings, explain what you see to be the relationships between client assessment, interventions, outcomes, and evidence-based practice. What progress has therapeutic recreation made in each of these areas, and what still needs to be done?

2. How does therapeutic recreation fit into the five categories of healthcare outcomes? How do our assessments and interventions contribute to these outcomes? What research or literature do you have to support these claims?

3. How well do our assessments provide internal validity evidence? How well do they provide external validity evidence? How sensitive to change are most of our instruments? How many of them are patient-centered?

4. Provide examples of clinical situations that illustrate Figures 9.1, 9.2, and 9.3. How well does therapeutic recreation measure up to other healthcare professions?

5. Explain the relevance of assessment and outcome measures to clinical decisions. How do they contribute to patient management?

6. What role do you or would you like to play in improving TR assessment and outcome measurement? When will you start?

References

Arrowsmith, H. (1999). A critical evaluation of the use of nutrition screening tools by nurses. *British Journal of Nursing, 8*(22), 1483–1490.

Belsey, J. and Snell, T. (2001). What is evidence-based medicine? Retrieved November 9, 2002, from http://www.evidence-based-medicine.co.uk/

Blankertz, L. and Cook, J.A. (1998). Choosing and using outcome measures. *Psychiatric Rehabilitation Journal, 22*(2), 167–174.

Brailer, D.J. and Kim, L.H. (1996). From nicety to necessity: Outcome measures come of age. *Health Systems Review, 29*(5), 20–23.

Connors, G.J., Allen, J.P., Cooney, N.L., DiClemente, CC., Tonigan, J.S., and Anton, R.E. (1994). Assessment issues and strategies in alcoholism treatment matching research. *Journal of Studies on Alcohol, 12*, 92–100.

Coye, M.J. (2001). No Toyotas in healthcare: Why medical care has not evolved to meet patients' needs. *Health Affairs, 20*(6), 44–56.

DePoy, E. and Gitlin, L.N. (1998). *Introduction to research: Understanding and applying multiple strategies.* St. Louis, MO: Mosby.

Durbin, J., Cochrane, J., Goering, P., and Macfarlane, D. (2001). Needs-based planning: Evaluation of a level-of-care planning model. *Journal of Behavioral Health Services and Research, 28*(1), 67–80.

Elliott, R. (1992). A conceptual analysis of Lambert, Ogles, and Masters' conceptual scheme for outcome assessment. *Journal of Counseling and Development, 70*(4), 535–539.

Fischer, C.T. (2000). Collaborative, individualized assessment. *Journal of Personality Assessment, 74*(1), 2–14.

Fritz, J.M. and Wainner, R.S. (2001). Examining diagnostic tests: An evidence-based perspective. *Physical Therapy, 81*(9), 1546–1564.

Granello, D.H., Granello, P.F., and Lee, F. (1999). Measuring treatment outcomes and client satisfaction in a partial hospitalization program. *Journal of Behavioral Health Services and Research, 26*(1), 50–63.

Granger, C.V. (1984). A conceptual model for functional assessment. In C.V. Granger and G.E. Gresham (Eds.), *Functional assessment in rehabilitation medicine* (pp. 14–25). Baltimore, MD: Williams & Wilkins.

Hatala, R., Holbrook, A., and Goldsmith, C.H. (1999). Therapeutic equivalence: All studies are not created equal. *Canadian Journal of Clinical Pharmacology, 6*(1), 9–11.

Hendryx, M.S., Dyck, D.G., and Srebnik, D. (1999). Risk-adjusted outcome models for public mental health outpatient programs. *Health Services Research, 34*(1), 171–195.

Jinnett, K., Alexander, J.A., and Ullman, E. (2001). Case management and quality of life: Assessing treatment and outcome for clients with chronic and persistent mental illness. *Health Services Research, 36*(1), 61–90.

Johnson, D.E.L. (1993). Scott & White measures "quality of health" in outcomes studies. *Healthcare Strategic Management, 11*(3), 7–9.

Kennedy, D. and Barter, R. (1995). Client assessment tool: A means to enhance nurse-client-physician collaboration. *Journal of Neuroscience Nursing, 27*(5), 312–318.

King, K.M. and Teo, K.K. (2000). Integrating clinical quality improvement strategies with nursing research. *Western Journal of Nursing Research, 22*(5), 596–608.

Kressel, D., DeLeon, G., Palij, M., and Rubin, G. (2000). Measuring client clinical progress in therapeutic community treatment. *Journal of Substance Abuse Treatment, 19*(3), 267–272.

Leiter, P. (1995). A national measurement tool for subacute outcomes. *Nursing Homes Long Term Care Management, 44*(4), 25–27.

Mason, M.M. (2000). Meeting the challenges of data collection in outcome systems. *Education and Treatment of Children, 23*(1), 75–95.

McCormick, B.P. and Funderburk, J. (2000). Therapeutic recreation outcomes in mental health practice. *Annual in Therapeutic Recreation, 9*, 9–20.

McGlynn, E.A. (1995). Quality assessment in reproductive health services. *Western Journal of Medicine, 163*(3), 19–27.

Mordock, J.B. (2000). Outcome assessment: Suggestions for agency practice. *Child Welfare, 79*(6), 689–710.

Nichols, S. (2001). Keynote: Therapeutic recreation practice: Art, science, or magic? In N.J. Stumbo (Ed.), *Professional issues in therapeutic recreation: On competence and outcomes* (pp. 153–158). Champaign, IL: Sagamore.

Parsons, R., Bruce Higley, H., Wallock Okerlund, V., Thorstensen, C., and Gray, H. (1995). Assessing the needs of our elders. *Public Management, 77*(2), 14–16.

Peterson, C.A. and Stumbo, N.J. (2000). *Therapeutic recreation program design: Principles and procedures* (3rd ed.). Needham Heights, MA: Allyn & Bacon.

Proctor, E.K. (2001). Building and consolidating knowledge for practice. *Social Work Research, 25*(4), 195–197.

Reihman, J., Wolford, K., Knapp, W., MacCallum, J., and Murray, N. (1983). Treatment outcomes in a day-treatment program. *International Journal of Partial Hospitalization, 2*(1), 17–31.

Richardson, W.S. (1997). Evidence-based diagnosis: More is needed. *Evidence-based Medicine*. Retrieved November 1, 2002, from http://www.acponline.org/journals/ebm/mayjun97/needed.htm

Rosoff, A.J. (2001). Evidence-based medicine and the law: The courts confront clinical practice guidelines. *Journal of Health Politics, Policy, and Law, 26*(2), 327–368.

Russo, J., Roy-Byrne, P., Jaffe, C., and Ries, R. (1997). The relationship of patient-administered outcome assessments to quality of life and physician ratings: Validity of the BASIS-32. *Journal of Mental Health Administration, 24*(2), 200–214.

Stumbo, N.J. (2002), *Client assessment in therapeutic recreation services.* State College, PA: Venture Publishing, Inc.

Stumbo, N.J. and Peterson, C.A. (2004). *Therapeutic recreation program design: Principles and procedures* (4th ed.). San Francisco, CA: Benjamin Cummings.

Thomas, J.R. and Nelson, J.K. (2001). *Research methods in physical activity* (4th ed.). Champaign, IL: Human Kinetics.

Tramm, M.L. (1995). A methodological approach advances outcome measurement. *Behavioral Health Management, 15*(3), 36–37.

Tully, M.P. and Cantrill, J.A. (1999). Subjective outcome measurement—A primer. *Pharmacy World and Science, 21*(3), 101–109.

Wade, D.T. (1999). Editorial: Outcome measurement and rehabilitation. *Clinical Rehabilitation, 13*, 93–95.

Ware, J.E., Jr. (1997). Healthcare outcomes from the patient's point of view. In E.J. Mullen and J.L. Magnabosco (Eds.), *Outcomes measurement in human services* (pp. 44–67). Washington, DC: National Association of Social Workers.

Wetzler, H. (1992). Measuring quality of life. *Business and Health, 10*(11), 67.

Whitty, P., Steen, N., Eccles, M., McColl, E., Hewison, J., Meadows, K., Clapp, Z., and Hutchinson, A. (1997). A new self-completion outcome measure for diabetes: Is it responsive to change? *Quality of Life Research, 6*(5), 407–413.

Objectives-Based Approach to Evaluating the Effectiveness of Therapeutic Recreation Services

Cynthia Carruthers, Ph.D., CTRS
University of Nevada—Las Vegas

Professionally competent therapeutic recreation specialists (TRSs) want to know if the services that they are providing to their clients are making a positive contribution to their treatment. They strive to constantly improve the services that they provide to their clients. They can articulate to clients, family members, administrators and other treatment team members the specific outcomes that their services contribute to the health and well-being of those they serve. Proficient TRSs conduct outcome evaluations as an integral and essential part of their practice. They know that outcome evaluation is not an add-on and it is not someone else's professional responsibility. They know, finally, that the viability of the therapeutic recreation (TR) profession relies on a critical mass of professionals just like themselves.

For decades, there has been a plea for more efficacy evaluation and research in therapeutic recreation (Carruthers, 1997; Compton, 1984). That need is compelling. However, there is an equal need for widespread, systematic evaluations of the effectiveness of practice (Cone, 2001; Gabor, Unrau & Grinnell, 1998). While efficacy and effectiveness evaluation have commonalities, there are some key differences. Efficacy evaluation is methodologically very rigorous and examines the outcomes of interventions in ideal, highly controlled conditions (Cone, 2001; Stumbo, 2000). Because of its scientific rigor, including the use of control or comparison groups to account for other possible influences on the client treatment variables being investigated, consumers of the systematic evaluation results can have great confidence in the findings (Stufflebeam, 2000). When an evaluation study of the efficacy of a TR intervention or program is conducted, an attempt is made to determine if there is a cause-and-effect relationship between the intervention and client outcomes. For example, a researcher might examine whether a leisure education program causes clients to become more active in constructive leisure activities and satisfied with their quality of life. Due to its rigor, efficacy evaluation requires fairly extensive research skills and resources.

Effectiveness evaluations investigate interventions as they occur in actual routine practice conditions (Nolan & Mock, 2000). Effectiveness evaluation is less concerned with being able to provide scientific support for cause-and-effect relationships and more concerned with answering fundamental practice questions, such as what outcomes are associated with the provision of an intervention (Martin & Kettner, 1996). In effectiveness evaluation, the actual outcomes associated with involvement in an intervention or program are compared to the intended outcomes (Gabor, Unrau & Grinnell, 1998). The effectiveness of the program, then, is the degree to which a program or intervention achieves its articulated goals and objectives (Schalock, 2001). Due to the lack of control of extraneous factors, it cannot be inferred that the program *caused* the accomplishment of the client objectives. For example, if no control groups were used in a study of the relationship between involvement in a leisure education program and increased leisure activity and improvement in quality of life, it is impossible to rule out that a documented increase in these variables was not caused by medication, more restful sleep, or the interventions of other professionals. In the monitoring of client outcomes in health and human services, often it is only possible to conclude that the client's behavior has changed in the intended direction (Gabor, Unrau & Grinnell, 1998). Interventions that are theoretically grounded and consistently associated with positive changes in intended client behaviors are sufficiently justified in most health and human service settings (Gabor, Unrau & Grinnell, 1998; see also Chapter 4). If resources permit, these interventions can be investigated later using more sophisticated and rigorous designs.

For many TR practitioners, evaluation seems rather daunting. As a result, a paradox exists. TR practitioners have stated that the development of a research base demonstrating the effectiveness of therapeutic recreation is the profession's greatest challenge (Hamilton & Austin, 1992), yet they also articulate that they feel ill-prepared to do it, and therefore avoid it (Savell, Huston & Malkin, 1993). As a result of this lack of involvement in evaluation, the quality of client care provided by TR professionals, as well as the advancement of the TR profession, are compromised. The purpose of this chapter is to describe ways in which TR professionals can begin to evaluate the effectiveness of their practice relatively easily. Luckily for TRSs who provide a theoretically grounded and systematically developed program, effectiveness evaluation is a natural extension of their programming efforts.

Determination of Outcomes

As stated previously, effectiveness evaluation determines the extent to which a program meets its intended goals and objectives. Throughout the process of program design and evaluation, there must be clear and linear linkages among all components of the system, including the agency's goals, and the TR program's statement of purpose, comprehensive program goals, specific program goals and objectives, interventions, outcomes, and assessment.

The goals for the comprehensive TR program are based on the needs of the clients and the service mandate of the agency (Stumbo & Peterson, 2004). A number of TR service models exist that describe the nature of services and their intended outcomes (Voelkl, Carruthers & Hawkins, 1997). While there are a number of different TR service models that might shape the selection of the goals of the comprehensive TR program, many of the models include goals that address the provision of services that improve the physical, cognitive, emotional, social, and leisure functioning of clients. On the comprehensive TR program level, goals delineate the intention of the program, but do not represent client objectives or client outcomes (Stumbo & Peterson, 2004). In order to evaluate the effectiveness of a program in attaining its intended outcomes, complete performance measures or behavioral objectives must be specified (Schalock, 2001). In therapeutic recreation, the delineation of performance measures occurs within the specific program, rather than at the comprehensive program level.

There is a strong and logical linkage between the comprehensive program goals and the specific programs. For each comprehensive program goal, the TRS determines the specific programs that will be used to operationalize the intent of the comprehensive program goals (Stumbo & Peterson, 2004). For example, a comprehensive program goal in a long-term care facility might be "to provide services that maintain or improve the cognitive functioning of residents." Specific programs might include 24-hour reality orientation, reminiscence and life review, sensory stimulation, mental exercises and activities, and remotivation (Hawkins, May & Rogers, 1996). A comprehensive program goal in a residential program for people with addictions might be "to provide services that improve the emotional functioning of residents." Specific programs might include coping skills, anger management, and expressive arts. A comprehensive program goal in a school-based program for adolescents with developmental disabilities might be "to provide TR services that improve students' level of perceived freedom in leisure, and ability to overcome barriers to leisure involvement." Specific programs might include leisure skills, leisure resources, social skills, and leisure awareness. TRSs should develop specific program areas for which there is sound theoretical and research support. It is also extremely important to include consumers of TR services in the program development process. If the TR goals and their operationalization through programs are not perceived as valuable by clients and others, the TR program in that agency will never be considered a relevant or necessary service.

Ultimate Goals and Instrumental Objectives

Once the TRS has decided on the types of programs to be offered, the intended outcomes for each specific program are delineated. The two types of specific program outcomes that are most amenable to measurement in practice are ultimate goals and instrumental objectives (Cone, 2001; see Chapter 4). When used in TR practice, an ultimate goal represents the purpose of the specific program. For example, the ultimate goal of a reality orientation program implemented in a long-term care facility may be to increase the residents' orientation to person, place, and time. The ultimate goal of the mental activities and exercises program may be to improve residents' memory and concentration. The ultimate goal of a coping skills program for people with addictions might be to improve the coping skills necessary for successful addictions recovery. The ultimate goal of a leisure skills program for adolescents with developmental disabilities might be to increase students' perception of competence in leisure. However, the ultimate goal of the treatment team to which therapeutic recreation belongs may have long-term goals, such as to improve functional independence, reduce depression, increase abstinence, or decrease recidivism. TRSs must be able to articulate how their specific program goals and interventions advance these treatment team goals, although their measurement is likely to occur on the team level. Figures 9.1, 9.2, and 9.3 (pp. 170–171) illustrate these relationships.

Instrumental objectives often are referred to as performance measures or behavioral objectives in the TR literature. For each specific TR program, the TRS identifies the behaviors that clients will need to attain on their way to accomplishing their ultimate goal. The instrumental objectives allow for measurement of different levels or stages of change relative to the ultimate goal (Schulte, 1997). Instrumental objectives represent building blocks through which therapists reach the intended outcome of the specific program (Cone, 2001). Once the instrumental objectives or performance measures are delineated, the content and process (i.e., interventions) of the specific programs are developed (Stumbo & Peterson, 2004). Again, TRSs should refer to the theoretical and research literature to determine the most salient objectives, content, and process for their specific programs. According to Cone (2001), when therapeutic interventions are based on theory, instrumental objectives become obvious, "evaluation results are more easily interpreted, and their implications for practice are more clearly understood" (p. 95). Effectiveness evaluation using performance measures allows the TRS to determine how clients are responding during the program and their level of progress toward attainment of the ultimate goal of the program.

Writing Performance Measures or Instrumental Objectives

Performance measures have three parts: behavior, condition, and criteria (Stumbo & Peterson, 2004). The *behavior* represents the evidence that the clients have acquired the knowledge, skills or affects (including cognitions) that are intended by the specific program (Gabor, Unrau & Grinnell, 1998; Stumbo & Peterson, 2004). The behaviors included for measurement reflect the TRS's theory of action (Caldwell, 2001). In other words, an assumption is made that the behaviors that form the core of the performance measures represent the essential behaviors or minimal amount of evidence that will reflect positive change toward the ultimate goal. For example, the specific behaviors targeted by a coping skills program for individuals in recovery from alcoholism might include the following behaviors:

- to recognize and change negative thoughts that interfere with enjoying life,
- to focus on and enjoy the present moment,
- to identify personal behavioral stress management strategies,
- to acquire skill in relaxation techniques,
- to focus on personal progress and self-acceptance rather than perfection,
- to learn to interact more comfortably with others,
- to develop friendship skills,
- to improve assertiveness skills,
- to identify coping strategies for high-risk leisure situations,
- to understand the steps in constructive leisure decision making,
- to identify leisure interests that promote enjoyment of a chemically free lifestyle, and/or
- to identify ways of overcoming barriers to involvement in satisfying leisure activities.

The selection of these coping behaviors is based on the Wills and Shiffman conceptual framework of the stress-coping process (Carruthers & Hood, 2002;

Hood & Carruthers, 2002). In this example, the evaluative assumption made is that if the clients can accomplish these behaviors, they would be better able to cope with their lives. The process and content of the program are targeted directly at facilitating the attainment of these behaviors. The research evidence is very clear that many individuals with alcoholism have significant problems with coping that can undermine their recovery and serves as the initial justification for conducting the TR coping skills program (Carruthers & Hood, 2002).

The *condition* portion of a performance measure specifies the situation or circumstances under which the behavior will occur and be measured (Stumbo & Peterson, 2004). Conditions specify the social contexts, timelines, and resources that are necessary for the successful demonstration of the behavior. Conditions that approximate real-life or natural situations are often a better measure of whether or not a client can actually apply the skills. However, orchestrating real-life situations in which a behavior can be demonstrated is often more difficult and time-consuming. For example, asking clients to demonstrate an assertiveness technique in a role-play situation (i.e., condition) is easier to arrange than monitoring their assertiveness skills when they are with their families. Other examples of conditions that might be used in TR performance measures include

- While in the TR family group…
- While attending an Alcoholics Anonymous meeting…
- After two weeks in the leisure skills program…
- When engaged in a cooperative activity with a peer…
- While engaged in a leisure activity of their choice…
- On a written examination…
- On a homework assignment….
- When given the necessary equipment…
- After completion of the coping skills program…

Again, the closer the condition is to the context in which the behaviors are ultimately to be practiced, the more confidence the therapist can have that the client will actually be able to use the skill in real life, thus the more valid the performance measure.

The *criterion* portion of the performance measure is what makes it truly measurable. It specifies the "exact amounts and nature of the behavior that can be taken as *evidence* that the objective has been met" (Peterson & Stumbo, 2000, p. 268). The criterion statements must be clear and precise enough that two therapists observing the same behavior would arrive at the same conclusions about the attainment of the objective. The key is to focus criterion measurement on the simplest, most straightforward behaviors that adequately represent the attainment of the objective.

Peterson and Stumbo (2000, pp. 268–270) have identified six types of criteria that are often used in TR practice. The criteria include

- number of trials, commonly written as "*x* out of *y* attempts;"
- level of accuracy, as in "throw a ball within one foot of a target;"
- amount of time for the behavior to occur, such as "push wheelchair without stopping for five minutes;"
- percentages or fractions of the time that a client will be able to perform the behavior, such as "use I-language statements correctly 25% of the time;"
- form of the behavior such as required in movement or the arts, for example, "Perform Salute to the Sun yoga routine using the proper form, as described in the *Hatha-Yoga Handbook*;" and
- procedures and characteristics which specify a series of simple behaviors which will demonstrate the achievement of a more complex behavior.

An example of a procedure would be

> While self-monitoring through a homework assignment on the unit, the client will demonstrate the ability to stop irrational, negative thoughts that interfere with enjoying life by
>
> 1. identifying a strong, uncomfortable feeling (such as anxiety, fear, anger), as it is occurring;
> 2. identifying the thought that preceded the feeling, and determine if it is rational;
> 3. changing the thought (if it is irrational); and
> 4. experiencing relief from the uncomfortable feeling, as judged appropriate by the TRS.

Many TR performance measures use this procedures-and-characteristics type of criteria.

Using Performance Measures To Evaluate Effectiveness

The use of performance measures or instrumental objectives to evaluate effectiveness is a type of formative evaluation. The purpose of formative evaluation is to assess the response of clients to treatment and to encourage "ongoing adjustments in treatment to reflect the current status of clients" (Cone, 2001,

p. 49). If clients are not making sufficient progress, the interventions are modified to better address the treatment needs of the client. The judgment as to whether or not the clients are making sufficient progress is based on their attainment of the performance measures. Again, instrumental objectives serve as a series of building blocks to attain the ultimate goal of the program. Ongoing performance measurement is conducted.

At regular, preestablished points in a specific program, performance measures are collected for all of the clients in the program. For example, after one week in the coping skills program, the ability of each of the clients to stop their irrational, negative thoughts is assessed. If TRSs find that 90% of the clients in the program have demonstrated the ability to change their irrational thoughts, they have evidence that the coping skills program is effective to date. On the other hand, it the TRSs found that only 20% of the clients in the program have successfully mastered the ability to change their negative thoughts, they would probably judge it ineffective and modify the intervention for the clients. This process is repeated for each performance measure in the specific program.

At the end of the specific program, the TRS also can analyze aggregate data to gather preliminary evidence about the overall effectiveness of the program. For example, the TRSs implementing a coping skills program could examine all of the clients' attainment of each of the twelve performance measures developed for the program. They might find that the clients' attainment of the performance measures ranged from 85% to 97%. They could report that the majority of the clients demonstrated behavioral attainment of the objectives of the program. This type of data begins to provide justification for the intervention based on effectiveness. The monitoring of performance measures is considered an exploratory evaluation design (Gabor, Unrau & Grinnell, 1998). This design allows TRSs to monitor client attainment of a program's objectives, refine interventions when appropriate, and report on the attainment of the objectives.

In the previous coping skills program example, can the TRSs argue that the high level of client attainment of the performance measures indicates that the client experienced an improvement in coping skills (the ultimate goal of the program)? Yes and no. If the performance measures, taken together, have a strong theoretical relationship to the coping skills construct and similar results are obtained with multiple groups of clients over time, TRSs are justified in making some preliminary statements about the clients' improvement in coping skills. However, a descriptive program evaluation design would provide stronger evidence for attainment of the ultimate specific program goal, because it measures the ultimate goal directly. According to Cone (2001), high-quality effectiveness evaluation requires the direct assessment of both instrumental objectives and ultimate goals.

Using Ultimate Goals To Evaluate Effectiveness

While exploratory effectiveness evaluation studies using performance measures are extremely important for providing evidence-based practice, descriptive designs allow the TRS to measure the overall *changes* that occurred in clients associated with a specific program or intervention (Gabor, Unrau & Grinnell, 1998). Descriptive evaluation designs require the use of a pretest and posttest. Because descriptive designs include both baseline and posttreatment measures, they are stronger and provide more information than those that involve only posttreatment measures (Speer, 1998). While descriptive evaluation studies are not as rigorous as explanatory evaluation studies that use random assignment of subjects and control groups to explore causality, they can be conducted in routine practice conditions and provide practical and useful information for quality improvement activities (Cone, 2001).

TRSs use assessments to determine the placement of clients into specific programs. Assessment "refers to the use of standard techniques, procedures, and instruments to generate information about clients to assist in structuring TR interventions" (Sylvester, Voelkl & Ellis, 2001, p. 116). Good assessments provide a solid baseline measure of the behaviors (e.g., knowledge, ability, cognition/affect) that are targeted for change through specific programs. Ideally, the same assessments that are used for program placement can be used as a posttreatment or outcome measure (see Chapter 9). Therefore, a good assessment should measure the behaviors that represent the ultimate goal of a specific program. For purposes of descriptive evaluation, assessment data can serve as both the pretest and posttest measure. This assessment data can be obtained through interviews, behavioral observation, self-administered surveys, or client records review (Stumbo & Peterson, 2004).

In order for an assessment to be useful as a pretest–posttest measure, it must be valid and reliable for its intended purpose (Stumbo & Peterson, 2004). According to Peterson and Stumbo, the "validity of an assessment refers to the extent to which it meets its intended purpose. It concerns what the test measures and how well it does it" (2000, p. 207). When TRSs are examining the validity of a measure for collecting baseline data in order to place a client in a specific program, they examine two different types of evidence (Sylvester, Voelkl & Ellis, 2001). The first type of evidence is content related. Content-related evidence addresses the relevance and representativeness of the items or components of the assessment (Sylvester, Voelkl & Ellis, 2001). For example, when evaluating the relevance of a coping skills assessment, TRSs would ask themselves the question: "Do the items on the assessment relate theoretically and directly to the coping skills construct that is intended to be measured?" When evaluating the representativeness of the items or components of the coping skills assessment, TRSs would ask themselves the question: "Do all of the items, taken together, capture fully all of the crucial dimensions of the coping skills construct?" Because the intended purpose of assessment is baseline measurement, program placement, and outcome evaluation, there should be a clear, linear link between the coping skills assessment and the goals, objectives, content and process of the coping skills program. In other words, there must be consistency in the theory that guides assessment and program development.

Criterion-related evidence is the second type that is used to evaluate the validity of an assessment (Sylvester, Voelkl & Ellis, 2001). Criterion-related validity refers to the degree to which the scores on an assessment of one construct are similar to the scores on an assessment of a similar or theoretically related construct (i.e., criterion measure). When the two scores are highly correlated in the direction that would be expected theoretically, it is evidence that the assessment has criterion validity. For example, theoretically one might assume that high scores on a coping skills measure would be correlated with high scores on a resiliency measure, as well as the ability to remain in recovery from alcoholism. Likewise, theoretically one might assume that high scores on a perceived freedom in leisure measure would be correlated with high leisure satisfaction, as well as leisure participation patterns. If the correlations are high and in the anticipated direction, they provide evidence that the measures are valid for program placement into a coping skills program or leisure education program, respectively.

Reliability addresses the degree of consistency and accuracy of an assessment. *Reliability* represents the degree to which an assessment stably and truly measures what it is intended to measure, rather than something extraneous (i.e., error; Sylvester, Voelkl & Ellis, 2001). For example, an unstable coping skills measure could not serve as an adequate baseline. If clients' coping skills scores vary appreciably from test to test with no external explanation for the changes, it would be impossible to attribute future changes in the posttest scores to involvement in a specific program. Similarly, conditions under which the assessment is conducted can introduce imprecision and error. For example, lack of standardization of assessment conditions and instruction, vague and imprecise descriptors of behaviors that create inconsistency within and among therapists, and distracting testing conditions can all interfere with an assessment's ability to capture the "true" score of clients. The reliability of an assessment instrument will impact significantly its value as a baseline and posttreatment measure.

Usually, the psychometric properties of validity and reliability for standardized tests are documented by their publishers. The use of standardized tests can lend credibility to an effectiveness evaluation study, because of the rigor involved in their development and refinement. Therefore, whenever possible, it is advantageous for TRSs to use standardized assessments for their baseline and outcome measurements. Unfortunately, there are very few standardized assessments developed specifically for therapeutic recreation (Stumbo & Peterson, 2004). Oftentimes, TRSs must develop assessment instruments for use in their own agencies (Stumbo, 2002). It is absolutely essential that the assessments clearly, logically, and completely measure the construct or behaviors intended, and do so with precision and dependability.

Once the pretest and posttest data have been collected, a comparison is made between each client's baseline score and posttreatment outcome score. According to Martin and Kettner, "If a client demonstrates either measurable movement toward desirable conditions, status, behaviors, functioning, attitudes, feelings, or perceptions or measurable movements away from undesirable conditions, status, behaviors, functioning, attitudes, feelings or perceptions, then the client has experienced a quality-of-life change" (1996, p. 77). Martin and Kettner have identified four different ways that pretest–posttest improvement outcome data can be presented as numeric counts without extensive statistical analysis:

1. the number of clients who demonstrated measurable improvement (e.g., 78 clients measurably improved their coping skills);

2. the percentage of clients who demonstrated measurable improvement (e.g., 87% of the clients measurably improved their coping skills);

3. the number of clients who demonstrate the target level of clinical improvement (e.g., 67 clients demonstrated clinical improvement in their coping skills); and

4. the percentage of clients who demonstrate a target level of clinical improvement (e.g., 74% of the clients demonstrated clinical improvement in their coping skills).

When measurable improvement is counted, positive change of any magnitude is included. Clinical improvement requires the determination of the amount of change that must occur in order for the goal of the program to be accomplished. One example of clients showing clinical improvement are those who were below a clinical cutting score at baseline (i.e., their score is below an acceptable level and indicates a problem), but above it at posttreatment (i.e., indicating significant change). The cutting score can be determined in a variety of ways, and is usually based on some normative criteria (Witt & Ellis, 1989).

A publisher of an assessment may provide national norms that serve as the cutting score. Few TR assessments have national norms available, however. When national norms are not available, four relevant alternatives have been proposed by Witt and Ellis (1989). First, comparisons can be made to others who complete the instrument at the same time. The TRS might decide, for example, that clients whose scores fall within the bottom 25th percentile on the coping skills assessment would benefit from the coping skills program. If those clients score above that cutoff score on the posttest, they would be judged as having made clinical improvement. Second, comparisons can be made to others who live in the local community or other clients who have received services from the agency. The TRS can develop local or agency norms that will aid in identifying those have the greatest problems and would benefit most from a program. Clients scoring above that norm after treatment would be judged as having made clinical improvement. Third, normative data from other agencies or communities serving a similar population might serve as the comparison for determining the cutting score. Again, clinical improvement would be evidenced by surpassing that score posttreatment. Lastly, clinical judgment can be used to determine clinical improvement. For example, a TRS using the Leisure Competence Measure (LCM; Kloseck & Crilly, 1997) might determine that any clients scoring below 6 or 7 (indicating independent functioning) on a subscale require intervention in that area. However, some clients may have scored a "1" on the scale, indicating "total dependence with total assistance;" while others may have scored a "4," indicating "modified dependence with minimal assistance." While both clients may benefit from intervention, one would not necessarily expect the individual with total dependence of "1" to accomplish a score of 6 (the original cutting score) by the conclusion of treatment. However, the client with the original score of "4" might readily accomplish a score of "6" by discharge. Therefore, a therapist might define clinical improvement as a change score, rather than an absolute score (e.g., two-level improvement in score on the LCM). If the client scoring a "1" on the LCM subscale scores a "3" at discharge, it would be determined that the client had made clinical improvement. The criteria for clinical improvement must be established prior to data collection, regardless of which method is chosen.

The use of a descriptive evaluation design to measure outcomes helps TRSs to measure and articulate the outcomes of their services. Strong descriptive evaluation is dependent on theoretically based, valid, and reliable assessment that can establish solid baselines and effectively measure client change relative to the ultimate goal of the program. Good evaluation results are dependent on the degree to which the specific programs effectively and efficiently address the problem behaviors (e.g., knowledge, abilities, cognition/affect) identified through assessment. The use of measurable improvement or clinical improvement data to evaluate change in the client allows TRSs to determine if clients involved in their programs are attaining the intended ultimate goal of the specific program.

Effectiveness evaluation compares actual client change with intended client changes (Gabor, Unrau & Grinnell, 1998). Through an exploratory evaluation design, TRSs can use performance measures to monitor their clients' movement toward the ultimate goal of a specific program. Through a descriptive design, TRSs use sound pretests and posttests to measure the clients' improvement relative to the ultimate goal of the program. The use of performance measures and pretests-posttests provides evidence of the level of effectiveness of the TR program.

While there has long been a plea for efficacy evaluation in therapeutic recreation, effectiveness evaluation is also essential for the advancement of the profession. Imagine what would happen to the field if every TR professional began to systematically measure the progress and change that occurs in the clients that they serve. Weak TR interventions would be modified or eliminated. Effective TR interventions would be disseminated, replicated, and celebrated. The quality of care to clients would improve. TRSs would have the satisfaction of knowing that they were providing an effective service to their clients. The value of therapeutic recreation would become more apparent to consumers. Exploratory and descriptive evaluation would be commonplace and would set the stage for more rigorous efficacy evaluation. Professionally, everything would just get better.

Discussion Questions

1. Identify two differences between efficacy and effectiveness evaluation.

2. How does the use of control groups contribute to the researcher's ability to determine cause-and-effect (e.g., the specific interventions that may be responsible for a change in the client's behavior)?

3. Identify the differences between ultimate goals and instrumental objectives. Why are both necessary?

4. Define the three parts of a performance measure. Give an example of an appropriate performance measure for an intervention designed to increase a child's ability to engage in cooperative play activities with peers.

5. Why is it important to determine the validity and reliability of an assessment before using it as a pretest-posttest?

6. Describe four different ways that numeric counts can be used to present pretest-posttest improvement outcome data.

7. When national norms to establish cutting scores are not available, what alternatives can be used by the TRS to establish cutting scores?

References

Caldwell, L. (2001). The role of theory in therapeutic recreation: A practical approach. In N.J. Stumbo (Ed.), *Professional issues in therapeutic recreation: On competence and outcomes* (pp. 349–364). Champaign, IL: Sagamore.

Carruthers, C. (1997). Therapeutic recreation efficacy research agenda. *Annual in Therapeutic Recreation, 7*, 29–41.

Carruthers, C. and Hood, C. (2002). Coping skills for individuals with alcoholism. *Therapeutic Recreation Journal, 36*, 154–171.

Compton, D. (1984). Research priorities in recreation for special populations. *Therapeutic Recreation Journal, 18*, 9–17.

Cone, J. (2001). *Evaluating outcomes: Empirical tools for effective practice.* Washington, DC: American Psychological Association.

Gabor, P., Unrau, Y., and Grinnell, R. (1998). *Evaluation for social workers: A quality improvement approach for the social services.* Boston, MA: Allyn & Bacon.

Hamilton, E. and Austin, D. (1992). Future perspectives of therapeutic recreation. *Annual in Therapeutic Recreation, 3*, 72–79.

Hawkins, B., May, M., and Rogers, N. (1996). *Therapeutic activity intervention with the elderly: Foundations and practices.* State College, PA: Venture Publishing, Inc.

Hood, C. and Carruthers, C. (2002). The use of coping skills theory in therapeutic recreation services. *Therapeutic Recreation Journal, 36,* 137–153.

Kloseck, M. and Crilly, R. (1997). *Leisure Competence Measure: Adult version professional manual and users guide.* London, ON: Leisure Competence Measure Data System.

Martin, L. and Kettner, P. (1996). *Measuring the performance of human service programs.* Thousand Oaks, CA: Sage.

Nolan, M. and Mock, V. (2000). *Measuring patient outcomes.* Thousand Oaks, CA: Sage.

Peterson, C. and Stumbo, N. (2000). *Therapeutic recreation program design: Principles and procedures* (3rd ed.). Needham Heights, MA: Allyn & Bacon.

Savell, K., Huston, A., and Malkin, M. (1993). Collaborative research: Bridging the gap between practitioners and researchers/educators. In M. Malkin and C. Howe (Eds.), *Research in therapeutic recreation: Concepts and methods* (pp. 77–98). State College, PA: Venture Publishing, Inc.

Schalock, R. (2001). *Outcome-based evaluation* (2nd ed.). New York, NY: Kluwer Academic.

Schulte, D. (1997). Dimensions of outcome measurement. In H. Strupp, L. Horowitz, and M. Lambert (Eds.), *Measuring patient changes in mood, anxiety, and personality disorders* (pp. 57–80). Washington, DC: American Psychological Association.

Speer, D. (1998). *Mental health outcome evaluation*. San Diego, CA: Academic Press.

Stumbo, N. (2000). Outcome measurement in healthcare: Implications for therapeutic recreation. *Annual in Therapeutic Recreation, 9,* 1–8.

Stumbo, N. (2002). *Client assessment in therapeutic recreation services*. State College, PA: Venture Publishing, Inc.

Stumbo, N.J. and Peterson, C.A. (2004). *Therapeutic recreation program design: Principles and procedures* (4th ed.). San Francisco, CA: Benjamin Cummings.

Stufflebeam, D. (2000). Foundational models for 21st century program evaluation. In D. Stufflebeam, G. Madaus, and T. Kellaghan (Eds.), *Evaluation models: Viewpoints on educational and human services evaluation* (2nd ed.; pp. 33–83). Norwell, MA: Kluwer Academic.

Sylvester, C., Voelkl, J., and Ellis, G. (2001). *Therapeutic recreation: Theory and practice*. State College, PA: Venture Publishing, Inc.

Voelkl, J., Carruthers, C., and Hawkins, B. (1997). Special issue on therapeutic recreation practice models: Guest editors' introductory comments. *Therapeutic Recreation Journal, 31*(4), 210–212.

Witt, P. and Ellis, G. (1989). *The Leisure Diagnostic Battery: Users manual and sample forms*. State College, PA: Venture Publishing, Inc.

Program Evaluation:
Collecting Data to Measure Outcomes

Mark A. Widmer
Brigham Young University

Ramon B. Zabriskie
Brigham Young University

Mary Sara Wells
University of Utah

Each of us participates in various programs on a regular basis. We take classes or take part in training at work. We might be involved in sports leagues or other free time activities where programs are designed and implemented for our enrichment and enjoyment. Every time we go to a restaurant, we evaluate the food, the service, and the atmosphere. In other words, we evaluate the restaurant's program. Even when going to the dentist we are involved in a program. A dentist's goal is not as simple as promoting healthy teeth and gums. They must demonstrate and document that the program is in compliance with professional, state, and federal guidelines. They must also be competitive in terms of costs and effectiveness. In addition, a dentist's program should be concerned with the patients' overall satisfaction. Patients should feel comfortable and at ease—a difficult proposition for dentists because people generally do not enjoy dental work. The process should be streamlined to eliminate long periods of waiting. Patients should be given a clear and precise report on their condition and, when needed, the treatment options.

It is part of human nature to reflect on and evaluate our experiences. Did the experience meet my needs or expectations? Was I treated kindly by the staff? Did it take too long or cost too much? In the case of the dentist, if we have a toothache a week later, we would have to go back again for another checkup. If we find a cavity was missed, our evaluation of the program would probably be fairly critical. Most of us would be looking for a new dentist. If our experience was repeated with other patients, this dentist might soon be out of work.

Like the dentist, therapeutic recreation (TR) programs are evaluated by participants. In addition, TR programs are under the scrutiny of many stakeholders, including funding agencies, external accreditation bodies, and others who might refer clients. Program evaluation plays a critical role in creating and maintaining high-quality care and in providing outcome-based evidence to meet evaluative and accountability needs.

The purpose of this chapter is to discuss program evaluation in the TR context and specifically address methods for measuring program outcomes. For an in-depth perspective on this subject, see Schulberg and Baker (1979) and Hadley and Mitchell (1995). This chapter will discuss why program evaluation is needed and how to do it. The basic principles associated with program evaluation will be presented along with ideas for measuring program outcomes in TR settings. Therapeutic recreation specialists (TRSs) work in diverse settings. Agency and client needs and goals vary from situation to situation. Consequently, the application of the principles this chapter introduces will depend on the setting and clients each agency serves. This chapter will help TRSs see how the principles apply in their specific TR setting.

The chapter begins by defining program evaluation and explaining the critical role it plays in TR programs. This is followed by a brief description of the program evaluation process. Most of the chapter, however, will focus on the principles associated with conducting outcome evaluations. Practical examples are provided from TR practice. The examples are intended to illustrate challenging tasks TRSs face as they evaluate program outcomes.

What Is Program Evaluation?

The concept of program evaluation in recreation and therapeutic recreation is not new (Kendall & Norton-Ford, 1982; Latchaw & Brown, 1962). Recent changes in the healthcare industry have created a greater interest in program evaluation generally, and outcome measurement specifically. Program evaluation is a proactive process of gathering useful information about a program and its components, then evaluating this information to make informed decisions about program modification (Wever, 1991). Outcome measures are a component of program evaluation that focus on quantifying changes in a patient's status (Burman, Rosen, Hurt & Kolarz, 1998). Ideally, outcomes research employs scientific methods. The process begins with a careful conceptualization of the program. This conceptualization then serves as a foundation for the rest of the process which includes "collecting, analyzing, and interpreting data to make or support decisions about a service program" (Hadley & Mitchell, 1995, p. 61).

Why Perform Program Evaluations and Outcome Studies?

Lee and Sampson (1990) state that the two most important reasons for program evaluation are improvement and accountability. Improvement refers to changes that might be made in the program to increase the effectiveness and efficiency of services to ensure clients receive the highest care with the available resources. Accountability has to do with the extent to which the program's goals are achieved, and whether allocated resources are being used efficiently.

Improvement of the services provided to clients is arguably the most important function program evaluation plays. The world around us is always changing. Great programmers know this and look for new and innovative ways to bring about positive change. They are curious, creative, and motivated to implement new techniques. They are also humble enough to have their work scrutinized and listen to suggestions openly. Program evaluation can facilitate meaningful changes. Changes may range from fine-tuning programming to eliminating program components. For example, a TR program for people with spinal cord injuries might include components on leisure identity, leisure awareness, leisure skills, and leisure resources. Experimental methods can be employed to determine if the elimination of any component(s) impacts outcomes. The results may suggest the elimination or consolidation of components would cut the time and cost of treatment without adversely affecting outcomes. On the other hand, if the program goals are not being met, it might suggest the revision and improvement of certain components.

Most agencies have a number of groups or stakeholders who have an interest in the quality of programming. Stakeholders may include participants and their families, insurance companies, governing boards, and agencies providing regulatory oversight (e.g., JCAHO). Evaluating whether the stated client goals are being achieved by a program may be determined through the use of outcome studies. In situations where program effectiveness is low, steps may be taken toward improvement. Evidence supporting program effectiveness may be used to justify the continuation or expansion of a program, to support accreditation, or to support marketing efforts.

In addition to improvement and accountability, program evaluation may also provide an additional benefit. Another, though less frequent, result of program evaluations is the opportunity to build on existing theory or to develop new theory (Jacobs-Lowery, 2001). Strong programs are built on sound conceptual or theoretical foundations. Evaluating the application of theory often leads to insights and refinement. Results from a theory-based program that are not in accordance with the stated mechanisms of the model may suggest changes or additions to strengthen the theory. These changes also lead to improved treatment effectiveness. Other results may suggest ideas for new theories that can be developed to direct future programs.

A Program Evaluation Model

A number of program evaluation models have been proposed. One example is Alexander's (1979) Rational Planning Model which consists of a seven-step process (see Figure 11.1).

In Alexander's model, the process begins by defining the problem in broad terms. This first step is accomplished by comparing the current state of the program to the ideal or desired state. The difference between these two states represents the problem. With the problem identified, the process seeks to move the program from the current to the desired state. Although current program evaluation focuses on continual improvement rather than identifying problems, the process is similar. The second step involves specifying the program goals and objectives. Peterson and Stumbo (2004) point out that all TR programs should be based on client needs. These goals should be in the form of general outcome statements. More specific measurable objectives should focus on "the specific targeted behaviors around which the rest of the program system is designed" (Peterson & Stumbo, 2000, p. 112).

The third step, analysis of future trends, focuses on taking into account any factors that might later impact the program. Examples include budget cuts or increases, staff cuts or increases, new facilities or equipment, and changes in the number or types of program participants. These factors may either support or undermine the program. The possible effects should be carefully considered in the evaluation process. The fourth step involves the development of alternative strategies to deal with each future trend scenario. The fifth step, implementation analysis, questions the viability of conducting a program evaluation in the current environment. For example, the agency may not have the resources or staff to conduct a program evaluation. Perhaps the political environment is such that staff and or administrators would not be supportive of an evaluation for fear of the results. Specific examples exist in TR settings where program administrators feared an evaluation would lead insurers to question the efficacy of the program and possibly discontinue funding.

It is interesting that Alexander's (1979) model includes a number of steps before the evaluation process begins. Clearly, following these steps will help avoid many problems that can be encountered throughout the evaluation process. If it appears that an evaluation is viable, the problem and goals have been identified, and future trends planned for, the sixth step is to design the evaluation. Based on the goals and objectives identified in step 2, evaluation

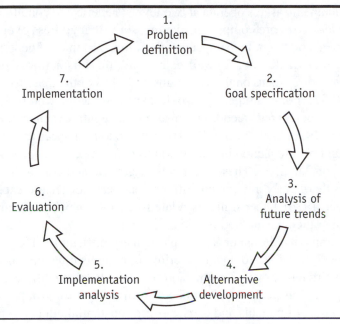

Figure 11.1 Rational Planning Model (adapted from Alexander, 1979)

criteria are established. This involves writing specific criteria that will be used as measures of the program's success. Measures to quantify the criteria then must be found or developed (this will be discussed later in greater detail). Data is then systematically collected and analyzed. The results are used to develop possible program alternatives that will facilitate resolution of the problem identified in step 1. The seventh and final step in the process is to select and implement the best alternative. The entire evaluation process is a positive, systematic journey that works to ensure high-quality TR programs. Implementation of the new alternatives signals the beginning of the process again. Strong, effective agencies are continually involved in this cyclical process of evaluation and change.

One of the most challenging components of the process is the identification and measurement of individual patient outcomes, or outcome measures. Changes in a client's clinical status are perhaps the most salient of all indications of program effectiveness. Measuring these changes is also the most sophisticated component of the program evaluation process. Measuring outcomes takes time, money, and expertise (Kane, 1997). This is because well-done outcome research involves the scientific method. In other words, the most rigorous outcome research employs experimental designs and randomly assigns participants to treatment and control groups in order to isolate the effect of treatment. Kane suggests "clinical research worships at the shrine of RCT [Randomized Clinical Trials]" (Kane, 1997, p 5).

Outcome measures operate at two levels: generic and condition specific. *Generic measures* are comprehensive measures that address overall effects on treatment condition. In therapeutic recreation, examples of generic measure might include quality of life, well-being, and life satisfaction. *Condition-specific measures* focus on the symptoms and signs of the treatment condition (Kane, 1997). For example, one would expect someone who is depressed to have low perceived freedom in leisure or a negative explanatory style (Seligman, 1990; Witt & Ellis, 1989). Other condition-specific symptoms or signs might be a reduction in motivation to participate in hobbies or leisure activities or flat affect. These examples of generic and condition-specific variables tie directly into the conditions necessary for leisure experiences (Neulinger, 1976). Other similarly related variables may be measured when examining outcomes in therapeutic recreation.

Experimental design or RCT is particularly difficult for TR practitioners to employ. First of all, to do an experiment, patients must be randomly assigned to different groups. Treatment groups may be given different variations of a program, but treatment is withheld from the control group. This takes large numbers of patients and carries some substantial ethical implications. Another practical problem stems from the fact that in most cases, TR services are only one element of the treatment services represented by treatment team members. Both of these issues present major barriers to the measurement of outcomes in therapeutic recreation. Given these limitations, consider this example of an ideal situation where a program is able to employ an experimental design. Following this presentation, suggestions for other outcomes methods will be provided.

Identifying Outcomes to Evaluate

The first step in determining what should be evaluated directly ties into the conceptualization of the program. Practitioners must know what they are attempting to accomplish when designing the program. This is one of the reasons theoretically based programs are essential to therapeutic recreation as Caldwell explains in Chapter 4. Theory can provide clear explanations about how to change human cognitions and behavior because it attempts to explain human phenomena. Without a sound conceptual or theoretical framework, programs will not have a central focus and mechanisms of change will not be delineated and implemented. Consequently, goals will be less directed and the methods of accomplishing these goals will be more ambiguous.

One example of how theory can guide a program in determining its desired outcomes can be found in a family recreation program for at-risk youth. The program was based on systems and self-efficacy theories and was intended to improve family functioning. Improved family functioning is expected to mediate adolescent participation in at-risk behaviors. Systems theory serves as a guide for determining the format of the program. Most programs for at-risk youth focus exclusively on the child and his or her behaviors. Systems theory, however, suggests that the actions of members within a family system can be highly contingent upon one another, forming a circular, interconnected process (Steinglass, 1987). Adolescent at-risk behaviors are often symptomatic of larger problems that typically involve the family as a whole, rather than merely the individual. For this reason, systems theory led the programmers to design interventions for the entire family. This particular program was, subsequently, developed as a TR experience for the families of at-risk youth. In other words, rather than working to achieve individual change, the outcomes in the program were expected to reflect change across the entire family system.

Building on the principles of systems theory, self-efficacy theory serves as a foundation for the goals and procedures which were developed. Self-efficacy theory suggests that individuals who perceive themselves as capable of a task are more likely to accomplish it (Bandura, 1977). Collective efficacy refers to the efficacy of individuals to complete tasks as a group (Bandura, 1997). This theory clearly describes the mechanisms involved in increasing and generalizing efficacy. In other words, the theory describes how efficacy can be increased in an activity such as building a fire without matches. It further describes the mechanisms by which the increased efficacy in fire building can be transferred or generalized to increased efficacy in more salient aspects of life, such as family problem solving.

Self-efficacy theory provides principles that serve as a programming guide to ensure that goals and objectives are accomplished. The overall goal of the program was to help reduce adolescent participation in at-risk behaviors. Research has suggested that negative parent-adolescent conflict often contributes to these behaviors. According to self-efficacy theory, families who perceive themselves as able to resolve conflicts in a healthy manner will be more likely to accomplish this task. The program was, consequently, designed to increase collective efficacy during a recreation experience which could be generalized to family conflict resolution.

In addition to specific outcomes related to collective efficacy, systems theory was again used to determine further program goals and objectives. The Circumplex Model (Olson, Russell & Sprenkle, 1979), based on systems theory, suggests family functioning is a combination of family cohesion and adaptability. Communication is the medium that moderates these two factors. Dysfunctional families are likely to be extremely high or low in cohesion and adaptability while healthier families are likely to be more moderate in these areas. Healthy communication can help poorly functioning families become stronger by bringing cohesion and adaptability to more moderate levels. A program that is intended to strengthen families in order to reduce at-risk behaviors may accomplish this by improving healthy communication between parents, adolescents, and siblings. Challenging family recreation was employed in this program as a modality for promoting healthy family communication and more specifically, positive parent-adolescent communication. The challenging recreation included a rustic family camp, a handcart trek, and a survival trek. Each program lasted four days. Families learned a variety of outdoor skills such as building a bow-drill fire and the construction of shelters.

Understanding what a program was designed to accomplish provides practitioners with the information they need for evaluation. A successful program will reach its goals as evidenced by demonstrating measurable outcomes. In this case, the theories indicated that the *outcomes* to be addressed and evaluated were increased collective conflict resolution efficacy and positive communication.

Are You Looking at Consumer/Client or Staff Perceptions?

Another concern in program evaluation is who should be evaluated. Practitioners need to determine whose perception is the most important. Outcome measures may focus on the perceptions of clients, staff, or other interested stakeholders, such as parents, spouses, accreditation bodies, and insurance companies, to determine the program's effectiveness. In the previous example, program evaluators decided to use multiple perspectives in obtaining data to measure outcomes. The participants completed self-report questionnaires and responded to in-depth interviews. Questionnaires were designed to measure individual perceptions of family capabilities and parent-adolescent communication. Interviews focused on family functioning. Staff also completed field notes by responding to questions regarding the differences they noticed in the families between the beginning and end of the experiences (McCoy & Thompson, 2000). These notes were used to determine how the families had changed as a result of the recreation experience from the perception of the trained staff member. They answered specific questions regarding family communication and interaction.

Data Collection and Standardized Procedures

Data collection can be done in a variety of ways including psychometric assessments, interviews, and observation. The most effective technique, which is also the most difficult and time-consuming, is to use all three methods in a triangulated approach. In each case, the data must be collected systematically.

Psychometric Assessment

The first method of collecting data is through psychometric assessments. Practitioners can either choose to use established measures, or when appropriate, develop their own. In both cases, steps need to be taken to ensure each instrument's reliability and validity of inferences. Standardized psychometric tools are published with information regarding the reliability and validity of inferences for certain groups. Other situations exist in which established assessment tools are either not available or are not appropriate. In these cases, new measures need to be developed. Several steps must be taken, however, to ensure that the instruments are sound.

An example of how this is completed can be found in the measurement tools developed for measuring outcomes of the family recreation program. Self-report questionnaires were developed to measure collective challenging recreation efficacy, collective conflict resolution efficacy, and parent-adolescent communication. The first step in this process involved defining the construct to be measured (DeVellis, 1991). This was based on the theoretically driven goals and objectives of the program.

The next steps in the process are to determine the format of the scale and then to develop questions. It is helpful to make sure that questions are designed to maximize variability of responses while maintaining similar format. This will help to increase reliability. Developing questions requires the practitioners to ensure that the questions are relevant to the domains of interest and that each domain is equally represented in the construct being measured.

These steps to ensure reliability and content validity were both used in the development of efficacy questionnaires for the family recreation program. Questions on the two instruments were written following Bandura's (1997) guidelines for efficacy scale construction. Bandura gives specific directions on the appropriate format for efficacy questionnaires. Evidence of content validity was then established through the use of expert reviewers. In regards to collective challenging recreation efficacy, experts in recreation and measurement read through the list of items to make sure the construct was appropriately represented. Questions for the collective conflict resolution efficacy instrument were written following methods of group conflict resolution recommended by Goldstein (1988), and were then analyzed by measurement experts.

The development of the parent-adolescent communication instrument used in the family recreation study provides an example of the next step in the process: administering the questionnaire to a test group (DeVellis, 1991). After determining the format and developing questions, program evaluators conducted a pilot study to reduce the number of scale items and calculate reliability estimates. One hundred thirty-three individuals completed the questionnaire. Through item analysis, the results allowed researchers to reduce the items on the questionnaire from 96 to 57, thereby making the scale more reasonable to complete by participants while maintaining representativeness, relevance, and reliability.

The next step in developing assessments to be used in outcome measurement is to gather criterion-related evidence of validity. This is done by administering the test of interest with other tests that should be systematically related to the test of interest. The existence of hypothesized relationships provides criterion-related evidence of validity. Construct validity has been defined as "the extent to which the scores on a test are an indicator of the theoretical construct of interest" (Suen, 1990, p. 145). Construct validity can be examined by administering the test of interest to groups that are known to be high on the construct and groups that are known to be low on the construct. Scores that reflect the known differences between groups are evidence that support making valid inferences from test scores. An example of this process is found in the development of the collective conflict resolution efficacy questionnaire used in measuring the outcomes of the family recreation program. The study examined collective conflict resolution efficacy in families with at-risk youth who reported high levels of family conflict. Researchers compared scores from this sample known to have high levels of conflict with scores from a sample of the general population to determine if the test could accurately measure the difference between the two groups. Results revealed significant differences between the groups. This suggests that the questionnaire was indeed able to discriminate between the two samples, thus providing evidence supporting construct validity.

Interviews

Interviews represent the second component of triangulated measurement in outcomes. Types of interviews range from highly structured to unstructured. Structured interviews follow a rigid format with specific, ordered, and predetermined questions. These interviews lend themselves to higher levels of reliability but are limited in scope and richness. At the other end of the spectrum, unstructured interviews target a general area, but the interaction is open as the responses vary. Unstructured interviews follow the natural flow of conversation. The area of interest is specified at the beginning, and the direction of questioning develops as the interview progresses. Semi-structured interviews maintain enough structure to be reliable, with enough flexibility to gather rich meaningful information. This format employs pre-determined content and questions. The questions, however, are open-ended, allowing the interview to follow the direction within the comfort of the individual. When conducting interviews, it is important to remember to probe with follow-up questions that allow the practitioner, who is conducting the interview, to more fully understand the individual's point of view. Identifying the best subjects to interview in a program evaluation is critical. For example, TRSs at a program for adolescents with eating disorders may chose to interview the adolescents, their parents, or both. If the outcome is tied to problems at home related to eating behavior, the parents may be the best source of information. If the outcome is tied to weight gain and client well-being, interviewing the client may be most appropriate. Subject selection depends on who can provide the most valuable information related to the outcomes.

Interviews were used in the family recreation program as another form of measurement in the study of outcomes. Themes were formulated in advance of the study. The themes focused on family perceptions of communication, problem-solving ability, and overall satisfaction with the program. Both parents and adolescents were interviewed in an effort to obtain the fullest range of perception.

Observation

The final aspect of triangulated measurement is evaluation through observation. This can be done either qualitatively or quantitatively. Qualitative observation consists of staff viewing specific behaviors then recording these behaviors in the client's chart or in a research document. Quantitative observation tends to be more systematic. It involves the careful selection and description of target behaviors. Methods for data collection are identified, and then the behaviors may be recorded. Several techniques for data recording are available. Typical methods include

- continuous recording (i.e., constantly recording whether or not the behavior is occurring),
- interval sampling (i.e., recording whether or not the behavior is occurring at specified intervals of time),
- duration (i.e., recording the length of time the behavior occurs during an observation), and
- latent sampling (i.e., the time that passes between the stimulus and when the desired behavior occurs). (Peterson & Stumbo, 2004)

New technology is available which makes quantitative observation easier to conduct. Interactions and behaviors can now be recorded, and then viewed by staff at a later, more convenient date. Computer programs exist that allow evaluators to code certain behaviors and to analyze their frequency (Smith & Mead, 1996).

Qualitative observation techniques were used in the family recreation study. TR student researchers worked under the direction of the TR staff. Following each day of the experience, student researchers reflected on and then responded to a set of questions regarding each family's behavior and interactions. They also noted any other relevant information about the families' experiences. This provided the TR staff with information from a third party about how the families were responding to their experiences.

Clinically Relevant Behaviors

Family therapy offers another unique approach to using observation in measuring outcomes. The approach seems particularly applicable to the practice and evaluation of therapeutic recreation. Family therapists have developed a procedure to teach therapists proper therapeutic techniques. The process involves teaching therapists to identify clinically relevant behaviors and providing them with specific feedback about how they should respond (Smith, Mead & Kinsella, 1998). This has resulted in a computerized rating system called the Clinically Relevant Behavior Tracker (CRB; Smith & Mead, 1996). In family therapy, specific behaviors seen as clinically relevant are identified as part of the treatment plan goals. Couples are videotaped and therapists use the CRB Tracker software to code these clinically relevant behaviors.

A recent outcome study, conducted by the authors, evaluated the effectiveness of two TR programs designed to promote marital strength. An experimental design was employed where couples were randomly assigned to one of three groups. The first two groups participated in different recreation interventions, and the third group served as a control. Outcomes were measured using psychometric instruments and observation of clinically relevant behaviors. As couples struggle to complete the task and become frustrated, they might choose a variety of methods to solve the task. For example, complete verbal and physical withdrawal of a partner is a clinically relevant behavior that indicates low levels of adaptability and cohesion. On the other hand, stopping and discussing the problem while making eye contact, or affectionate physical contact is a behavior that represents high levels of adaptability and cohesion. Data were collected at the beginning and end of the programs, and involved videotaping couples while they completed an initiative game. Researchers then compared the frequency of the clinically relevant behaviors to determine the effectiveness of the program.

The CRB approach to outcome measurement may be easily applied in TR programs. Consider for example, a client who has recently had a traumatic brain injury. The TRS will establish goals and objectives to address needs related to the following characteristics: paresis or weakness in a part of the body, expressive language difficulties, receptive language problems (i.e., difficulty processing information), short-term memory deficits, emotional lability and disinhibition, and limited attention span (Brain Injury Association of America, n.d.). The TRS would then identify clinically relevant behaviors related to each goal that would represent progress toward goals or elimination of the problems. TR sessions would periodically be videotaped and then analyzed using the CRB Tracker. Finally, the TRS would review the results to determine if the client's clinically relevant behaviors changed over time, thus determining the extent to which the desired program outcomes were achieved.

Measuring Outcomes Without a Comparison Group

While experimental designs are the best choice for program evaluation, they are often difficult to conduct for practical and ethical reasons. Recruiting subjects for control groups is challenging. Withholding treatment from a control group creates a serious ethical dilemma. This creates a need for other options in outcome measurement. The easiest of these is to track client changes from admission to discharge like the previous example. Much of the same process can be used for nonexperimental as well as for experimental design. The process begins with determining the desired outcome and whose perspective will be used in the evaluation process. Data collection and standardization procedures should follow. Determining the effectiveness of TR programs without using a comparison group necessitates a pretest-posttest design. Baseline data through an assessment of the variables (e.g., behaviors) of interest need to be obtained before the treatment begins. Another set of data is collected following the program using the same assessment methodology. Outcomes are determined by comparing the two data sets. Although any changes in the outcome variable may be the result of treatment, without a control this is a tenuous assumption.

This is, however, an effective means of evaluating programs when an experimental design is not feasible, yet, some limitations exist which lower the practicality of the descriptive design. The primary difficulty with this type of outcome evaluation is the lack of control over other variables that may affect client status. The observed changes may not actually be the result of the TR program. Another variable may have led to the changes instead. For example, a long-term treatment program for adolescents engaging in substance abuse may demonstrate a decrease in a certain behavior following treatment, and TRSs may attribute this change to their interventions. Factors that were not a part of the TR program, however, may have actually led to these changes. Other aspects of the treatment team may have been effective in creating change, or the natural maturation of the individuals may have led to change in behavior. This possibility to incorrectly attribute treatment outcome is one reason that it is preferable to evaluate programs using an experimental design whenever possible.

An outcome study on a therapeutic wilderness program provides an example of a situation where an experimental design was not possible and outcomes were studied using a pretest-posttest design (Widmer, Smith & Wells, 2000). In this situation an experimental design was not feasible for several reasons. Many stakeholders were involved in the study. Each had their own needs and interests. Outcomes were selected that best represented the needs of the stakeholders. The program administrators wanted to evaluate treatment outcomes as quickly as possible in order to convince third-party payers to reimburse for treatment. Insurance companies were also interested in knowing the results as soon as possible. The urgency of the study limited opportunities to employ an experimental design. They did not want to take the time to recruit subjects and conduct the study. Rather, they wanted to use the existing admission assessment data as a baseline in a pretest-posttest design. Another restricting factor was the availability of the control group. Obtaining a control group for the study would have required finding a group that was in need of treatment, but was not receiving it at the time. One option would have been to withhold treatment from part of the sample. Withholding treatment from people seeking help is unethical and inappropriate and may expose the agency and therapists to significant legal liability. Another option, although unlikely and difficult to implement, would be to use a similar treatment facility as a comparison group.

The desire for immediate results and lack of a control group led the researchers to use a pretest-posttest design to determine (to the extent possible) if the therapeutic wilderness program was successful in treating adolescents with behavioral and emotional problems. Clients had completed a social history/assessment form upon entering the program, and researchers developed a posttest questionnaire which was comparable to the baseline data collected from this assessment. One of the agency's desired outcomes was long-term improvements in the original treatment concerns such as substance abuse, oppositional defiance, and family conflict. Long-term changes were, therefore, measured by assessing changes in clients at six weeks and at one year following treatment. The data gathered in this process provided the therapeutic wilderness program with documentation of specific outcomes for the insurance company. More importantly, the information was also useful in determining what areas of the program needed to be strengthened, and it generated new ideas for improving the services given to clients.

Client and Staff Satisfaction

Effective treatments are an important consideration when measuring outcomes, but they are often not the only variable of interest. In many cases, critical outcome measurement focuses on more global issues such as client satisfaction. For clients, "satisfaction is considered an indicator of quality of care" (Maciejewski, Kawiecki & Rockwood, 1997, p. 67). Satisfaction is seen as the individual's evaluation of the provider's performance. It may include a variety of service aspects such as convenience, technical quality, staff interaction, cost, environment, and the length of treatment. Research suggests that satisfaction with communication between the staff and patient is one of the best predictors of overall satisfaction (Kane, 1997).

Client satisfaction should be measured for a number of reasons. First, the clients are the primary purpose and focus of programs. They can play an important role in defining how TR programs are delivered. Clients may have the best perspective on what aspects of a program are helpful. Patients' evaluations "affect many things, including future behavioral intentions, word-of-mouth communications and referrals" (Maciejewski, Kawiecki & Rockwood, 1997, p. 75). A number of issues should be considered when evaluating client satisfaction. Individuals interested in pursuing this subject should consider consulting Maciejewski, Kawiecki, and Rockwood's chapter in *Understanding Healthcare Outcomes Research* edited by Robert Kane (1997).

Summary

This chapter reviewed the basic principles of program evaluation. After defining program evaluation and explaining the role it plays in therapeutic recreation, the rational planning model (Alexander, 1979) was presented. This model provides an example of the process. The model was followed by a more detailed discussion of outcome measures. As illustrated in a family recreation program and a wilderness therapy program, program evaluation can be a challenging process. The process, however, brings with it significant rewards for the agency, the staff, and the clients.

Because of the diversity among agencies that provide TR services, the challenges of conducting program evaluation also vary. Individuals interested in measuring outcomes in their particular setting should modify principles from this chapter to best serve their needs. Overall, outcome-based program evaluation is an ongoing cyclical process that ensures practitioners are providing the highest quality of care possible, while maintaining accountability to both internal and external sources.

Discussion Questions

1. How is program evaluation related to theory-based programming?

2. How could a TRS use each of the three aspects of the triangulated measurement to assess the leisure functioning of an adolescent with cognitive disabilities?

3. How could a TRS support evidence of validity of inferences for a questionnaire he or she created to measure the improvements made following a skiing program designed to reduce depression in individuals with disabilities?

4. What are the strengths and weaknesses of using experimental design when evaluating TR programs?

5. Explain why comparison groups are difficult to attain when evaluating TR programs.

6. How would a TRS use the Rational Planning Model to improve the impact of a leisure education program designed for individuals with developmental disabilities?

References

Alexander, E. (1979). Planning theory. In A.J. Cantanese and J.C. Snyder (Eds.), *Introduction to urban planning* (pp. 106–119). New York, NY: McGraw-Hill.

Bandura, A. (1977). Self-efficacy: Toward a unifying theory of behavioral change. *Psychological Review, 84*, 191–215.

Bandura, A. (1997). *Self-efficacy: The exercise of control.* New York, NY: W.H. Freeman.

Brain Injury Association of America. (n.d.) Electronic references. Retrieved January 3, 2003 from http://www.biausa.org/Pages/consequences%20of%20brain%20injury.html

Burman, W., Rosen, C., Hurt, S., and Kolarz, C. (1998). Toto, we're not in Kansas anymore: Measuring and using outcomes in behavioral healthcare. *Clinical Psychology: Science and Practice, 5*(1), 115–133.

DeVellis, R.F. (1991). *Scale development: Theory and applications.* Newbury Park, CA: Sage.

Goldstein, A.P. (1988). *The PREPARE curriculum: Teaching prosocial competencies.* Champaign, IL: Research Press.

Hadley R. and Mitchell, L. (1995). *Counseling research and program evaluation.* New York, NY: Brooks/Cole.

Jacobs-Lowery, R.L. (2001). A formative evaluation of an adolescent development program: The logic model process (Doctoral dissertation, Rutgers University, 2001). *Dissertation Abstracts International, 62*, 3379.

Kane, R.L. (1997). *Understanding healthcare outcomes research.* Gaithersburg, MD: Aspen.

Kendall, P. and Norton-Ford, J. (1982). Therapy outcome research methods. In P. Kendall and J. Butcher (Eds.), *Handbook of research methods in clinical psychology* (pp. 429–460). New York, NY: Wiley & Sons.

Latchaw, M. and Brown, C. (1962). *The evaluation process in health education, physical education, and recreation.* Englewood Cliffs, NJ: Prentice Hall.

Lee, L.J. and Sampson, J.F. (1990). A practical approach to program evaluation. *Evaluation and Program Planning, 13*, 157–164.

Maciejewski, M., Kawiecki, J., and Rockwood, T. (1997). Satisfaction. In R.L. Kane (Ed.), *Understanding healthcare outcomes research* (pp. 67–89). Gaithersburg, MD: Aspen.

McCoy, J.K. and Thompson, B. (2000). Qualitative research with young informants. In S. Frost Olsen (Chair), *Talk to me about it: Issues involved in interviewing children and young adolescents.* Symposium conducted at the National Council on Family Relations, Minneapolis, MN.

Neulinger, J. (1976). The need for and implications of a psychological conception of leisure. *Ontario Psychologist, 8*(2),13–20.

Olson, D.H., Russell, C.S., and Sprenkle, D.H. (1979). Circumplex model of marital and family systems: Cohesion and adaptability dimensions, family types, and clinical applications. *Family Process, 18*, 3–28.

Peterson, C.A. and Stumbo, N.J. (2000). *Therapeutic recreation program design: Principles and procedures* (3rd ed.). Needham Heights, MA: Allyn & Bacon.

Schulberg, H. and Baker, F. (1979). *Program evaluation in the healthcare fields* (Vol. II). New York, NY: Human Sciences.

Seligman, M.E.P. (1990). *Learned optimism.* New York, NY: Alfred A. Knopf.

Smith, R.C. and Mead, D.E. (1996). CRB Tracker. Unpublished software program. St. Louis, MO, and Provo, UT: Authors.

Smith, R.C., Mead, D.E., and Kinsella, J.A. (1998). Direct supervision: Adding computer-assisted feedback and data capture to live supervision. *Journal of Marital and Family Therapy, 24*(1), 113–125.

Steinglass, P. (1987). A systems view of family interaction & psychopathology. In T. Jacob (Ed.), *Family interaction and psychopathology: Theories, methods, and findings* (pp. 25–65). New York, NY: Plenum.

Stumbo, N.J. and Peterson, C.A. (2004). *Therapeutic recreation program design: Principles and procedures* (4th ed.). San Francisco, CA: Benjamin Cummings.

Suen, H.K. (1990). *Principles of test theories.* Hillsdale, NJ: Lawrence Erlbaum.

Wever, M.F. (1991). The evaluation process. In R.L. Boucher and W.J. Weese (Eds.), *Management of recreational sport in higher education* (pp. 319–328). Carmel, IN: Brown & Benchmark.

Widmer, M.A., Smith, S.H., and Wells, M.S. (2000). Therapeutic wilderness program: Findings of an outcome study. *Abstracts from the 2000 Symposium on Leisure Research* (Phoenix, AZ; p. 68). Ashburn, VA: National Recreation and Park Association.

Witt, P.A. and Ellis, G.D. (1989). *The Leisure Diagnostic Battery: Users manual and sample forms.* State College, PA: Venture Publishing, Inc.

Outcomes Measurement as a Tool for Performance Improvement

Chapter

12

Bryan P. McCormick
Indiana University

The purpose of this book is to provide a comprehensive overview of identifying, producing, and measuring outcomes in therapeutic recreation (TR) practice. Although outcome measurement is a useful tool in determining the effectiveness of services for individual clients, it is also a critical tool in assessing the overall performance of the services of a discipline, unit, or organization. Although performance improvement is a somewhat recent phenomenon in healthcare, it is likely to remain a key focus in the future (McLaughlin & Kaluzny, 1999). The purpose of this chapter is to link the use of outcomes to larger issues of performance improvement (PI) in health and human services. Thus this chapter identifies how outcome measurement in TR practice can be used to ensure that therapeutic recreation provides valued and accountable services (Thompson, 1996). In order to understand how performance improvement has come to be such an important management principle in health and human services, the chapter begins with a brief review.

Alphabet Soup: From Quality Assurance (QA) to Performance Improvement (PI)

Performance improvement (PI) is a result of an evolution of practices related to evaluating service quality in health and human services. Given that this evolution has been relatively rapid, it can be assumed that continued evolution is probable. In other words, today's PI is likely to be known by another acronym in the relatively near future. So, how can one both understand PI and be prepared for future changes? One avenue is to examine the evolution of concepts of service quality evaluation in health and human services.

Although Sluyter (1998) lamented that "unfortunately our traditional approach to monitoring and improving the performance of human service organizations relies to a great extent on external judgments, made by some more or less independent licensing or accrediting body" (p. 5), the tracing of concepts of monitoring and evaluating performance in external accrediting bodies is instructive. For example, in tracing its own history, the Joint Commission for the Accreditation of Healthcare Organizations (JCAHO, 1991) noted that until 1975 JCAHO (then the Joint Commission on the Accreditation of Hospitals or JCAH) standards contained no specific guidelines for assessing and improving the quality of care. Scalenghe (1991) stated that the underlying belief of the pre-1975 standards was that as professionals, healthcare providers would implicitly maintain a high level of care.

Quality Assurance (QA)

In 1975 JCAH published a supplement to the *Accreditation Manual for Hospitals* that contained a standard related to the quality of professional services. This standard required that hospitals demonstrate that their services were "consistently optimal" by continually evaluating care through reliable and valid measures. One of the important aspects of this first standard on quality was that it required measurable criteria.

In 1979 the JCAH standards incorporated a chapter on quality assurance (QA) in the *Accreditation Manual for Hospitals*. The focus of QA activities outlined in this new chapter was on the identification of problems impacting patient care outcomes. While this increased activities system-wide, hospitals had difficulties in implementing the standards (JCAHO, 1991). One such difficulty was that the approach taken by many healthcare providers was to seek out problems or deficiencies in care. As a result, in 1985 revisions were made to JCAHO's QA standards to de-emphasize problem focus and emphasize "monitoring and evaluation of important aspects of care" (JCAHO, 1991, p. 8). This shift to monitoring aspects of care reflected current thinking on the assessment of quality in health services (cf. Donabedian, 1982, 1986).

Although the focus of the 1985 standards was on the ongoing evaluation of important aspects of care, implementation was still a problem. JCAHO (1991) noted that there were difficulties in identifying "optimal care," and a lack of knowledge of what information to collect as indicators of optimal care. In addition, QA activities were still carried out largely by a QA department with little real participation at the organizational level. Finally, there was a widespread perception by healthcare providers that QA activities were being undertaken just to satisfy external bodies, such as JCAHO. At the same time, a few hospital systems had begun to adopt a relatively new management philosophy based on the principles of Total Quality Management (TQM).

McLaughlin and Kaluzny (1999) noted that the principles of TQM, as applied in healthcare, were usually termed Continuous Quality Improvement (CQI).

Continuous Quality Improvement (CQI)

Dienemann (1992) noted that CQI used a different philosophy of management from QA approaches. CQI was based on assumptions that "the most costly problems are due to the system being unnecessarily complex, rigid, or otherwise unresponsive" (Dienemann, 1992, p. 20), and not the result of poor clinician performance. In addition, attainment of an "optimal" level of quality was irrelevant, thus searching out problems and eliminating them ceased to be the focus of monitoring and evaluation. As a result of this shift in managerial philosophy, standards issued by JCAHO during the early 1990s (e.g., JCAHO, 1992) reflected the underlying principles of this newer approach to monitoring and evaluating important aspects of care. JCAHO standards related to CQI de-emphasized attaining an optimal level of care, and instead emphasized continual improvement of service quality. Although the new CQI approach minimized previous managerial views that problems were the result of poor individual performance, the continuing pressures on healthcare services mandated another shift in managerial thinking in healthcare as well as in JCAHO's standards.

Performance Improvement (PI)

The publication of the 1996 *Accreditation Manual for Hospitals* (JCAHO, 1996) indicated that the Joint Commission was no longer using "quality" as a measure of service—they were now interested in "performance." In addition, performance was to be measured by outcomes. JCAHO (1997) identified the role of outcomes measurement in performance improvement stating that "one of the main components of any agency's [accreditation] survey is the focus on performance improvement, which includes the measurement and assessment of quantifiable data based on resident outcome" (p. 5). The shift in JCAHO standards reflected a change in the overall managerial philosophy in health and human services that was known as improving organizational performance (IOP), or performance improvement (PI). Sluyter (1998) defined performance improvement as an organization's "overall effectiveness in meeting the identified needs of each of its constituent groups through systematic efforts that continuously improve its ability to address those needs effectively" (p. 9). In other words, performance improvement relates to an organization's ability to (a) identify the needs of each constituent group, and (b) systematically strive to improve its ability to meet those needs.

So, what can be learned by this evolution from QA to CQI to PI that will help TR professionals in anticipating future changes? One clear theme in this evolution is that consumerism among health and human service recipients has increased the demands for accountability among providers. A variety of customers are increasingly demanding "proof" that the services provided are worth their time and money. It is unlikely that the need to meet the expectations of a variety of constituent groups (e.g., clients, payers, other care providers) will disappear in the future. Thus, TR professionals will continue to need to consider the expectations of not only their clients, but also a number of other constituents impacted by their services.

The second clear theme is that the evaluation of health services had moved from ensuring the appropriate structures of care, to the appropriate processes of care, to the appropriate outcomes of care. The future will continue to base decisions about the quality of health and human services on outcomes. This is not to say that structures and processes will no longer be considered, but they will be subordinate to outcomes.

Finally, there has been a clear evolution in the nature of what constitutes "proof" of meeting client needs. Prior to 1975, the proof of high-quality services rested largely with the individual assessment of the care provider (almost exclusively physicians). If the care provider perceived that the care was clinically successful, it was appropriate care. Under PI, appropriateness of care is determined by measurable outcomes using statistical methodology (Kazandjian & Lied, 1999). The future is likely to only intensify the emphasis on data-driven decision making. Health and human service professions that are able to employ basic quantitative methodologies will be well-equipped to participate in their own destinies. To repeat an often-used phrase in performance improvement: "In God we trust—all others send data."

Changing Managerial Philosophy and Changing Outcomes

Arguably, one of the greatest changes imposed on evaluating the quality of health services brought about by the evolution from QA to PI has been on the nature of outcomes considered to be important. Spath (1996) identified that historically outcomes "centered on results that most interested clinicians" (p. 4). As noted in the previous brief historical review, outcomes were typically defined by care providers based on their own views of important changes in client status as a result of care. However, both CQI and PI significantly expanded how outcomes were conceptualized (McLaughlin & Kaluzny, 1994; Sluyter, 1998). As early as 1990 there were indications in the healthcare literature that medical outcomes needed to include the service recipient's point of view as well (cf. Geigle & Jones, 1990). Ware (1992) stated that "a medical outcome has come to mean the extent to which a change in a patient's functioning or well-being meets the patient's needs or expectations" (p. 3). The inclusion of patient perception of need or expectation signaled the beginning of the broadening of outcomes as related to the quality of health and human services. The previous chapters on valued client outcomes (Chapters 5 & 6) reflect this inclusion of consumer perspective in defining relevant outcomes of TR services.

Yet the PI approach even broadens the realm of relevant outcomes beyond the care provider and direct care recipient. Remember that PI is based on the identification and satisfaction of the needs of a variety of stakeholder groups. Thus a performance improvement approach must consider outcomes valued by a multitude of stakeholders. These include not only clients and their family members, but also a variety of other "customers" that are impacted by a service (Sluyter, 1998). Sluyter cited three basic groups of customers. First, there are external customers. These are the ultimate customers and are represented by clients and their families.

The second group is comprised of internal customers. Internal customers are groups of people internal to the organization. Employees and volunteers are examples of internal customers. This group also includes those who rely on one another within the organization as examples of customers. For example, other disciplines may rely on the therapeutic recreation specialist (TRS) for assessment information.

Finally, Sluyter identifies stakeholders as a group of customers with a special interest in the organization. This group only benefits indirectly from the organization. Sluyter (1998) stated that "stakeholders may include funders of programs, accreditation or licensing agencies, advocacy groups, and the community at large" (p. 16). For example, if a TR professional was operating an adult daycare which was funded in part through community giving (e.g., the United Way), the funding organization would represent a stakeholder in the performance of the adult daycare. The implication is that whenever a TRS seeks to use outcomes as the basis for performance improvement, he or she must be sure to consider outcomes that are valued by a variety of stakeholders.

In addition to the need to be aware of a variety of customers' expected outcomes, the expansion of relevant outcomes beyond the perspective of the service provider has resulted in a number of classification schemes of outcomes. One of the first outcome classification approaches was offered by Stewart (1992) based on the Medical Outcomes Study (MOS). The MOS resulted in the SF-36 Health Survey (Ware, Snow, Kosinski & Gandek, 1993). The SF-36 categorized outcomes into (a) clinical status, (b) physical function and well-being, (c) mental function and well-being, (d) social/role function and well-being, and (e) general health perceptions and satisfaction. The reader should see that many of these categories of outcomes are relevant to TR practice.

Another approach to the classification of outcomes can be seen in JCAHO's (1999) identification of outcome measures relevant to accreditation. They cited the three general categories of (a) health status, (b) patient perceptions of care, and (c) clinical performance outcomes. *Health status* outcomes reflect the functional well-being of specific populations, both in general and in relation to specific conditions, such as physical functioning, bodily pain, social functioning, and mental health. *Patient perceptions of care* outcomes include satisfaction measures that focus on the delivery of care from the patient's and/or family's perspective. JCAHO noted examples such as satisfaction with patient education, medication use, pain management, communication regarding plans and outcomes of care, prevention of illness, and improvement in health status in this category of outcomes. Finally, *clinical performance outcomes* reflect more of an intermediate outcome of the processes of a service than an ultimate outcome. This category of outcomes reflects the outcomes of processes of care such as the appropriateness of clinical decision making. For example, one outcome of the process of assessment in therapeutic recreation is the creation of a prioritized list of needs (Austin, 1999). It would be possible to review the outcomes (defined as an accurate identification of needs) of the TR assessment process to identify the clinical performance characteristics. If the list of needs generated by the assessment process was not relevant to the client's situation, one could identify that there was a poor outcome in the process of clinical decision making.

Role of Outcomes in Performance Improvement

How does one go about using TR outcomes to improve performance? To answer this question one must consider both the nature of therapeutic recreation and health and human services generally. The fact that therapeutic recreation is a *service* distinguishes it from other professions that provide *products*. One of the key differences is that in service industries the service is produced, consumed, and evaluated by the consumer almost simultaneously. As a result, the nature of the service cannot be measured as easily as in manufacturing industries. In addition, in manufacturing products there is often a time lag between the production, consumption (or use), and evaluation of quality of the product. Thus improving performance in service industries requires different approaches from that of manufacturing industries. The implications of this difference are that once the service has been delivered, it is too late to take it back. Adding more inspectors or supervisors to maintain quality services just won't cut it. Instead we [service providers] need a different paradigm for how quality is produced in services and how we must manage and improve it. (Sluyter, 1998, p. 29)

The crux of this difference is that in service industries, performance is the result of a multitude of processes. These processes ideally result in outcomes that meet the needs of consumers. JCAHO (1997) clarified the link between outcome measurement, processes results, and performance improvement. "Performance improvement concentrates on the processes organizations use and their attempts to continuously improve the efficiency and effectiveness of these processes" (p. 11). Most importantly, without a particular outcome in mind, improvement of a process becomes difficult. With no outcome in mind, it is difficult to determine if changes to a process have been effective. When one anticipates what outcomes can be expected and what outcomes were achieved, one can more effectively determine if changes have been successful.

As noted at the beginning of this chapter, performance improvement is essentially an evaluative activity. The goal is to ensure that TR services and the overall organization are successfully meeting the needs of their customers. Schalock (2001) indicated that evaluative processes are decision oriented. This means that the findings of an evaluative process are used to inform decisionmakers, give guidance for revision, and provide feedback to customers about the process in question. In this framework, the role of outcome measurement is to provide a data-based foundation for decision making. JCAHO (1997) characterized the process as follows: "Measure the outcomes and determine what needs to be fixed in the process. Change the process and confirm that it was improved. Finally, determine whether the outcomes have improved as a result of the process changes" (p. 17).

Organizational Relevance and TR Outcomes

One of the key concepts that should be noted in the previous discussion is that performance improvement is an organization-wide activity. Unlike previous management approaches that tended to be department or discipline specific, PI is clearly focused on the improvement of *organizational* performance. This does not mean that services or disciplines such as therapeutic recreation cannot undertake performance improvement initiatives. Yet this organizational focus does imply that discipline- or service-specific performance improvement initiatives must be connected to organizational initiatives. In other words, if the outcomes that are being tracked by a TR department do not have clear relevance to organizationally valued outcomes, information on the performance of the TR service will be of little interest to the organization. Thus one of the keys to meaningful outcome measurement and performance improvement is to wed TR outcomes to valued institutional outcomes (McCormick & Funderburk, 2000). For example, if the organization uses the SF-36 (Ware, Snow, Kosinski & Gandek, 1993) or the Functional Independence Measure (FIM; Uniform Data System for Rehabilitation, 2002) as an organizational outcome measure, then outcome measures in TR services should have a clear connection to one or more of the domains in these measures. If the outcomes being tracked within the TR service are clearly related to valued organizational outcomes, then the TR service is more likely to be seen as an integral component of the overall services of the organization.

Summary

This chapter identified the role of outcomes measurement in performance improvement. In general, outcomes are a critical component for any performance improvement initiative. At the same time, a few key points should be remembered as related to TR practice, outcome measurement, and performance improvement. First, outcomes must be considered broadly in terms of the preferences of a variety of customers. Singular reliance on clinical status outcomes may produce a service that is effective, but unwanted. In addition, outcomes must be not only valued by constituent groups, but they also must be demonstrable. McCormick and Darnsteadt (1999) warned that as a profession therapeutic recreation too often focuses on "how and what service to provide...without considering how to demonstrate the effects of these services" (p. 77). Outcome *measurement* provides such a link between service provision and accountability. Lastly, PI activities in a TR service must be in concert with the outcomes valued by the larger organization. TR professionals must be aware of the interests of the larger organization, and ensure that their services are central to the mission of the organization.

Discussion Questions

1. What was the underlying assumption about maintaining the quality of services prior to JCAHO's introduction of quality standards in 1975. Do you think this was a reasonable assumption?

2. Quality assurance was problem-focused. What were some of the weaknesses of such an approach?

3. How did quality assurance (QA) differ from continuous quality improvement (CQI)?

4. How does performance improvement (PI) differ from continuous quality improvement (CQI)?

5. What is accountability, and how can TR specialists demonstrate the quality of their services?

6. List five outcomes of TR services that could be measured.

References

Austin, D.R. (1999). *Therapeutic recreation processes and techniques* (4th ed.). Champaign, IL: Sagamore.

Dienemann, J. (1992). Approaches to quality improvement. In J. Dienemann (Ed.), *Continuous quality improvement in nursing* (pp. 15–43). Washington, DC: American Nurses Publications.

Donabedian, A. (1982). *The criteria and standards of quality*. Ann Arbor, MI: Health Administration Press.

Donabedian, A. (1986). Criteria and standards for quality assessment and monitoring. *Quality Review Bulletin 14*, 99–108.

Geigle, R. and Jones, S.B. (1990). Outcomes measurement: A report for the field. *Inquiry, 27*, 7–13.

Joint Commission on Accreditation of Healthcare Organizations. (1991). *The transition from QA to CQI*. Oakbrooke Terrace, IL: Author.

Joint Commission on Accreditation of Healthcare Organizations. (1992). *Accreditation manual for hospitals*. Chicago, IL: Author.

Joint Commission on Accreditation of Healthcare Organizations. (1996). *Accreditation manual for hospitals*. Chicago, IL: Author.

Joint Commission on Accreditation of Healthcare Organizations. (1997). *Using outcomes to improve performance in long-term care and subacute settings*. Oakbrook Terrace, IL: Author.

Joint Commission on Accreditation of Healthcare Organizations. (1999). *Framework for core measures*. Retrieved from http://www.jcaho.org/perfmeas_frm.html

Joint Commission on Accreditation of Hospitals. (1975). *Accreditation manual for hospitals*. Oakbrook Terrace, IL: Author.

Kazandjian, V.A. and Lied, T.R. (1999). *Healthcare performance measurement*. Milwaukee, WI: ASQ Quality Press.

McCormick, B.P. and Darnsteadt, J. (1999). Quality and performance improvement: Implications for therapeutic recreation. *Annual in Therapeutic Recreation, 8*, 70–80.

McCormick, B.P. and Funderburk, J. (2000). Therapeutic recreation outcomes in mental health practice. *Annual in Therapeutic Recreation, 9*, 9–19.

McLaughlin, C.P. and Kaluzny, A.D. (1994). Defining total quality management/continuous quality improvement. In C.P. McLaughlin and A.D. Kaluzny (Eds.), *Continuous quality improvement in healthcare* (pp. 3–10). Gaithersburg MD: Aspen.

McLaughlin, C.P. and Kaluzny, A.D. (1999). Defining quality improvement: Past, present and future. In C.P. McLaughlin and A.D. Kaluzny (Eds.), *Continuous quality improvement in healthcare* (2nd ed.; pp. 3–33). Gaithersburg, MD: Aspen.

Scalenghe, R. (1991). The Joint Commission's "agenda for change" as related to the provision of therapeutic recreation services. In B. Riley (Ed.), *Quality management: Applications for therapeutic recreation* (pp. 29–42). State College, PA: Venture Publishing, Inc.

Schalock, R.L. (2001). *Outcome-based evaluation* (2nd ed.). New York, NY: Plenum.

Sluyter, G.V. (1998). *Improving organizational performance*. Thousand Oaks, CA: Sage.

Spath, P.L. (1996). The evolution of medical effectiveness and outcomes management initiatives. In P.L. Spath (Ed.), *Medical effectiveness and outcomes management* (pp. 3–7). Chicago, IL: American Hospital Publishing.

Stewart A.L. (1992). The medical outcomes study framework of health indicators. In A.L. Stewart and J.E. Ware, Jr. (Eds.), *Measuring functioning and well-being: The medical outcomes study approach* (pp. 12–24). Durham, NC: Duke University.

Thompson, G.T. (1996). Structuring your department to manage coverage and reimbursement. In D. Wagner, B. Kennedy, and A. Pritchard (Eds.), *Recreational therapy: The next generation of reimbursement* (pp. 1–18). Hattiesburg, MS: American Therapeutic Recreation Association.

Uniform Data System for Rehabilitation. (2002). *Functional independence measure*. Amherst, NY: Author.

Ware, J.E., Jr. (1992). Measures for a new era of health assessment. In A.L. Stewart and J.E. Ware, Jr. (Eds.), *Measuring functioning and well-being: The medical outcomes study approach* (pp. 3–11). Durham, NC: Duke University.

Ware, J.E., Jr., Snow, K.K., Kosinski, M., and Gandek, B. (1993). *SF-36 Health Survey manual and interpretation guide*. Boston, MA: New England Medical Center.

Conveying the Possible With Client-Directed Outcomes and Social Marketing

Susan "BOON" Murray, Ed.D., CTRS
University of Wisconsin—La Crosse

When you hear the term *marketing outcomes* what comes to mind? How do therapeutic recreation specialists (TRSs) feel about promoting and justifying their programs and services to participants, colleagues, agencies, and funding sources "in a manner that highlights efficacy" (Broida, 2000, p. 1)? How can TRSs authentically present their potential to facilitate healing to any audience—especially therapeutic recreation (TR) participants? How can TRSs promote outcomes to colleagues in other health and human services and to funding sources so they broaden their concept of "medicine" to value the TR approach?

The first goal of this chapter is to explore these questions by challenging whether the TR focus on outcomes is therapist-directed or truly client-directed in light of a controversial book by cofounders of the Institute for the Study of Therapeutic Change (Duncan & Miller, 2000). The second goal is to demonstrate how to analyze attributes and benefits of therapeutic activities to articulate client-valued program outcomes with some help from social marketing principles. The third goal is to present practical ideas for conveying TR outcomes via program announcements, program protocols, and professional resources in a profession polarized by valuing either leisure or health as its central theme.

Reframing the TRS's Stance via Client-Directed Outcomes

Broyard (1992), while hospitalized for cancer treatment, wrote in his journal, "The important thing is the patient, not the treatment" (p. 68). Textbooks in many health and human services professions focus exclusively on the therapist's frame of reference. One result is that clients may receive help and resources without being involved in decision making. The professional's privileged frame of reference stems from being socialized to give allegiance to theoretical models, to specialize in an expert language consumers may not understand, and to credit skill in facilitating modalities as the specialist's success. But who really does the hard work of growth and change?

Clients, not therapists, make treatment work. Duncan and Miller (2000) debunk the myth of the "guru therapist" and recast the client as the "star of the therapeutic drama" in *The Heroic Client: Doing Client-Directed, Outcome-Informed Therapy* in the context of mental health. They identified four factors of change that create positive outcomes "regardless of the theoretical orientation or professional discipline of the therapist" (pp. 56–57). These include:

- the clients' manifestation of inner strength by seeking help, along with having social supports, which accounts for 40% of positive outcome;

- the clients' partnership with their therapist in collaboration to reach each client's goals, which contributes 30% to positive outcome;

- the clients' expectation that there are solutions to problems and the instillation of hope, which contributes 15% to positive outcome; and

- the consideration of alternative models and techniques that allow choice when one form of therapy is not working, which contributes 15% of positive outcome. (Duncan & Miller, 2000, pp. 56–57)

Many treatments and approaches work. Clients make the most of what works in the modalities presented to address their issues and their regeneration (Hubble, Duncan & Miller, 1999). In fact, clients have their own theory of change in tandem with their lifelong learning, how they view what is at stake for them, and how it can be resolved. A growing number of attribution studies regarding outcomes in mental health recommend that therapists who formulate approaches tailored to each individual's unique needs, rather than asserting theories of human behavior to fit diagnostic criteria, establish a stronger alliance to promote change and growth. Duncan and Miller recommend a sensitivity shift to client-directed change and viewing the client as the "engine of change" (p. 67). In other words, it may not be that "evidence-based practice…should guide delivery of service" (Lee & Yang, 2000, p. 21), but rather that TRSs should better acquaint themselves with clients' dreams and goals, and how clients utilize their resources. A given situation may call for a focus on existential or functional outcomes based on the client's view, the setting, and other factors such as who else is helping. Means and ends may coincide within the same activity which complicates and challenges the TRS's role identity to facilitate change or insight. For example, planting a tree, piecing a quilt, or making a memory box could all be *means* for survivors and their terminally ill loved one to make sense of that person's impending death as legacy building (O'Keefe, 1993). At the same time, each of these activities may be an *end* in itself, an existential outcome, as the individual's way to memorialize their life purpose and their continuity. TRSs socialized by their training to view their role as leisure development or health promotion may not allow a tolerance for ambiguity that invites exploring the client's priorities in the realm of functional or existential outcomes.

Of course, clients are not always clear about what they want, especially if they are not accustomed to envisioning possibilities due to a cycle of dependency, or if they are experiencing the shock of crisis. However, if it is desirable to make therapeutic recreation a more collaborative and outcome-oriented experience, TRSs can begin conversations with clients as the framing of an alliance as "an intimately interpersonal event committed to the client's goals" (Duncan & Miller, 2000, p. 149). In this collaborative conversation, the TRS lets the client take the lead. Duncan and Miller (2000) offer the following practical guidelines:

1. Explore clients' undiscovered personal theories of change by having them describe their experiences and what they want in *their* language—take notes and share them with clients to elevate the importance of what they express.

2. Ask questions that evoke how clients think change may occur, and how clients see the specialist and the change process as helping to attain their goals.

3. Elicit examples from clients where they have been successful making change.

4. Amplify clients' evolving theories of change by being curious and committing to clients' worldviews as they identify solutions and approaches to intervention.

5. Track outcome data in clients' language and share it at each session—score and interpret all data *with* clients and invite comments on the relevance of interventions.

Building on Duncan and Miller's idea of a "conversation," the TRS can develop a genuine partnership with clients by paying more attention to the universal hunger for personal significance, along with attending to the client's "presenting problem." This means to ask TR clients what they long for as goals of their existence—their *existential* outcomes (James & James, 1991). Do they long for good health and vitality? to know and understand their purpose and significance? While assessment receives renewed attention by emphasizing functional outcomes in the clinical practice of therapeutic recreation (Stumbo, 2002), tools that incorporate an individual's environment and social support systems may be more complementary to individualized planning:

- person-centered planning tools such as Circle of Support and MAPS (Making Action Plans; Falvey, Forest, Pearpoint & Rosenberg, 1997);
- personal futures planning (Smull & Harrison, 1992);
- portfolios as autobiographical profiles of abilities, dreams, and goals (Galambos, 1995); and
- ecological inventories (Jacobson & Wilhite, 1999; Snell, 1987).

Of prime significance, these tools do not deny a person's vulnerabilities or impairments but change the perception of the client to a person with potential. Checking TR methods and theories with participants for a first-person view is prerequisite to avoiding third-person dominated models of practice. How TRSs use language to refer to and write about clients either marginalizes or emancipates them and is fundamental to their sense of becoming the engineers of change.

As TRSs develop outcomes literature and training materials for the profession, they might consider new ways of documenting client-directed outcomes such as participant and family member testimonials regarding therapeutic change and how it occurs as portrayed in *The Benefits Are Endless...* (NTRS, 2000). This training video presents outcome vignettes where clients and families speak and reflect as authorities on their TR experience, demonstrating one strategy for conveying TR effectiveness to audiences. In fact, videos where participants and their family members specify health or leisure outcomes could be content analyzed as qualitative methodology, thus allowing a forum for client-directed outcomes to be verified as human science research. This type of evidence might be classified as collaborative research or action research (Reason & Rowan, 1981) or lived experience research (Ellis & Flaherty, 1992). While published manuscripts with clients and families as lead authors and coauthors could affirm client-directed approaches, only one example of this is found in TR literature (Wise & Hale, 1999).

In summary, shifting priority to client-directed outcomes is one strategy for the TRS to incorporate into marketing TR outcomes. Turning to social marketing approaches is another.

How Social Marketing Aids Promotion of Outcomes

Another method for redirecting therapeutic recreation to promote client-directed outcomes is social marketing since it involves prioritizing clients' requirements and using language perceptively. Social marketing originated to promote behavior change as healthful outcomes for prevention and health maintenance. It has been applied to promoting leisure benefits although it is not specifically identified as "social marketing" for this purpose, but instead referred to as benefits-based awareness (BBA), benefits-based programming (BBP), and benefits-based management (BBM; O'Sullivan, 1999). The underlying concept is to reposition public awareness to focus on outcomes as the effects of meaningful activity rather than just being aware of activities or interventions themselves.

Since TRSs often meet their clients in group sessions, many programs are designed and delivered based on clients' identified needs. Social marketing begins with needs assessment and complements a principle of TR programming: "The need of the client determines the nature of programs provided" (Peterson & Stumbo, 2000, p. 27). "Very simply, social marketing is the use of commercial marketing techniques to promote the adoption of a behavior that will improve the health or well-being of a target audience or of society as a whole" (Weinreich, 1999, p. 3). The distinguishing feature of social marketing is that the action or behavior benefits the individual or society rather than the proponent's organization.

Social marketing is most appropriate when applied to sustaining health, facilitating personal growth as behavior change, increasing program use, or increasing participants' satisfaction with existing services. It is widely used for improving health (e.g., tobacco and alcohol cessation, reducing high cholesterol, advocating cancer screening); for injury prevention (e.g., from suicide, sexual assault, domestic violence); and for fostering community involvement (e.g., organ and blood donation, voting). Social marketing follows a systematic process:

1. Select and understand target markets;

2. Determine strategies by developing a marketing mix that combines the four Ps—*products* (e.g., behaviors to be changed), *price* (i.e., the "cost" of adopting desired behaviors and abandoning ineffective behaviors), *place* (i.e., where the target audience will perform the behavior or learn more about how to change), and *promotion* (i.e., key messages to influence behavior change and media channels where the message appears such as announcements or fact sheets);

3. Develop an evaluation and monitoring strategy; and

4. Compile a detailed implementation plan. (Kotler, Roberto & Lee, 2002)

This chapter does not address all four aspects, but instead focuses on the *promotion* aspect—how to utilize outcomes-based program announcements for TR participants, outcomes-based program protocols for colleagues and funding sources, and professional organization materials as key messages specifying improved health or leisure fulfillment.

The social marketing "product" is the behavior or offering one wants the target audience to adopt. In a TR context it may range from *physical products* such as using a journal for personal growth or memory enhancement, to *services* such as leisure education programs, to *practices* such as inclusion support, to *more intangible ideas* such as finding sanctuary in nature as spiritual comfort (Weinreich, 1999, p. 10). Participants should perceive that the product is a viable solution to their distress or will satisfy their needs. Of course, TRSs may need to build up awareness of how behavior can be improved or provide other necessary skills before promoting change (e.g., assertiveness training could precede self-advocacy). TRSs can use their expertise in activity analysis to refine "products" offered (e.g., making them easier to use, more effective, more attractive). For example, an electronic method of journaling may appeal to adolescents rather than a paper journal for privacy reasons. A follow-up support group for relapse prevention may be held in an online chat room for convenience and accessibility.

All "products" should be designed to appeal to the target audience. This involves choosing language carefully to convey a program or service in terms of specific benefits or outcomes the TRS is certain the target audience will value. One programmatic application of social marketing could be outcome-based program announcements that motivate participation.

Promoting Therapeutic Recreation With Outcome-Based Program Announcements

Outcomes are the actual benefits attained by participants during or after involvement in programs (O'Sullivan, 1999). Outcomes could be knowledge, skills, values, attitudes, behaviors, needs met, changes, and improvements. Outcomes can be short-term (e.g., increasing range of motion) or long-term (e.g., maintaining independence). Consider what makes modalities and facilitation techniques therapeutic or beneficial. General programs (e.g., stress management, exercise, adventure programs), population-specific programs (e.g., caregiver support, medical play), and even newly derived programs like Edenizing (Thomas, 1996) each have meaning in their own right. TRSs understand the inherent healing qualities of modalities because they have analyzed them via activity analysis. They also recognize that the goal of an intervention or program is also the effect or outcome. Therefore, TRSs who promote potential benefits that match participants' desires access their motivation and engagement.

TRSs can consider the most critical outcomes within their particular delivery system as the key messages. They can then match the message, and the means for delivering the message, to the specific target group (O'Sullivan, 1999). This may include printed materials such as consumer newsletters, program descriptions with research outcomes featured as pull quotes, electronic messages on websites, voice mail messages, or personal testimonials of participants. For example, Figure 13.1 (p. 240) is a program announcement promoting physical exercise as The Benefits of Chairobics: Sit To Be Fit which can be used to promote exercise in a rehabilitation setting for people with spinal cord injury. This flyer was designed to display client-valued outcomes by first creating a "benefit ladder" (Weinreich, 1999), and thus utilizes a social marketing approach. The designer first identifies the attribute that describes the activity (i.e., tone your body) and the benefit the participant will receive from the attribute (i.e., muscle strength). Then the designer probes participants and available literature about seated exercise to "ladder" additional benefits the target audience deems important, so that key messages are positioned as appealing outcomes (e.g., feeling in control).

Table 13.1 (p. 241) reveals the benefits ladder derived to feature selected attributes of the Chairobics program. This table also features examples of two other facilitation techniques and their attributes (i.e., social skills, bereavement support) as potentially participant-valued outcomes that could be displayed in program announcements. Benefits ladders to express outcomes may appear as program descriptions in newsletters or daily event posters as well. They could be derived as participants' self-articulated benefits which appear as part of a feature article in an agency newsletter or information packets given to new participants. Displaying announcements in high-traffic areas promotes outcomes and attunes families, staff, and observers to the therapeutic importance of programs.

Useful Outcomes Classifications for Leisure Benefits

Using a social marketing approach requires cultivating a benefits-based mindset, an initiative emphasized by NRPA and NTRS for the last twenty years. According to Driver and Bruns, benefits and outcomes are synonymous where the Benefits Approach to Leisure (BAL) has been operationalized to include (a) improved conditions or gains, (b) prevention of a worse condition,

The Benefits of Chairobics: Sit To Be Fit

Work Out With Wendy To . . .

✓ Breathe easier to reduce your stress and exercise your lungs

✓ Tone your body to build muscle strength and be more independent

✓ Work out with others to be part of a healthy trend and stay well

✓ Feel better, more alive and in control with more energy for other activities

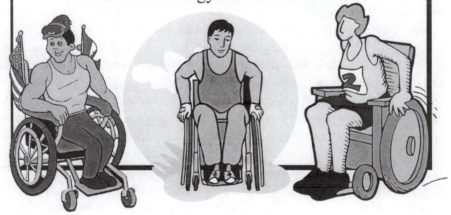

Figure 13.1 Outcome-based program announcement—The Benefits of Chairobics: Sit To Be Fit (65% of original size)

or (c) realization of a specific satisfying psychological experience (1999, p. 354). Because the tremendous social significance of leisure outcomes is not clearly understood, the benefits movement has been a purposeful effort to enumerate specific types of benefits attributed to leisure and to categorize them. Personal development, psychophysiological, social and cultural

Table 13.1 Benefits-based ladder for Chairobics

Activity: Chairobics

Attribute ➡	Benefit ➡	Benefit ➡	Benefit
Breathing better	Reduces stress	Increases lung capacity	Feel more relaxed
Tone your body	Builds muscle strength	Be more independent	Have more freedom; more opportunities
Workout with others	Being part of a healthy trend	Social approval of wellness ethic	Staying well and continuing to participate
Feeling better	Feel more alive	Feel more in control	Have more energy for other endeavors

Activity: Social Skills

Attribute ➡	Benefit ➡	Benefit ➡	Benefit
Greeting others	Evokes positive feeling	Lifts your mood	Feel less awkward in social situations
Making conversation	Express your opinions	Can get you what you want	Create reciprocal regard

Activity: Bereavement Support

Attribute ➡	Benefit ➡	Benefit ➡	Benefit
Drawing out feelings	Provides release	Accept loss and receive hope	Get energized to live life again
Supportive company	Validates grief reactions	Realize you're not alone	Is educational in learning new ways to cope

benefits, and environmental benefits have been studied, classified, and now form an integrated approach to leisure research. This same approach has been recently incorporated into specifying benefits as outcomes in therapeutic recreation *where the central theme is leisure* (Broida, 2000, 2001; NTRS, 2000). *Therapeutic Recreation—The Benefits Are Endless...Training Program and Resource Guide* (Broida, 2000) contains researched TR outcomes cross-referenced on a spreadsheet with a key by type of benefit, modality, population age, diagnostic group, and literature citation. Anecdotal "success stories" and a literature review illustrate categorically identified domains of benefits including (a) physical, (b) social, (c) psychological/emotional, (d) cognitive, (e) expressive, (f) recreation and leisure development, and (g) benefits to profession/staff and caregivers/parents/family. This training manual provides source material such as PowerPoint scripts and disability-related media to derive outcomes as key messages for three target audiences: (a) other TRSs, (b) health and human service colleagues, and (c) community audiences.

Useful Outcomes Classifications for Health Benefits

The *Benefits of Therapeutic Recreation: A Consensus View* (Coyle, Kinney, Riley & Shank, 1991) provides a typology of outcomes as six global benefits where the central theme is health. Researched benefits related to therapeutic recreation include physical health, cognitive functioning, psychosocial health, growth and personal development, personal and life satisfaction, and societal and healthcare outcomes (Shank, Kinney & Coyle, 1993). The *Benefits of Therapeutic Recreation: A Consensus View* (Coyle, Kinney, Riley & Shank, 1991) enumerates categorical benefits of activity-based interventions by population or setting. However, the originators of this classification stress that therapists should "make concerted efforts to report the outcomes of their research in ways that are seen as relevant to the broader healthcare system" (p. 318).

Marketing Outcomes With Program Announcements

Outcome-based program announcements should convey outcomes emphatically as action verbs that increase or decrease change (e.g., resolve your grief, stop feeling so alone) to directly engage participants. Using nonclinical language to express benefits to participants elevates clients to care partners by respecting their responsibility as the true catalyst of therapeutic change. Outcome-based program announcements contain four basic elements (see Figure 13.1, p. 240; also Figure 13.4, p. 248):

- **A title** captures attention by framing therapeutic activity with a benefits-based slogan to convey a memorable sense of behavior change or re-creation. It should be featured as bold display type (18–36 points). Individuals or groups of peers can brainstorm program titles to project the essence of desired outcomes.
- **An invitation to join a named facilitator** personalizes the invitation to "come out and play" for change or renewal.
- **A bulleted list of potential outcomes presented in participant-friendly language** highlights them as remarkable and makes them easy to read at a glance by setting the font in 14 to 24 point type. Using nonclinical, concise language that mirrors how clients converse creates anticipation. A benefits-based

announcement for children may utilize age-relevant phrasing such as "tell your feelings to your doll" to promote the emotional benefit of medical play along with children's drawings or artwork to enhance the message. Benefits should be displayed concisely as bulleted phrases. Consider using a benefits ladder to connect attributes of activity to a hierarchy of benefits when designing announcements (see Table 13.1, p. 241). Formatting the outcomes in the same font as the title and name of the facilitator enhances the readability. Selecting an easy-to-read, less decorative font is preferable, especially for clients with vision impairments.

- **Complimentary graphics attract readers to the announcement** by catching attention and uniting the program title with outcomes as a complete, action-oriented display (e.g., using clip art, photographs, symbols, texture, color). Alternatively, printing announcements on thematic, full-color background papers from office supply stores can create a mood or metaphor associated with an activity (e.g., the "road" to self-improvement). Graphics should be culturally sensitive and represent the client population.

In summary, benefits-based announcements can be quickly designed and displayed as standard 8 ½-by-11–inch formats. However, they can also be displayed as banners, or even replicas of a modality. For example, one TRS created a gigantic book cover using posterboard where enlarged storybook character cutouts proclaimed *The Benefits of Bibliotherapy...Learning To Live Happily Ever After*. Her social marketing slogan implies that reading or hearing storybooks "permits readers to rethink their own situations from a more detached and safe distance...when information is conveyed in an economical and emotionally memorable manner" (Gold, 1988. p. 137). Figure 13.2 (p. 244) offers a checklist for designing outcome-based program announcements.

Promoting Therapeutic Recreation With Outcome-Based Program Protocols

Outcome-based program protocols are companion documents to outcome-based program announcements that display therapeutic benefits of activity-based interventions to colleagues and funding sources. They are designed to convey the role of the TRS as well as facilitation components and best-practice, research, and organizational resources. Program protocols express

Please award points as follows for each item:
Gold—10 points, Silver—8 points, Lead—5 points, Not Yet—0 points

_____ 1. The title is benefits-based expressing an explicit outcome.
❏ Gold ❏ Silver ❏ Lead ❏ Not yet
Comments:

_____ 2. The title is expressed rhythmically as a slogan that makes the outcome memorable.
❏ Gold ❏ Silver ❏ Lead ❏ Not yet
Comments:

_____ 3. The title is displayed in a legible font as the largest element on the page.
❏ Gold ❏ Silver ❏ Lead ❏ Not yet
Comments:

_____ 4. The facilitator is announced by name.
❏ Gold ❏ Silver ❏ Lead ❏ Not yet
Comments:

_____ 5. Explicit benefits of participation are featured in the language of participants as an age-appropriate, reader-friendly expression of target audience.
❏ Gold ❏ Silver ❏ Lead ❏ Not yet
Comments:

_____ 6. A benefits ladder is utilized to convey outcomes _or_ multiple effects are enumerated.
❏ Gold ❏ Silver ❏ Lead ❏ Not yet
Comments:

_____ 7. Benefits are concisely displayed as functional or existential outcomes in a style that is easy to read at a glance (e.g., bullets, numbers, clusters).
❏ Gold ❏ Silver ❏ Lead ❏ Not yet
Comments:

_____ 8. Graphics complement the text to enhance the key message and overall effect.
❏ Gold ❏ Silver ❏ Lead ❏ Not yet
Comments:

_____ 9. Culturally sensitive graphics do not marginalize or offend any potential audience.
❏ Gold ❏ Silver ❏ Lead ❏ Not yet
Comments:

_____ 10. All text is error-free in mechanics (e.g., spelling, punctuation, grammar).
❏ Gold ❏ Silver ❏ Lead ❏ Not yet
Comments:

_____ 11. Only one font is utilized throughout the announcement for stylistic coherence.
❏ Gold ❏ Silver ❏ Lead ❏ Not yet
Comments:

_____ **TOTAL (Possible Points: 110)**

Use scoring feedback to revise your outcomes-based program announcement.

Figure 13.2 Quality check for outcome-based program announcements

the magnitude of facilitating an intervention as comprehensive or specific program activity. For example, aquatic therapy is a comprehensive program that can be delineated as a generalized protocol, whereas Watsu (i.e., water shiatsu) is a specific type of aquatic therapy that could warrant a more precise protocol, especially in delineation of facilitation components. An outcome-based program protocol describes and explains benefits of a particular intervention at-a-glance so that interdisciplinary colleagues, administrators, and funding sources understand what will be provided as a therapeutic endeavor. Sylvester, Voelkl, and Ellis (2001) outline controversies and limits of protocols. They caution that standardization conflicts with the individuality of clients, underscoring the ethical necessity to first consider each client's goals. They also note how standardized protocols may not be multiculturally sensitive. However, protocol design may continue to be a viable way to convey diverse interventions and services *if* the designer makes an effort to integrate cultural sensitivity. The program protocol What is Tape Art? (see Figure 13.3, pp. 246–247) is a companion document to The Benefits of Tape Art: Sticking To Re-Creation (see Figure 13.4, p. 248), an outcome-based program announcement for participants. The Tape Art protocol stresses "cultural" flexibility by accounting for variation in how facilitators respond to patients' energy level and mood.

A program protocol can be displayed concisely with bulleted elements and five categorical headings (see Figure 13.3). Distinct from program announcements, these include:

- **A title and definition description** where the title is posed as a question (i.e., What Is Tape Art?) creates interest in activity as intervention by preparing readers for a clear-cut explanation. Bulleted definitions or characterizations can concisely convey the nature of the activity and its multiple aspects. The description can be quoted directly and cited, or paraphrased when retrieved from original sources such as textbooks or Internet sites.

- **Settings and populations** are a logical enumeration of where and with whom the activity might be useful since some program activities are more setting-specific than others (e.g., reminiscence in geriatric settings, medical play for hospitalized children). Program resources often reveal a variety of settings where outcomes can be articulated.

- **Goals/benefits/participant and program outcomes** specify a larger list of inherent goals as outcomes in clinical language unlike a program announcement that uses nonclinical language. These are derived categorically through activity analysis and can be displayed congruently to reveal a measure of change

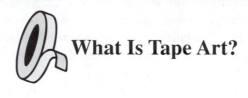

What Is Tape Art?

Tape Art is...

• Drawing life-size images with adhesive tape to make silhouettes without preliminary sketches

• Focusing on giving people a healing art experience, not a product

• Personalizing living space and animating the environment with murals or drawings

• Engaging patients in interacting in their environment by directing or creating drawings

• Giving people a chance to express themselves and show their individuality

• Appealing to all ages and abilities, adjustable for anyone's level of energy

Settings where Tape Art may heal include...

• Hospitals (e.g., intensive care units, isolation wards, patient rooms, recreation areas)

• Prisons and juvenile detention centers

• Residential treatment centers for youth

• Schools

• Arts festivals, annual celebrations, or disaster or mass trauma sites (e.g., the Oklahoma City bombing)

• Community centers, day treatment centers, assisted-living residences

Goals/therapeutic benefits/participant and program outcomes of Tape Art may include...

• Giving participants or patients something positive to focus on without using too much energy

• Giving participants a sense of control over their environment by speaking through art rather than words (e.g., kids in crisis express the unspeakable in tape drawings— see "Sticking to Therapy")

Figure 13.3 Outcome-based program protocol—What Is Tape Art?

- Encouraging collaboration/interaction with peers, staff, family, and friends through art making

- Being spontaneous and fostering free creativity in activity that is not rule-bound

- Having a pleasant and rewarding art experience with a dramatic result

- Creating a tool for dialogue to process a participant's lifestyle or clinical issues

Facilitation components of a Tape Art experience, event, or program may include...

- Purchase artist tape from local vendors (e.g., hardware stores).

- Notify administrators, staff, and custodians that Tape Art is harmless, and its low-grade adhesive backing can be removed from any surface. The vibrant blue tape is crepe-paper based, and can be torn and molded with ease.

- Remove tape after 24 hours, except in hospitals because removing it may lessen the healing benefits. Wipe the tape clean with disinfectant if Tape Art is left up in a hospital or institution.

- Alter or rework the creation by lifting up the tape and trying again.

- For the very young, very ill, or absent-at-surgery patient, family and staff can create a picture based on an image the patient will like. For the "up-and-at-'em, full-o'-beans patient" or visiting family, collaborative drawing can be encouraged in the patient's room or recreation areas.

- Create "murals on request" for the patient who is too ill to participate

- Invite reluctant participants to "direct" the drawing; or extend an energy-compromised patient's imagination by physically completing a Tape Art drawing.

- Facilitate drawings with dialogue or intuitive creativity and respond to a participant's energy and mood.

- Cofacilitate groups making murals or drawings followed by processing as debriefing.

Best practice, research, and online resources for Tape Art include...

- Welcome to the World of Tape Art: http://www.tapeart.com

- Roth, W.B. (1997). Sticking with therapy: Kids using tape art to tell their stories. *Healing Magazine, 2*(2), 12–18. Basic instructions for drawing with tape appear in this article.

Figure 13.3 (continued) Outcome-based program protocol—What Is Tape Art?

The Benefits of Tape Art

Sticking to Re-Creation

With BOON Murray, CTRS, by…

- Taping your art out in a fun and dramatic art experience
- Drawing freely and easily with tape making larger-than-life silhouettes
- Freely altering and reworking your drawing as you go
- Speaking through your feelings "on tape!"
- Making your mark safely applying tape and removing it from any surface
- Turning floors, wall, halls, and doors into temporary murals
- Personalizing your space by making your own mural
- Making a group mural with peers or staff, or direct the drawing
- Strolling the gallery of tape murals to appreciate other tape artists' images
- Discussing your finished Tape Art mural with the group so everyone recognizes what it means

Visit www.tapeart.com

Figure 13.4 Outcome-based program announcement—The Benefits of Tape Art: Sticking to Re-Creation (65% of original size)

(e.g., "improved circulation, increased insight," "reduced anxiety, decreased loneliness"). As planning progresses, a protocol designer can refer to stated elements to derive measurement evidence of client or program progress.

- **Facilitation components** form a detailed listing of any process-related activity including assessment, planning, and team evaluations/consultations, as well as subcategories of activity (e.g., processing as debriefing is a definitive component of adventure therapy sessions).

- **Best-practice, research, and online resources** display definitive sourcebooks for interdisciplinary integration of modalities such as *Learn to Meditate* (Fontana, 1999), a how-to guide listed as a best-practice resource in a protocol titled *What is Meditation?* Listing a national trade association as a research-based resource enhances an evidence-based practice identity when representing a therapeutic modality (e.g., The Delta Society represents animal-assisted therapy).

Designers can self-assess or peer review outcome-based protocols using a quality check (see Figure 13.5, p. 250). In addition to program announcements and protocols, TRSs can promote outcomes as key messages targeted to audiences such as legislators and as recruitment of professionals to the field of therapeutic recreation; this requires turning to professional organizations.

Professional Organization Resources for Promoting Outcomes

The American Therapeutic Recreation Association (ATRA) and National Therapeutic Recreation Society (NTRS) both provide materials such as event accessories to celebrate and promote therapeutic recreation, as well as signature documents for public distribution to convey outcomes, at nominal fees to offset printing costs. For example, ATRA provides packets that contain position statements on cost-benefits for TRSs to hand directly to legislative representatives as an initiative of the Public Policy Team (Baumann, 2002). Every TRS pressed to articulate outcomes and relevant interventions to prospective employers during job interviews might utilize *Recreational Therapy: A Summary of Health Outcomes* as a handout or career portfolio document (ATRA, 1994). This outcome-oriented document summarizes research cited in *Benefits of Therapeutic Recreation: A Consensus View* (Coyle, Kinney, Riley & Shank, 1991) along with programmatic activities for physical medicine, older adults, psychiatric disabilities, pediatrics, and developmental disabilities. NTRS distributes complementary copies of *Therapeutic Recreation Specialists: The Quality of Life Professionals* (Wenzel, 2000) defining TR service provision and describing a day in the life of a TRS, as well as professional preparation and career opportunities.

The *Therapeutic Recreation—The Benefits Are Endless...Training Program and Resource Guide* (Broida, 2000) is designed to help TRSs consistently promote their practice in terms of benefits and outcomes produced, to

Please award points as follows for each item:
Gold—10 points, Silver—8 points, Lead—5 points, Not Yet—0 points

_____ 1. Protocol begins with "What is… [name of program/intervention/activity/service]?"
❏ Gold   ❏ Silver   ❏ Lead   ❏ Not yet
Comments:

_____ 2. The name of the protocol designer is announced.
❏ Gold   ❏ Silver   ❏ Lead   ❏ Not yet
Comments:

_____ 3. An easily understood, bulleted description/definition is either cited or paraphrased and not plagarized.
❏ Gold   ❏ Silver   ❏ Lead   ❏ Not yet
Comments:

_____ 4. Relevant settings or populations for intervention are indicated.
❏ Gold   ❏ Silver   ❏ Lead   ❏ Not yet
Comments:

_____ 5. Benefits are stated simultaneously as goals and outcomes to reveal what makes the activity therapeutic.
❏ Gold   ❏ Silver   ❏ Lead   ❏ Not yet
Comments:

_____ 6. Detailed facilitation components are displayed that are unique to the program activity and incorporate the TR process (i.e., assess, plan, implement, evaluate).
❏ Gold   ❏ Silver   ❏ Lead   ❏ Not yet
Comments:

_____ 7. Best-practice, research, and online resources are displayed including professional organizations that promote the activity and conduct evidence-based research, articles or media about a TR context, and instructional media or supplies for facilitation.
❏ Gold   ❏ Silver   ❏ Lead   ❏ Not yet
Comments:

_____ 8. All text is error-free in mechanics (e.g., spelling, punctuation, grammar).
❏ Gold   ❏ Silver   ❏ Lead   ❏ Not yet
Comments:

_____ 9. Graphics enhance the overall layout and complement the nature of the activity/program/intervention/service being presented.
❏ Gold   ❏ Silver   ❏ Lead   ❏ Not yet
Comments:

_____ 10. Only one font is used throughout the protocol for stylistic coherence and readability.
❏ Gold   ❏ Silver   ❏ Lead   ❏ Not yet
Comments:

_____ **TOTAL (Possible Points: 100)**

Use scoring feedback to revise your outcomes-based protocol.

Figure 13.5 Quality check for outcome-based protocols

develop and justify programs based on documented benefits as outcomes, and to manage programs in a manner that highlights efficacy. This copyrighted resource allows users to integrate variable levels of technology into promotion depending on their proficiency in presentation mechanics or their agency resources. For example, users might customize PowerPoint scripts or utilize ready-made overhead transparencies to market outcomes to three targeted audiences. Although clients are overlooked as a potential audience in this material, PowerPoint presentations could be tailored to introduce clients to TR services or modalities in order to increase their comfort with what to expect and what satisfaction they might derive. In fact, these presentations could be modified in collaboration with clients within a local agency (with documentation of informed consent to use clients' testimonials and photographs).

Summary

Professionals who choose therapeutic recreation as a calling can never tire of explaining the field and its outcomes when the context for practice varies across a broad array of populations, settings, and therapeutic purposes. Social marketing principles can help TRSs derive client-valued outcomes using a benefits ladder to convey key messages in outcome-based program announcements and program protocols. Recent professional organization materials and training tools can help TRSs articulate client-directed outcomes, as well as meaning and purpose, to participants, colleagues, funding sources, and third parties.

Discussion Questions

1. Do you believe that TR practice promotes client-directed outcomes or therapist-directed outcomes? How does this affect marketing outcomes?

2. Think of an example where you selected an organized program to bring about a positive change in your own behavior. What attracted you to that program? What message does that send for TRSs when marketing their programs to potential participants?

3. Discuss examples of TR programs with which you are familiar and explain whether the central theme is health promotion or leisure fulfillment for outcomes. What marketing strategies are employed to promote these outcomes?

4. Discuss the ways you could utilize a benefits ladder to convey outcomes of TR programs to various stakeholders (refer to Table 13.1, p. 241).

5. Discuss aspects of language to consider when designing program slogans that appeal to potential participants.

6. How would you communicate outcomes to participants versus outcomes to colleagues or funding sources?

References

American Therapeutic Recreation Association. (1994, September). *Recreational therapy: A summary of health outcomes*. Hattiesburg, MS: Author.

Baumann, D. (2002, July/August). ATRA in action: Taking the message home in 2002 is set for August. *ATRA Newsletter, 18*(4), 4.

Broida, J. (Ed.). (2000, October). *Therapeutic recreation—The benefits are endless...Training program and resource guide*. Ashburn, VA: National Therapeutic Recreation Society.

Broida, J. (Ed.). (2001). *Therapeutic recreation—The benefits are endless... Training program and resource guide: Part II/Resource guide supplement*. Ashburn, VA: National Therapeutic Recreation Society.

Broyard, A. (1992). *Intoxicated by my illness*. New York, NY: Fawcett Columbine.

Coyle, C.P., Kinney, W.B., Riley, B., and Shank, J. (Eds.). (1991). *Benefits of therapeutic recreation: A consensus view*. Ravensdale, WA: Idyll Arbor.

Driver, B.L. and Bruns, D.H. (1999). Concepts and uses of the benefits approach to leisure. In E.L. Jackson and T.L. Burton (Eds.), *Leisure studies: Prospects for the twenty-first century* (pp. 349–367). State College, PA: Venture Publishing, Inc.

Duncan, B. and Miller, S. (2000). *The heroic client: Doing client-directed, outcome-informed therapy*. San Francisco, CA: Jossey-Bass, Inc.

Ellis, C. and Flaherty, M.G. (Eds.). (1992). *Investigating subjectivity: Research on lived experience*. Newbury Park, CA: Sage.

Falvey, M., Forest, M., Pearpoint, J., and Rosenberg, R.L. (1997). *All my life's a circle—Using the tools: Circles, MAPS & PATHS*. Toronto, ON: Inclusion Press.

Fontana, D. (1999). *Learn to meditate: A practical guide to self-discovery and fulfillment*. San Francisco, CA: Chronicle Books.

Galambos, D. (1995). *Planning...To have a life*. Toronto, ON: Sheridan College Learning Materials Services.

Gold, J. (1988). The value of fiction as therapeutic recreation and developmental mediator: A theoretical framework. *Journal of Poetry Therapy, 1*(3), 135–148.

Hubble, M.A., Duncan, B.L., and Miller. S.D. (1999). *The heart and soul of change: What works in therapy*. Washington, DC: American Psychological Association Press.

Jacobson, S. and Wilhite, B. (1999). Residential transitions in the lives of older adults with developmental disabilities: An ecological perspective. *Therapeutic Recreation Journal, 33*(3), 195–208.

James, J. and James, M. (1991). *Passion for life: Psychology and the human spirit*. New York, NY: Penguin Books.

Kotler, P., Roberto, N., and Lee, N. (2002). *Social marketing: Improving the quality of life*. Thousand Oaks, CA: Sage .

Lee, Y. and Yang, H. (2000). A review of therapeutic recreation outcomes in physical medicine and rehabilitation between 1991–2000. *Annual in Therapeutic Recreation, 9,* 21–34.

National Therapeutic Recreation Society. (2000). *Therapeutic recreation—The benefits are endless...* [Video]. Ashburn, VA: Author.

O'Keefe, C. (1993, September). *The role of legacy building in chronic illness.* Paper presented at the annual meeting of the American Therapeutic Recreation Association, Baltimore, MD.

O'Sullivan, E. (1999). *Setting a course for change: The benefits movement.* Ashburn, VA: National Recreation and Park Association.

Peterson, C.A. and Stumbo, N.J. (2000). *Therapeutic recreation program design: Principles and procedures* (3rd ed.). Needham Heights, MA: Allyn & Bacon.

Reason, P. and Rowan, J. (1981). *Human inquiry: A sourcebook of new paradigm research*. New York, NY: John Wiley & Sons.

Shank, J., Kinney, W., and Coyle, C. (1993). Efficacy studies in therapeutic recreation research: The need, the state of the art, and future implications. In M. Malkin and C.Z. Howe (Eds.), *Research in therapeutic recreation: Concepts and methods* (pp. 301–335). State College, PA: Venture Publishing, Inc.

Smull, M.W. and Harrison, S.B. (1992). *Supporting people with severe reputations in the community*. Alexandria, VA: National Association of State Mental Retardation Program Directors.

Snell, M.E. (1987). *Systematic instruction of persons with severe handicaps.* Columbus, OH: Charles E. Merrill.

Stumbo, N.J. (2002). *Client assessment in therapeutic recreation services.* State College, PA: Venture Publishing, Inc.

Sylvester, C., Voelkl, J., and Ellis, G.D. (2001). *Therapeutic recreation programming: Theory and practice*. State College, PA: Venture Publishing, Inc.

Thomas, W. (1996). *Life worth living: How someone you love can still enjoy life in a nursing home—The Eden Alternative in action*. Action, MA: VanderWyk & Burnham.

Weinreich, N.K. (1999). *Hands-on social marketing: A step-by-step guide*. Thousand Oaks, CA: Sage.

Wenzel, K. (2000). *Therapeutic recreation specialists: The quality of life professionals*. Ashburn, VA: National Therapeutic Recreation Society.

Wise, J. and Hale, S. (1999). Strengthening and generalizing self-efficacy in a male with a spinal cord injury. *Therapeutic Recreation Journal, 33*(4), 333–341.

Outcome Measurements From a Therapeutic Recreation Practitioner's Perspective

Diane Etzel-Wise, M.A., CTRS
Central Missouri State University

Norma J. Stumbo, Ph.D., CTRS
Illinois State University

As mentioned in the previous chapters, being able to define and measure important outcomes is a major challenge for all healthcare professionals. As health services move toward evidence-based care, the mandate to measure outcomes grows. But how are therapeutic recreation specialists (TRSs) responding to this mandate? Is "outcomes" just a buzzword soon to be gone from the healthcare vocabulary, or should practitioners be emphasizing measuring outcomes and reorganizing their daily, weekly, and monthly schedules to accommodate this process? Are some practitioners tracking outcomes for therapeutic recreation (TR) interventions now? If so, what instruments are they using? If not, what issues prevent practitioners from tracking outcomes? What role does professional preparation play in addressing practice outcomes? How can professional organizations assist members in identifying and implementing outcome measurement processes that move the profession forward in the healthcare arena? TR practitioners, educators, supervisors, and organizational leaders have chanted this litany of questions for several years, although the language may change slightly depending on the climate within healthcare.

The purpose of this chapter is to provide a brief background of practitioners' viewpoints of outcomes in TR service delivery. This chapter focuses on outcome measures used in practice, barriers to measuring outcomes, and the role of preprofessional education and professional organizations in promoting outcomes.

Therapeutic Recreation: Daily Activities and Lifetime Achievements

After spending anywhere from four to six hours in direct treatment service with clients, at least one to two hours with documentation and one to two hours in clinical staff meetings, outcome measurement, data collection, and reporting may not be at the top of the typical TRS's to-do list. However, even a glimpse at the bigger picture of healthcare provides a clear focus on the need to do so. Outcome definition and measurement simply must be done— it must become a priority every day.

Beyond time constraints, we know that outcome measurement remains a challenge. Slade addressed some of the difficulties within mental health services:

> Outcome could result from self—rather than professional help, the link between intervention and outcome is not straightforward, outcomes are not always positive, outcomes may be influenced by the absence rather than presence of an intervention, and outcome may differ from different perspectives. There is as yet no consensus about an agreed definition of outcome for individual patients. Further complexity arises when evaluating outcome in mental health services. Three levels of mental health service can be identified: specific treatments, combinations of treatments (such as a community mental health centre), and population-wide treatments (all programmes for a defined population, such as managed care organization)....The outcome data needed to inform each level are very different. (Slade, 2002, p. 743)

Within therapeutic recreation, one of the largest problems in measuring outcomes and achieving evidence-based practice is the lack of high-quality and outcome-oriented research (Bedini, 2001; Carruthers, 1997/98; Compton & Dieser, 1997; Malkin, 1993; Mannell, 1983; Witt, 1988). This is not a new problem, nor one that will ebb quickly. In some respects part of this problem can be attributed to a (perhaps perceived) practitioner-scholar chasm. However, several recent attempts have been made to provide possible solutions.

One possible solution was provided by Savell and Huston (1991) and Savell, Huston, and Malkin (1993) who encouraged and suggested how to "bridge the gap" between practitioners and researchers-educators. A second solution has been presented by a number of TR authors—that of using program evaluation data as a method of measuring outcomes (Patrick, 1997, 2001; Shank, Coyle & Kinney, 1993; Shank, Coyle, Kinney & Lay, 1995; Shank & Kinney, 1991; Widmer, 2001; Widmer, Zabriskie & Wells, 2003).

However, no movement will be made at all until more practitioners and supervisors commit to a larger "buy-in" for the need and begin to discover for themselves that outcomes are difficult, but doable. Until that happens on a large-scale basis, the field of therapeutic recreation will continue to experience difficulties in obtaining reimbursement, maintaining or adding positions, receiving support from its administrators, and earning the respect of healthcare colleagues.

To help the profession move forward, practitioners will need to maintain an intervention focus (i.e., specific programs aimed at predetermined client outcomes; Shank & Coyle, 2002; Stumbo & Peterson, 2004), while adding a combined research/administrative role. Several actions are needed on the part of the professional to accomplish this synthesis of roles.

First, professionals must become aware of and use internal professional standards. Internal standards of practice, such as those from the American Therapeutic Recreation Association (ATRA, 2000; http://www.atra-tr.org) and the National Therapeutic Recreation Society (NTRS, 1995; http://www.nrpa.org), give clear guidance on the mandate for systematically designing, implementing, and evaluating intervention programs to achieve client outcomes. Basic program evaluation and research skills are a necessity. In addition, professionals should keep abreast of standards required by the Joint Commission on Accreditation of Healthcare Organizations (JCAHO; http://www.jcaho.org) and the Rehabilitation Accreditation Commission (CARF; http://www.carf.org).

Second, practitioners need to hone strategic planning skills for both long- and short-term planning, as well as time management skills. The aim is to spend more time on the activities (e.g., daily, weekly, monthly, yearly) that will make the biggest difference. Problem solving, decision making, and prioritizing become hourly events to ensure that the "big rocks" (such as measurement of client outcomes) become a reality (Covey, 1989).

A third helpful initiative on the part of the practitioner is learning the healthcare outcome terminology in order to improve communication with other disciplines. Chpaters 1 through 3 in this text define some of the most prevalent terms used in outcome measurement. Knowing the language is extremely helpful in augmenting the collection of system-wide outcome data and carving a unique niche for TR's contribution to overall effort. TRSs have much to learn, but also much to contribute.

Case Example of a TRS's Efforts

It goes without saying that many TRSs are highly successful in targeting important outcomes and then using appropriate procedures to measure the extent of their achievement. Most of these TRSs are contributing to a larger agency-wide effort of outcome measurement. Jim Barrett, TRS/CTRS, is one such individual. Jim works with the Spinal Cord Injury Team at Pitt County Memorial Hospital in Greenville, North Carolina, and had the following to say about TR outcome measurement:

> We use UDS FIM to track FIM Gain, Average Length of Stay (LOS), and LOS Effectiveness. We compare to ourselves, trending quarter to quarter to quarter and with regional and national data. I coordinate the Spinal Cord Injury (SCI) Team [including] all the therapists and nurses through the process. I report the summary and action plans in a Program Evaluation Committee that has leaders from all programs and disciplines. The biggest challenge is that staff from all disciplines [become] defensive if our scores are lower than the national comparison. We tend to say our patients are different: "We had more quadriplegic patients, we had more behavioral issues, we had more angry patients, and so forth." As team leader, I try to view the findings at face value and… create action plans that address the lower scores, especially if we see trends over a period of time.
>
> We use the Jackson Organization Patient Satisfaction Survey to look at scores of the questions as well as overall satisfaction. Our facility looks at the overall satisfaction globally.…Our SCI Team wants to have a good overall score. We look at the different questions with Jackson and get to compare our SCI scores (by quarter) over a five-quarter comparison. Special attention is given to scores that have increased (or decreased) by .15 on a five-point scale per quarter over a three-quarter time frame. We also have items recognized as opportunities to celebrate "success" and areas where improvement efforts should be focused. The team develops an action plan, which we carry out throughout the next quarter…
>
> Another big challenge with FIM and Jackson Patient Satisfaction is the timeliness of the data. We will get the July, August, September FIM report and the Jackson Survey in November or December. Our discussion on the data will be in December, and I will report on the data in Program Evaluation in January 2003. Our action plans are always based on data two to four months old so I feel that we are constantly playing catch-up. We have completed a nine-question Rehab internal day of discharge survey that gives us more immediate feedback. (J. Barrett, personal communication, 2002)

This communication is shared to illustrate the degree to which outcome measurement requires an understanding of current standards, strategic planning and time management skills, and competence in outcome terminology. Competence in basic program evaluation and research is essential. The next section of this chapter will discuss the results of an informal survey of TR practitioners and their perceptions of and competence in measuring outcomes.

Results of an Informal Survey: Practitioner's Perspective on Outcomes

The American Therapeutic Recreation Association, at the time of this writing, is collecting informal information about how TR professionals are faring in the current outcomes-focused environment. Below is a sample of initial comments from 72 respondents that have been collected with a brief five-question survey; comments from the membership were gathered until May 2003.

Outcome Measures

The first question on the survey asks what outcome measures are used by the responding TRSs. One-third of the respondents indicated that they currently tracked and reported TR outcomes and/or rehabilitation services' outcomes in their facilities. Instruments used to track outcomes by the respondents included

- Leisure Competence Measure (LCM; Kloseck, Crilly, Ellis & Lammers, 1996)
- Functional Independence Measure (FIM; Guide for Uniform Data Set for Medical Rehabilitation, 1996)
- Beck Depression Inventory (BDI; Beck 1978)
- Jackson Patient Satisfaction Survey (Jackson Group, 2002)
- Incapacity Status Scale (Reding, LaRocca & Madonna, 1987)
- Minimum Data Set (MDS; Center for Medicare and Medicaid Services, 2002)
- Press Ganey Satisfaction Surveys (Press Ganey Associates, 2002)
- Geriatric Depression Scale (Yesavage et al., 1983)
- Mini-Mental State Examination (MMSE; Folstein, Folstein & McHugh, 1975)

Only the Leisure Competence Measure is unique to TR practice. All other outcome measures are used in tandem with other healthcare providers.

Slade (2002) listed the outcome measurement principles that were identified in a systematic review within mental health. They include:

- Standardized measures should be used.
- Relevance to informing practice should be emphasized.
- Multiple perspectives should be used.
- Standardized methods should be used.
- Data collection should be cheap and simple.
- Measures should be relevant to the patient group.
- Treatment received should be characterized.
- Feedback should be quick, easy, and meaningful.
- Aggregated data should be compatible with benchmarks.
- Meaning of measures should be comprehensible.
- Data should be collected longitudinally.
- Case mix (e.g., diagnosis) should be assessed.
- Measures should show means/processes of change.
- Measures should fit with psychopathology theories.
- Outcomes chosen should be multidimensional.
- Costs should be included.
- Data on treatment leavers who exit before targeted outcomes are reached should be collected.
- Usefulness to measure individual differences should be considered. (Slade, 2002, p. 746)

Barriers

The remaining two-thirds of the respondents indicated they currently did not track outcomes and identified several barriers to outcome measurement. The most common barrier cited was "lack of time." Related to the limited time issue were high volumes of admissions and discharges, lack of adequate staff numbers, and lack of time or resources for analysis. The second major constraint was "lack of knowledge." The respondents indicated they lack knowledge about the definition of outcomes, tools, statistical processes, and tracking methods.

The third major barrier was "lack of administrative support." Situational barriers included "team-based services—not tracking by individual disciplines," "Set-up of unit," "Not in agreement on outcome approach in our department," "My practice is on a contractual basis," and "We need to revamp our assessment process."

The barriers to outcome measurement mentioned by TRSs parallel those noted in other professions such as nursing (Evans & Pearson, 2001), medicine (Evidence-Based Medicine Working Group, 1992; Glasziou, Irwig, Bain & Colditz, 2002; Wade, 1999), social work (Proctor, 2001), and mental health (Slade, 2002). We should not assume that other professions have adequate time for outcomes measurement and we are the only profession that does not. All healthcare professionals face the same challenges of time limitations, economic constraints, and (at least perceived) disincentives from administration.

Professional Preparation

Of the respondents currently tracking outcomes, about one-half perceived that their undergraduate programs prepared them adequately. Of the respondents *not* currently tracking outcomes, about one-half perceived they were adequately prepared in their undergraduate or graduate programs. Some of the aforementioned barriers prevented the nontracking respondents from measuring outcomes at the present time.

Interestingly enough, the data from this questionnaire can be illustrated through a matrix of possibilities and answers (see Figure 14.1). Of those who recieved adequate undergraduate education to measure outcomes, only 50% did so. Of those who did not receive adequate education, 50% somehow managed to measure outcomes despite not learning the process as an undergraduate. So it would appear that those who felt outcomes were important to measure did so both because and in spite of their undergraduate educational experiences. This supports the documented notion that supplying information does not guarantee its absorption (Glanville, Haines & Auston, 1998; Hall, 2000; Johnson & Griffiths, 2001; Wolf, 2000).

Once again, therapeutic recreation is not the only healthcare profession to grapple with these issues. In fact the most well-documented struggle has been within the medical field as they move from a traditional to an evidence-based, scientific delivery of services (Glanville, Haines & Auston, 1998; Johnson & Griffiths, 2001; Wolf, 2000). Every profession is confronting the need to advance from an "art" to a "science" (King & Teo, 2000; Nichols, 2001; Rosoff, 2001).

	Adequate Education	Inadequate Education
Measure Outcomes	50% of respondents	50% of respondents
Did Not Measure Outcomes	50% of respondents	50% of respondents

Figure 14.1 Illustration of educational preparation and measurement of outcomes in practice

Role of Professional Organizations

When survey respondents were asked what assistance would be helpful from their professional organizations, they identified the following three main categories: (a) education, (b) models/tools/instruments, and (c) a research agenda. Under education, respondents requested more sessions (i.e., nationally, regionally and especially *locally*), educational resources, one-day sessions/ training, tapes, and information on the organizations' website. Specific topic requests included: methods for establishing and tracking outcomes, data collection procedures, rating effectiveness of data, and utilizing data cooperatively with other facilities.

In reference to models, tools and/or instruments, suggestions from respondents included identification or provision of models for specific diagnostic tracks (i.e., psychiatry, substance abuse, geriatric); creation of an easy-to-follow data collection model; or creation of an instrument with complete instructions for statistical analysis and interpretation. It was also suggested that a simple tool would be more widely used.

Finally, developing a research agenda was the requested by a small number of respondents.

These findings put TR professions at a peculiar juncture. Of the estimated 39,000 practicing TRSs, only 18,000 are certified by the National Council for Therapeutic Recreation Certification. Of those 18,000, only 4,000 are members of either of the two national membership organizations for therapeutic recreation. "They are us and we are them." Professional organizations do not exist independent of the professionals, and professionals who sit back and wait for information to fall into their laps are in danger of extinction. Each and every practicing professional is responsible for joining and supporting the organizations, creating and consuming current knowledge, and helping the profession remain viable, growth-oriented, and central. "We must remain committed to promoting TR interventions and outcomes that are designed and supported with sound statistical research data that clearly demonstrates our effectiveness" (Thompson, 2002).

Outcomes:
A Priority Focus for Professional
Organizations and Professionals

Both the American Therapeutic Recreation Association and the National Therapeutic Recreation Society have maintained a focus on outcomes or benefits of services provided to clients. It is well-understood that concerted and cooperative efforts are needed to ensure the profession's future success.

Although both organizations are active in this effort, due to space limitations, the American Therapeutic Recreation Association's efforts will be presented. ATRA has increased the offerings of outcomes-focused educational sessions and journal articles, with one entire volume of the *Annual in Therapeutic Recreation* focused entirely on outcomes and outcome measurements. In 2000–2001 an ATRA Outcomes Task Force was charged with developing an aggressive plan for the use of outcome measurements in the daily practice of TRSs. Goals included

- Conduct a thorough review of literature and examination of outcome models in the TR profession, healthcare, World Health Organization, disability, and other relevant arenas;

- Integrate program evaluation methods in daily practice of TRSs;

- Educate practitioners in the use of outcome models, measurements and methods in daily practice of therapeutic recreation;

- Implement treatment interventions that are based on efficacious, empirical data; and

- Establish a national database of professional efficacy research and outcomes information.

The ATRA Outcomes Task Force and their initiative provides but one example of the recent focus on outcomes. It also is well-understood that each professional needs to take personal and professional responsibility for the upkeep of the knowledge base.

Here are some specific suggestions for TR professionals and students:

- Perform your job with an eye toward creating a professional identity.

- Ensure that clients' needs remain first and foremost in your actions.

- Use the tools of the profession, such as the standards of practice and the codes of ethics.

- Upgrade your current competence through continuing education opportunities, from books, to newsletters, to workshops, to classes, to the Internet.
- Network with other professionals who also are committed to upgrading their skills.
- Maintain records of clients' successes and barriers to independence.
- Absorb and information from colleagues in other disciplines.
- Work cooperatively as a respected member of the service team.
- Contribute your expertise, energy, and time to a professional organization.
- Maintain your status as a Certified Therapeutic Recreation Specialist.

If every TR professional became committed to these ten actions, we would become the model for every other healthcare profession. Wouldn't that be cool?

Summary

Putting outcome measurement into practice is a sometimes difficult and challenging task. This chapter highlights some of the actions to take and barriers encountered by TR professional in their efforts to identify, produce, and measure outcomes. Data from an informal survey are presented to highlight some of these concerns and successes. This chapter also presented the recent creation of the ATRA Outcomes Task Force and its initiatives. Each and every professional and student is urged to develop outcome competencies. It is hoped that this book aids in this effort.

Discussion Questions

1. Discuss some of the barriers to identifying, producing, and measuring outcomes in therapeutic recreation. How do those differ from other healthcare professions?

2. Discuss some of the solutions to identifying, producing, and measuring outcomes in therapeutic recreation. How are these the same as other healthcare professions?

3. What outcomes should therapeutic recreation focus on exclusively, and which should we focus on cooperatively with other healthcare professions?

4. What actions to improve the state-of-the-art of outcomes in therapeutic recreation will you commit to completing within the next 6 to 12 months?

References

American Therapeutic Recreation Association. (2000). *Standards for the practice of therapeutic recreation and self-assessment guide*. Alexandria, VA: Author.

Beck, A. (1978). *The Beck inventory*. Philadelphia, PA: The Center for Cognitive Therapy.

Bedini, L.A. (2001). Status of therapeutic recreation research. In N. Stumbo (Ed.), *Professional issues in therapeutic recreation: On competence and outcomes* (pp. 335–348). Champaign, IL: Sagamore.

Carruthers, C. (1997/98). Therapeutic recreation efficacy research agenda. *Annual in Therapeutic Recreation, 7*, 29–41.

Center for Medicare and Medicaid Services. (2002). Minimum data set (MDS). Retrieved December 30, 2002, from http://cms.hhs.gov/medicaid/mds20/man-form.asp

Compton, D.M. and Dieser, R. (1997). Research initiatives in therapeutic recreation. In D.M. Compton (Ed.), *Issues in therapeutic recreation: Toward a new millennium* (2nd ed.; pp. 299–326). Champaign, IL: Sagamore.

Covey, S.R. (1989). *Seven habits of highly effective people*. New York, NY: Fireside.

Evans, D. and Pearson, A. (2001). Systematic reviews: Gatekeepers of nursing knowledge. *Journal of Clinical Nursing, 10*(5), 593–599.

Evidence-Based Medicine Working Group. (1992). Evidence-based medicine: A new approach to teaching the practice of medicine. *Journal of the American Medical Association, 268*, 2420–2425.

Folstein, M., Folstein, S., and McHugh, P. (1975). Mini-mental state: A practical method of grading the cognitive state of patients for the clinician. *Journal of Psychiatric Residence, 12*, 189–198.

Glanville, J., Haines, M., and Auston, I. (1998). Finding information on clinical effectiveness. *British Medical Journal, 317*, 200–203.

Glasziou, P., Irwig, L., Bain, C., and Colditz, G. (2001). *Systematic reviews in healthcare*. Cambridge, UK: Cambridge University Press.

Guide for the Uniform Data Set for Medical Rehabilitation. (1996). *Independence Measure (FIM instrument) Version 5.1*. Buffalo, NY: State University of New York at Buffalo.

Hall, K. (2002). Research in progress: Developing the protocol for a systematic review of literature on effective literacy teachers and their teaching. *Reading, Literacy, and Language, 36*(1), 44–47.

Jackson Group, Inc. (2002). *Jackson patient satisfaction survey*. Retrieved October 20, 2002, from http://thejacksongroup.com/index.cfm

Johnson, M. and Griffiths, R. (2001). Developing evidence-based clinicians. *International Journal of Nursing Practice, 7*, 109–118.

King, K.M. and Teo, K.K. (2000). Integrating clinical quality improvement strategies with nursing research. *Western Journal of Nursing Research, 22*(5), 596–608.

Kloseck, M. and Crilly, R. (1997). *Leisure competence measure: Adult version, professional manual and users' guide.* London, ON: Leisure Competence Measure Data System.

Kloseck, M., Crilly, R.G., Ellis, G.D., and Lammers, E. (1996). Leisure Competence Measure: Development and reliability testing of a scale to measure functional outcomes in therapeutic recreation. *Therapeutic Recreation Journal, 30*(1), 13–26.

Malkin, M.J. (1993). Issues and needs in therapeutic recreation research. In M.J. Malkin and C.Z. Howe (Eds.), *Research in therapeutic recreation: Concepts and methods* (pp. 3–24). State College, PA: Venture Publishing, Inc.

Mannell, R.C. (1983). Research methodology in therapeutic recreation. *Therapeutic Recreation Journal, 17*(4), 9–16.

National Therapeutic Recreation Society. (1995). *Standards for the practice of therapeutic recreation services.* Arlington, VA: National Recreation and Park Association.

Nichols, S. (2001). Keynote—Therapeutic recreation practice: Art, science, or magic? In N.J. Stumbo (Ed.), *Professional issues in therapeutic recreation: On competence and outcomes* (pp. 153–158). Champaign, IL: Sagamore.

Patrick, G. (1997). Making clinical research happen. In D.M. Compton (Ed.), *Professional issues in therapeutic recreation: Toward a new millennium* (2nd ed.; pp. 144–165). Champaign, IL: Sagamore.

Patrick, G. (2001). Perspective—Clinical research: Methods and mandates. In N. Stumbo (Ed.), *Professional issues in therapeutic recreation: On competence and outcomes* (pp. 401–418). Champaign, IL: Sagamore.

Press Ganey Associates. (2002). *Press Ganey satisfaction surveys.* Retrieved October 20, 2002, from http://www.pressganey.com

Proctor, E.K. (2001). Building and consolidating knowledge for practice. *Social Work Research, 25*(4), 195–197.

Reding, M.J., LaRocca, N.G., and Madonna, M. (1987). Acute hospital care versus rehabilitation hospitalization for management of nonemergent complications in multiple sclerosis. *Journal of Neurological Rehabilitation, 1*, 13–17.

Rosoff, A.J. (2001). Evidence-based medicine and the law: The courts confront clinical practice guidelines. *Journal of Health Politics, Policy, and Law, 26*(2), 327–368.

Savell, K. and Huston, A. (1991, September). Collaborative research: Bridging the gap between practitioners and researchers/educators. Paper presented at the American Therapeutic Recreation Association Annual Conference, Kansas City, KS.

Savell, K., Huston, A., and Malkin, M.J. (1993). Collaborative research: Bridging the gap between practitioners and researchers/educators. In M.J. Malkin and C.Z. Howe (Eds.), *Research in therapeutic recreation: Concepts and methods* (pp. 77–96). State College, PA: Venture Publishing, Inc.

Shank, J. and Coyle, C. (2002). *Therapeutic recreation in health promotion and rehabilitation*. State College, PA: Venture Publishing, Inc.

Shank, J., Coyle, C., and Kinney, W.B. (1993). Efficacy studies in therapeutic recreation research: The need, the state of the art, and future implications. In M.J. Malkin and C.Z. Howe (Eds.), *Research in therapeutic recreation: Concepts and methods* (pp. 301–336). State College, PA: Venture Publishing, Inc.

Shank, J., Coyle, C., Kinney, W., and Lay, C. (1995). Using existing data to examine therapeutic recreation services. *Annual in Therapeutic Recreation, 5*, 5–12.

Shank, J.W. and Kinney, W.B. (1991). Monitoring and measuring outcomes in therapeutic recreation. In B. Riley (Ed.), *Quality management: Applications for therapeutic recreation* (pp. 69–88). State College, PA: Venture Publishing, Inc.

Sheikh, R.L. and Yesavage, J.A. (1986). Geriatric Depression Scale (GDS): Recent evidence and development of a shorter version. *Clinical Gerontologist, 5*, 165–173.

Slade, M. (2002). What outcomes to measure in routine mental health services and how to assess them: A systematic review. *Australian and New Zealand Journal of Psychiatry, 36*, 743–753.

Stumbo, N.J. and Peterson, C.A. (2004). *Therapeutic recreation program design: Principles and procedures* (4th ed.). San Francisco, CA: Benjamin Cummings.

Thompson, G.T. (2002, September). Inaugural speech at the Annual Conference of the American Therapeutic Recreation Association, Keystone, CO.

Wade, D.T. (1999). Editorial: Outcome measurement and rehabilitation. *Clinical Rehabilitation, 13*, 93–95.

Widmer, M.A. (2001). Methods for outcome research in therapeutic recreation. In N. Stumbo (Ed.), *Professional issues in therapeutic recreation: On competence and outcomes* (pp. 365–382). Champaign, IL: Sagamore.

Widmer, M.W., Zabriskie, R., and Wells, M.S. (2003). Program evaluation: Collecting data to measure outcomes. In N.J. Stumbo (Ed.), *Client outcomes in therapeutic recreation services* (pp. 201–220). State College, PA: Venture Publishing, Inc.

Witt, P.A. (1998). Therapeutic recreation research: Past, present, and future. *Therapeutic Recreation Journal, 22*(1), 14–23.

Wolf, F.M. (2000). Lessons to be learned from evidence-based medicine: Practice and promise of evidence-based medicine and evidence-based education. *Medical Teacher, 22*(3), 251–259.

Yesavage, J.A., Brink, T.L., Rose, T.L., Lum, O., Huang, V., Adey, M., and Leirer, V.O. (1983). Development and validation of a geriatric depression screening scale: A preliminary report. *Journal of Psychiatric Research, 17*, 37–49.

About the Authors

Candace Ashton-Shaeffer, Ph.D., CTRS/TRS, is an Associate Professor at University of North Carolina at Wilmington. She has over 30 years experience in therapeutic recreation including ten years as a therapeutic recreation specialist in long-term care, community mental health, early intervention, and municipal recreation. Ashton-Shaeffer is a past-president of the National Therapeutic Recreation Society. Her research interests focus on leisure behavior and school-based therapeutic recreation services, and include studies on older women, older-adult athletes, elite wheelchair athletes, and therapeutic recreation as a related service for students with disabilities.

Linda L. Caldwell is Professor of Recreation and Park Management and Professor in Charge of Research for the School of Hotel, Restaurant, and Recreation Management at Penn State University. She earned her B.S. at Penn State (1976), her M.S. at North Carolina State University (1982), and her Ph.D. at the University of Maryland (1986). Much of Caldwell's research has centered around adolescents, leisure, and health. She is particularly interested in leisure education, prevention research, and the developmental affordances of leisure. Currently, Caldwell is the lead investigator on a NIDA-funded substance use prevention program that helps middle school youth learn to use their leisure time wisely. She also is involved with several international projects (Santiago, Chile; Cape Town, South Africa; Lome, Togo) that focus on developing youth competencies, healthy lifestyles, and democratic behavior through leisure.

Cynthia Carruthers, Ph.D., CTRS, LADC, is an Associate Professor at the University of Nevada, Las Vegas. Her areas of interest include positive psychology, recovery, coping, youth development, leisure education, community building, and program evaluation. Carruthers has served as Chair of the Research Committee for the American Therapeutic Recreation Association (ATRA) and Editor of the ATRA *Annual in Therapeutic Recreation*, as well as Associate Editor of the *Therapeutic Recreation Journal*.

Diane Etzel-Wise, M.A., CTRS, earned a B.A. in Recreation, an M.A. in Health Services Management, and accumulated comprehensive experience in mental health service delivery, consumer empowerment initiatives, psychosocial rehabilitation, supervision, and program design/development. Over the past 26 years of her career in therapeutic recreation, Etzel-Wise has worked for consumers at three Kansas mental health centers and numerous inpatient psychiatric or substance abuse treatment settings including the Menninger Clinic. She has served as an Assistant Professor at Central Missouri State University, Warrensburg, since 1997 and currently provides Basic Strengths and Recovery Model Training to community mental health centers through the University of Kansas School of Social Welfare. Etzel-Wise served as President of the American Therapeutic Recreation Association from 2000–2001 and created the Outcomes Task Force during her term. A native Kansan, her recreational pursuits include gardening, social and spiritual gatherings, and traveling. She lives with her husband, Pat, in a Lenexa, Kansas earth-bermed home.

Jan S. Hodges, Ph.D., CTRS, is an Assistant Professor in the Recreation and Leisure Studies Program at the University of North Texas, Denton. She has been in the therapeutic recreation profession for over 20 years, working in various service settings. Hodges has written and presented on topics related to outcomes in developmental disabilities services and community partici-pation by persons with disabilities.

Colleen Deyell Hood received her Ph.D. in Leisure Studies from the Univer-sity of Illinois and is currently an Associate Professor at Oklahoma State University. Her scholarly interests include therapeutic recreation professional development, leisure and addiction, coping skills theory, women and addic-tion, and social psychology of leisure. She has authored or coauthored a number of articles in the *Therapeutic Recreation Journal* and the *Annual in Therapeutic Recreation*. Hood has been involved in professional organiza-tions extensively, serving as Chair of the Protocol Development Committee of ATRA, coeditor of the *Therapeutic Recreation Journal* for NTRS, and president of the Canadian Therapeutic Recreation Association.

John M. Jacobson is a Rehabilitation Planning Specialist for the Department of Veterans Affairs (VA), Physical Medicine and Rehabilitation Central Office. He received a Bachelor of Science degree in 1971 and a Master of Science degree in 1977 in Recreation and Park Management with a Therapeutic Recre-ation option from the University of Oregon. He is a past board member of the National Council for Therapeutic Recreation Certification and the American Therapeutic Recreation Association. Jacobson was a national trainer for the VA's Functional Status and Outcomes Database, and presents nationally on topics including professional ethics, accreditation, rehabilitation manage-ment, and outcomes. His current position with the VA deals with rehabilita-tion policy, accreditation, and outcomes from a federal perspective.

Bryan P. McCormick, CTRS, is an Associate Professor in the Department of Recreation and Park Administration at Indiana University. He has made a number of presentations on outcome-based practices and theory-based practice. McCormick has served in leadership positions in both ATRA and NTRS, as well as state-level therapeutic recreation professional organizations.

Susan "BOON" Murray, Ed.D., CTRS, is Associate Professor of Therapeutic Recreation and coordinates internships at University of Wisconsin—La Crosse. Her doctorate is from Temple University where she facilitated journaling with patients to understand how their lived experience of acute physical rehabilitation and recovery affected their perceptions of therapeutic recreation and patienthood. Murray has presented and written about existential outcomes as mediating clients' self-discovery of purpose and meaning and an issue of role identity. As coeditor of Practice Perspectives from 1998–2001 for *Therapeutic Recreation Journal*, she introduced the genre of personal narratives as a way to sensitize readers to the humanity of doing therapeutic work, and a potential strategy of empowerment for adding clients' voices to the articulation of practice as a caring partnership.

Mason Peebles, M.S., CTRS, is a doctoral student pursuing a degree in higher education at the University of North Texas, Denton. His minor field of study is therapeutic recreation in which he also holds B.S. and M.S. degrees. Peebles is a teaching fellow in the Kinesiology, Health Promotion and Recreation Department and teaches physical activity, kinesiology, and recreation courses.

Jo-Ellen Ross, Ph.D., CTRS, is an Assistant Professor and Director of the Recreation Program at Chicago State University. She has been a CTRS for over 20 years and has worked as a practitioner in a wide variety of settings including acute and rehabilitation hospitals, social service agencies, schools, camps, and park and recreation agencies with individuals of all ages. Today, even as a full-time faculty member, Ross continues to practice therapeutic recreation. Her research interests include leisure behavior and its meaning in terms of inclusion and diversity, assistive technology, persons with disabilities, family, social networks, and transitions.

Dr. Carmen V. Russoniello has over 15 years experience as a recreational therapist, counselor, biofeedback therapist, and educator. He is a past president of the American Therapeutic Recreation Association and currently serves as Team Leader for the Association's Healthy People 2010 initiative. His research is focused on understanding the underlying psychophysiological processes evoked by recreation participation and the relationship of these processes to health. Russoniello is an Assistant Professor and currently teaches recreational therapy and biofeedback courses at East Carolina University.

Norma J. Stumbo is a Professor of Therapeutic Recreation at Illinois State University in Normal, Illinois, where she has been employed since 1984. She has authored, coauthored, and edited several books in therapeutic recreation including: *Therapeutic Recreation Program Design: Principles and Procedures* (Benjamin Cummings), *Client Assessment in Therapeutic Recreation*

(Venture Publishing, Inc.), and *Professional Issues in Therapeutic Recreation* (Sagamore Publishing). Stumbo also publishes extensively in the *Therapeutic Recreation Journal* and the *Annual in Therapeutic Recreation*. She presents internationally on a wide variety of topics including assessment, intervention programming, outcomes, and wellness.

Mary S. Wells is a therapeutic recreation Ph.D. candidate at the University of Utah, and an outcome and evaluation consultant to a large therapeutic wilderness program.

Mark A. Widmer, Ph.D. is an Associate Professor of Therapeutic Recreation at Brigham Young University, Provo, Utah.

Barbara Wilhite, Ed.D., CTRS, CPRP, is a Professor in the Recreation and Leisure Studies Program at the University of North Texas, Denton. Her practice, research, and teaching interests include therapeutic recreation, gerontology, sport and disability, experiential learning, and qualitative research approaches.

Ramon Zabriskie, Ph.D., is an Assistant Professor of Therapeutic Recreation at Brigham Young University, Provo, Utah.

Other Books by Venture Publishing, Inc.

The ABCs of Behavior Change: Skills for Working with Behavior Problems in Nursing Homes
by Margaret D. Cohn, Michael A. Smyer, and Ann L. Horgas

Activity Experiences and Programming within Long-Term Care
by Ted Tedrick and Elaine R. Green

The Activity Gourmet
by Peggy Powers

Advanced Concepts for Geriatric Nursing Assistants
by Carolyn A. McDonald

Adventure Programming
edited by John C. Miles and Simon Priest

Assessment: The Cornerstone of Activity Programs
by Ruth Perschbacher

Behavior Modification in Therapeutic Recreation: An Introductory Manual
by John Datillo and William D. Murphy

Benefits of Leisure
edited by B.L. Driver, Perry J. Brown, and George L. Peterson

Benefits of Recreation Research Update
by Judy M. Sefton and W. Kerry Mummery

Beyond Baskets and Beads: Activities for Adults with Functional Impairments
by Mary Hart, Karen Primm, and Kathy Cranisky

Beyond Bingo: Innovative Programs for the New Senior
by Sal Arrigo, Jr., Ann Lewis, and Hank Mattimore

Beyond Bingo 2: More Innovative Programs for the New Senior
by Sal Arrigo, Jr.

Both Gains and Gaps: Feminist Perspectives on Women's Leisure
by Karla Henderson, M. Deborah Bialeschki, Susan M. Shaw, and Valeria J. Freysinger

Client Assessment in Therapeutic Recreation Services
by Norma J. Stumbo

Conceptual Foundations for Therapeutic Recreation
edited by David R. Austin, John Dattilo, and Bryan P. McCormick

Dementia Care Programming: An Identity-Focused Approach
by Rosemary Dunne

Dimensions of Choice: A Qualitative Approach to Recreation, Parks, and Leisure Research
by Karla A. Henderson

Diversity and the Recreation Profession: Organizational Perspectives
edited by Maria T. Allison and Ingrid E. Schneider

Effective Management in Therapeutic Recreation Service
by Gerald S. O'Morrow and Marcia Jean Carter

Evaluating Leisure Services: Making Enlightened Decisions, Second Edition
by Karla A. Henderson and M. Deborah Bialeschki

Everything From A to Y: The Zest Is up to You! Older Adult Activities for Every Day of the Year
by Nancy R. Cheshire and Martha L. Kenney

The Evolution of Leisure: Historical and Philosophical Perspectives
by Thomas Goodale and Geoffrey Godbey

Experience Marketing: Strategies for the New Millennium
by Ellen L. O'Sullivan and Kathy J. Spangler

Facilitation Techniques in Therapeutic Recreation
by John Dattilo

File o' Fun: A Recreation Planner for Games & Activities, Third Edition
by Jane Harris Ericson and Diane Ruth Albright

The Game and Play Leader's Handbook: Facilitating Fun and Positive Interaction
by Bill Michaelis and John M. O'Connell

The Game Finder: A Leader's Guide to Great Activities
by Annette C. Moore

Getting People Involved in Life and Activities: Effective Motivating Techniques
by Jeanne Adams

Glossary of Recreation Therapy and Occupational Therapy
by David R. Austin

Venture Publishing, Inc.
1999 Cato Avenue
State College, PA 16801
Phone: 814-234-4561
Fax: 814-234-1651
www.venturepublish.com